W9-CCP-465

Books by Dee Hardie

Views from Thornhill *(1988)*
Hollyhocks, Lambs and Other Passions *(1985)*

VIEWS
from
THORNHILL

VIEWS
from
THORNHILL

Of Family, Farm and Other Fancies

~~~~~~~~~~~~~~~~~~~~~~~~~~~~~~~~~~~~

Dee Hardie

Illustrations by
Elizabeth Hardie

Atheneum   1988   New York

Copyright © 1988 by Dee Hardie

These columns have previously appeared in the *Baltimore Sun,* 1966–1972, the *Roanoke Times* and the *Boston Herald-Traveler,* 1970–1972, *House & Garden,* 1980–1983, and *House Beautiful,* 1984–1987.

All rights reserved. No part of this book may be reproduced or transmitted in any form or by any means, electronic or mechanical, including photocopying, recording or by any information storage and retrieval system, without permission in writing from the Publisher.

Atheneum
Macmillan Publishing Company
866 Third Avenue, New York, N.Y. 10022
Collier Macmillan Canada, Inc.

Library of Congress Cataloging-in-Publication Data

Hardie, Dee.
  Views from Thornhill: of family, farm and other fancies/Dee Hardie.
    p. cm.
  "These columns have previously appeared in the Baltimore sun, 1966–1972, the Roanoke times and the Boston herald-traveler, 1970–1972, House & garden, 1980–1983, and House beautiful, 1984–1987"—T.p. verso.
  Continues: Hollyhocks, lambs and other passions. 1985.
  ISBN 0–689–11983–6
  1. Baltimore Region (Md.)—Social life and customs. 2. Farm life—Maryland—Baltimore Region. 3. Country life—Maryland—Baltimore Region. 4. Thornhill Farm (Md.) 5. Hardie, Dee. 6. Baltimore Region (Md.)—Biography.   I. Title.
F189.B15H37   1988
975.2′6—dc19   87–31773
                                                            CIP

Macmillan books are available at special discounts for bulk purchases for sales promotions, premiums, fund-raising, or educational use. For details, contact:

Special Sales Director
Macmillan Publishing Company
866 Third Avenue
New York, N.Y. 10022

Printed in the United States of America
DESIGNED BY LAURA HOUGH

For our grandchildren
with great expectations
and hopes of plenty

INTRODUCTION

This is a family collection, a collection of columns that have appeared in newspapers and magazines, spanning some twenty-one years and going from the usual growing pains of a young family in the past to my present days of glory as a grandmother.

It started on November 29, 1966, a Tuesday a little more than a month after my fortieth birthday. I obviously wanted to make a statement. I wrote a column about what I knew best: I wrote about myself. Looking back on it, I'm not sure why. Perhaps I was startled by being forty. Perhaps I thought it was about time I did something other than caring for four children, an old farmhouse, a most satisfactory husband. Whatever, the *Baltimore Sun* accepted me as a weekly columnist, and this desire to express myself continues. There are moments, granted, when I would do almost anything not to write: scrub the kitchen floor, polish brass, clean out closets. But once I get myself to the typewriter and I have figured out the first paragraph, I am at home with myself. Writing gives me pleasure, it gives me pride. And although I consider myself a private person, I have never regretted that when I was forty I went public.

My subject is always the same: my family, our life and times, our surroundings. Little wonder, really. As a very young girl, a very shy young girl who read late into the night by flashlight, my favorite author was Louisa May Alcott. One of our daughters is named Beth, which may have been borrowed, not so unconsciously, straight from *Little Women*. (I, on the other hand, always thought of myself as Jo.) And as a seventeen-year-old I was enthralled with John Galsworthy's *Forsyte Saga,* his intriguing web of family life that went on and on.

While my model authors wrote fiction, I write fact—about the everyday life at Thornhill Farm, the whims and fancies of the Hardie children, Todd, Louise, Tommy and Beth, and how they grew. I don't think they minded when I went on about what they wore on Halloween, or when I recorded their innocent pursuits. But then again I never did hold an editorial conference with a nine-year-old. I just tried to write what came naturally, the best ideas coming unannounced, just happening.

As I read these columns now, some seem dated, others seem timeless. There are names from the past—Francis Chichester; John-John, a little boy whose father was president; Green Stamps. (Remember Green Stamps?) Some years, like wine, are more provocative, more full-bodied. Some years have more columns than others. This is because I borrowed some of the column material for my first book, *Hollyhocks, Lambs and Other Passions: A Memoir of Thornhill Farm,* which was published by Atheneum in 1985.

In 1971 I was offered a job at *House & Garden* magazine, as the Baltimore contributing editor. Not as a columnist, but as a house detective. I found houses, we photographed them, I wrote the copy. I also wrote about travels, and whatever feature I could convince the editors they needed. Eventually I gave up my column in *The Baltimore Sun,* which I had written for seven years. And it wasn't until May 1980 that a personal column of mine appeared in *House & Garden.* There were reasons. Until then it hadn't been the right time for the magazine, or the right time for me.

House & Garden had always had columns. How to decorate, how to garden, what to eat. They added spice, a garnish to one's lifestyle. But they weren't a personal insight into life itself. Nor do I think the magazine was interested in that type of writing. In 1980, nine years after I started writing for the magazine, I decided to try to write about our family's life in the country. It had all become even more important to me. Anyone who has read my first book knows that our son Tommy died in 1975, at the age of nineteen. For me, this changed everything—how I wrote, how I lived, my priorities. After five years of grief, I figured Tommy would want me to get on with it. The first column I wrote was about his raspberries. It was accepted and from May 1980 on I was a monthly columnist for *House & Garden.* I happened to be there at the right time. The "family" was making a comeback, and "country" was definitely in.

I wrote this column for three years, until *House & Garden* changed their format. Without missing a month, I started writing for *House Beautiful* magazine in January 1983. Now titled *From Thornhill Farm,* the column continues.

And so do my readers, thank heavens. I receive letters from everywhere. I've learned about parts of America that I must admit I never knew existed. These letters are my geography lessons, these letters are instant friendship. The writers, since they read my column, know all about me, so they tell me about themselves. Sometimes I laugh, sometimes I cry. It's amazing how often priorities and families are the same. I remind the young of their mothers or their grandmothers, and I remind older readers of themselves. If ever I dare express the foolish notion that I might be different from anyone else, these letters put me in my place, very nicely so.

These readers have asked for another book, a collection of my columns. Some have even taken the trouble to paste my monthly columns into a scrapbook. I find this all very flattering, and surprising as well. I hope they enjoy these twenty-one years of the Hardie family.

Perhaps I am more sensitive to it, but I think there is a difference between the columns I wrote for newspapers before Tommy died, and those I wrote afterwards for magazines. In those early years, I think I was more fun. So very light-hearted. Life is still good, but there is someone missing. And that is always with me. Perhaps my later columns have more depth. I like to think so. Maybe a message every once in awhile—I'm not sure. I still just write what comes naturally. My readers seem to think I write of the "celebration of life." Perhaps I do. Perhaps after losing someone so very dear you realize even more how important it is to make *everything* count—even if it's merely having tea with your grandchildren. I___ look at every day in this way. I don't want to miss a thing! Big or small.

As I read again those early columns I was surprised to see how often I mentioned grandchildren. Even before we had any— even when our children were still teenagers! It must have been a deep-seated desire. Well, we now have three grandchildren, Albert, Edith and Meriwether, and they are the joys of my life. This book is for them, and for the others I hope will come into my life, this wonderfully new realm of grandmotherhood.

Dee Hardie

THORNHILL FARM
September 1987

VIEWS
from
THORNHILL

When I was twenty-one, unmarried, unburdened, with the whole world to see and to savor, I read in a slick magazine that you really aren't a woman until thirty. Remembering that, thirty wasn't bad. In fact, I suspect I was looking forward to it. Forty isn't bad either. It's just hard to believe.

It's even harder for my husband. The little girl he married sixteen years ago is now a forty-year-old woman. The shock shows whenever he's taking home our evening baby-sitters and he keeps saying, "Mrs. Hardie just turned forty, would you believe it!" I really wouldn't mind, except that all their mothers are younger. He, by the way, is five years older than I, but then he's better looking.

I could point out to him that Marie Antoinette lost her head at thirty-eight. But since I seemed to have lost mine often during my thirties, it wouldn't be much of a consolation to either of us.

It's easier to count when you're forty. For instance, forty plus twenty-five equals sixty-five, a terrifying thought! But at least you know where you stand—or hope to be standing later on.

When you're nineteen, you haven't got time to count; when you're twenty-nine or thirty-nine, you're on the brink and just don't bother. Round numbers are infinitely much better than round figures, another addition that seems to come with age.

I could have turned back the clock. In fact, I was told to do just that by a glamorous friend, age unknown. We'll call her Mrs.

Dorian Gray. Well, Dory Gray said the moment you move to a new place, as I did thirteen years ago, is the time to erase a few years. Who will know whether you're twenty-seven or twenty-five? Who will care, thought I? But to keep the records straight I wrote to my sister—younger by four years—to let her know she might think she was twenty-three, but she was barely twenty-one.

My New England conscience started reconsidering. It's a pretty good joke now. But what of the later years? No, I would rather be hopefully called an attractive forty than a ragged thirty-five—if anyone ever took the time to think about it.

Time magazine recently thought a lot about it. They've put me in my place, merely by siphoning off the years forty to sixty, designating them as the "middle ages." It is true many are younger, all those astronauts and Barbra Streisand. Bobby Kennedy, I might add, is a few months older.

More than fringe benefits, there are certain graces to being forty. You don't seem in such a hurry. You have time to figure out what you haven't done—or have done. This time around let the *younger* mothers decorate the school fair. No, I cannot collect another penny.

Our children, certainly out of diapers but not yet in the driver's seat, are a lovely age. Our house is at peace. Built in 1843 and rejuvenated by us in 1956, it does not need another new kitchen, nor can it stretch another cubic foot.

Part of the fun, and I do like occasions, is that I share my birthday with a great gang—General Eisenhower, Jimmy Doolittle and the Battle of Hastings. When you're inconspicuously, even remotely connected with history, it helps?

In sixteen years of marriage I have gained five pounds, four children, three tennis partners, two cars and one husband. I like where I am.

This just may be my Renaissance. Who knows, a mink coat might be looming in the future. I *am* old enough.

November 1966

About a month after we moved here to the country I met an elderly grande dame at tea who asked me where we lived. When I told her, she said, "Oh, so you're the ones who bought that lemon!" Well, that lemon has been our home for eleven years and it is the apple of our eye.

Our parents probably felt the same way as she did. Parents always want something better for their children. Our house *was* an eyesore, but to us it was love at first site. Henry Thoreau once wrote, "I would rather be all by myself on a pumpkin than crowded on a velvet cushion." We felt much the same way.

Living in this old farmhouse, built in 1843, we feel we have a part of history, filled with the presence of our family. We own fifty-nine acres of America, "more or less," as the deed reads, and it is all ours.

The four children particularly love our woods—ten acres of white oak, elm, hemlock and laurel. It was here during the Civil War that the owner, a Southern sympathizer, hid his horses from the Yankees. The children insist that on dark, gray days you can still hear hoofbeats.

Our house, half stone, half wood, is high on a hill in the center of this pie-shaped Thornhill Farm. We are always conscious of living on the land. Every window from every side of the house frames a slice of our life, and farm . . . the sheep in line, one after another, wandering down to the front pasture; the young ponies chasing one another over the fields; the winter pink skies at five in the afternoon with the almost-Oriental horizon of silhouetted trees; the very green of spring. . . .

Once everything works, there is nothing better than life in the country. Perhaps one of the happiest periods for the children came several years ago when the well went dry. Limited baths, of course, and no ancient handmaiden ever carried so much water as I. Living in the country *is* rewarding but it can also be hard work.

The thing to do is try to size up the country, rather than have the country outsize you. After eleven years we think we've learned a little. For example, every year our vegetable garden gets smaller. Starting off with a vast agricultural spread, ranging from rutabaga to melons, we now have only a tidy patch of lettuce.

We've tried as many animals; every shape except kangaroo, says a friend. But now it's only a flock of sheep and the ponies. One February, years ago, I even called my husband Tom, then in Mexico in the midst of some important board meeting or other, just to tell him that the pigs were out. The pigs were *always* getting out. We no longer have pigs.

After working so hard and long on an old house you may sometimes forget its real purpose: to shelter, not to show, a home, a hearth. The house mustn't become more important than the people within. And we've had lots of good times in this Thornhill Farm. A friend became a bride here and this is where our son Tommy was christened.

The wedding was held only a few weeks after we moved in. With the house still unfinished in many ways, I painted the living room white the day before the ceremony. Since we had no lawn at that point, we threw grass seed instead of rose petals and rice as the newlyweds left.

The christening was in June a year later for Tommy, and by then we had a lawn. We even had the baptismal water brought home by my mother-in-law from the River Jordan. She thought we should boil it, and boil it we did—completely away. So little Tommy, resplendent in a white suit and bare feet, was christened with water from his own farm.

December 1966

I n our family, you can never tell when we'll start thinking about Christmas cards.

More than just choosing them, we have to produce them, for we invariably send photographs of ourselves. Rain or sleet or missing teeth, that photograph gets taken. Every year. And every year I ask myself the same searching question . . . who in the world wants to see our children *again* this year?

Self-perpetuation always wins out, or is it self-indulgence? Anyhow I think we continue in the same old pattern because *we* like photographs of other people's children on Christmas cards. You see how the children have grown over the year, you see the changes, you also sometimes see the insides of their houses. That to me is more interesting than a Currier & Ives snow scene.

Some Christmas cards are so beautiful you can hardly bear to throw them away. Those benefiting the United Nations or some special purpose are definitely worthwhile. But could you please tell me what a black poodle with a sequined collar has to do with the spirit of Christmas?

We've never had any animals on our Christmas cards, only our four lively offspring. And it hasn't always been easy. Although the photograph turns out to be the main attraction, I feel there should be some feeling of Christmas, often very slight.

One year we had them hanging from a peach tree, along with some Christmas balls . . . another year all snug in our patch-work-quilted bed with stocking caps and wreaths around their necks. Then I felt we had to go a little further . . . a manger scene. Since this was going to be an indoor shot we got an outside photographer. Poor boy. And we did it a year ahead.

I particularly wanted the children with the newborn lambs. However, our lambs arrived in January and Christmas was the next December, hence we were really going to be organized *that* Christmas. Adorable lambs and little children; how could you miss?

We had the lambs and the children and hay all over the place, even a horse sticking his head through a barn window. We had everything except the Wise Men. But *we* weren't too smart. I had expected too much. We took that Christmas photo over again—instead, the children merely walking across a hill, with the magnificent Worthington Valley in the background.

About three summers ago we were in France, and this was the year we would be all "Noel" and Eiffel Tower—next to Baltimore's Washington Monument, my favorite landmark. Beth, our youngest, was not with us but I planned to superimpose her from the very top, along with some holly berries. The rest of us would be sitting in front.

On a sunny morning we raced to the Champ-de-Mars in Paris. Knowing full well our taxi driver wasn't Henri Cartier-Bresson, we explained that with this fine German camera all you have to do is click. *"Ne bougez pas, ne bougez pas,"* he kept saying. And move we did not. We didn't do anything but hope for the best.

It was with great expectations and the sound of carols in our ears that we later looked at the three rolls of developed film. What we saw was not a Christmas card . . . not even the Eiffel Tower, but the San Francisco Earthquake. That was the Year We Didn't Send a Christmas Card.

This year we're hoping for better things. Again this summer we tried to take our Christmas card photograph in Europe. In fact, by our colored slides it now looks like we were searching more for Christmas than for culture. If available, I probably would have used the Holy Grail as a prop.

We finally found the right background at the Alhambra in Granada, Spain—perfectly symmetrical Moorish windows of stained glass, with each child posed in an arched window. Only later did we discover we were in the caliph's harem!

Friends receiving our cards may have visions of sugarplums dancing in their heads, but to us, this year, harem-scarem means . . . "Merry Christmas!"

December 1966

W hen I was in college, the Home Ec majors specializing in domestic sciences were all fine girls, good girls—clean, neat, no makeup, every head in a hairnet. And we, the Liberal Arts majors, thought they were all very dull!

Now, eighteen years later, I'm eating crow and they're eating duck à l'orange. They can cook. I'm just learning.

They were smarter. They knew even then where they were going—right into a kitchen. Whereas I had hoped for a detour into the world of culture, not the cuisine. And by hook and by cook and my mother-in-law's help before dinner parties, I never had to take that slice of life too seriously—until now.

But after sixteen years of marriage and four children I am suddenly the family's cook, a bride in the kitchen.

I don't expect any sympathy; nor do I want it. I've had a lot of fun not being in the kitchen. Yet to ease my conscience just a little, I do have one good excuse: I was married in Paris.

Before flying to our wedding I packaged my luggage allowance of sixty-six carefully weighed pounds, which included *the* bridal cookbook, *The Joy of Cooking* (weight: one pound). But the very day I was leaving a handsome silver cigarette box arrived from Tom's college clubmates. Its weight: one pound. Guess which ingredient was left out.

I didn't need the cookbook anyhow. We had Marie Therese. For five dollars a week, the going rate, she turned our small apartment into a five-star restaurant.

I suppose I could have stayed a little closer to Marie Therese. But come on. If you were a bride, if you were in Paris, if you were twenty-four . . . would you have stayed in the kitchen?

Now it *is* my beat. And it really isn't so bad. I've gone through the rise and fall of soufflés; I can even make a pretty good apple pie—the touch of grated lemon rind makes the difference. And roast beef is a cinch. It's just that constant, everyday chore of cooking. One *must* have an appreciative audience.

My husband is a wonderful help. He'll eat anything . . . and usually does, just when I'm preparing it. He samples a little of this, a little of that. . . .

"Dee, it needs more garlic."

"But, Tom, the children don't like garlic!"

"Well, it needs something!"

You can see how interested he is. He even rips recipes out of newspapers and magazines, thinking I can whip them up on a moment's notice. Little does he realize that for *his* recipes it takes a day to do the marketing plus a road map to find that special shop that has that special ingredient which I hope I'll only need once.

I do put a lot of thought into my menus. And it does take time, as any woman will be only too glad to tell you.

I also like to decorate the table. Frankly, I still much prefer folding napkins into shapes of swans, as do the Danes, than folding in egg whites. But now I am the cook, and a little atmosphere should help. So we often have candlelight.

Comes the moment of truth. I've prepared a monument of a meal. I might even change for dinner—like taking off my apron. We sit down. The candles sparkle, the conversation starts. . . .

"You know, Mrs. MacNeille *makes* her own butter," says Todd as he spreads a quarter of a pound of oleo on his roll.

Beth pipes up. "Mrs. Howell doesn't care how many peanut butter and jelly sandwiches we eat as long as we wash our hands."

"I like tunafish better," adds Louise.

Tommy just looks and says, even if it's chicken: "There's too much fat."

I don't argue anymore. I just throw him a carrot and he goes back to his cave.

Fortunately, our daughters *like* to be in the kitchen; they *like* to cook. The other day Beth and Louise made some delicious fortune cookies. My fortune read, "Go to Hollywood—the walk will do you good."

Well, that's one way to get out of the kitchen.

January 1967

Naming a new child can often cause discussions more heated than the baby's formula. It certainly did in our case.

When it became evident fourteen years ago that we were to become parents for the first time, there were many words, even a few tears, in addition to the joy. Long lines of genealogy were studied, as well as the farthest limbs of the family tree. After all, names are very important. It's the first thing anyone knows about you.

Mothers care a great deal about this. Fathers don't care as much, but in the long run they still like to get in their two cents or, at least, a grandparent's name. (Some, hoping for reciprocal kindness, remember that rich great-uncle.)

That's perfectly all right as long as your wife likes your grandfather's or grandmother's name. John, Mary, Elizabeth or David are forever, but you've got to admit Hortense or Agatha or Horatio do show their age.

My husband said he didn't particularly care if his son, if it were a son, was named after him. That is, not until five days after the baby was home from the hospital. Then he changed his mind. But it was too late. At least I thought it was too late. (Fortunately our second son is our only offspring resembling his father, and the name's the same.)

Our first son has an old Maryland name that, in his case, has absolutely nothing to do with Maryland. His name is Todd. The T-o comes from Tom, my husband's name; and the d-d comes from my name, Dee. Manufactured yes, but better than looking in movie magazines. Who really wants to be Rock or Rip the rest of his life?

When in doubt there are always the dogs. Some of the nicest dogs I know in Maryland are named after grandparents. There is a noble pedigreed Chesapeake named Luke, a smaller spaniel who answers to Albert, and many female counterparts.

Actually, our spaniel Albert (pronounced *à la française,* "Al-bear") is named after my father, who takes it with the fun and affection it was meant. Sometimes this is reversed. We know a highly intelligent, beautiful young lady named after her father's boyhood dog.

Some parents have an easier choice, merely naming their children after the cities where they were born—for example, Portland, Rochester; and Florence Nightingale, who had the good luck to be in Italy at the time. There is a Philadelphia in our family, but my husband drew the line at that one. Consequently, our two daughters are happily called, after two great-grandmothers, Louise and Elizabeth.

Roman Catholic parents are also helped a bit. Since the

Council of Trent in 1563 they must give a saint's name to each child. This is certainly not difficult today as most common Christian names have now been borne by one or more saints.

Names can give you status or be stumbling blocks. It's just the way you look at it. And no matter how you plan or hope, it could all change the moment your child goes to school. You might call him Charlie but he may be Fats or Flash or Speedy or Butter-fingers the rest of his life.

I guess the best thing to do is relax and hope a rose by any other name will still smell as sweet.

Perhaps at birth you could give your children a "name certificate" guaranteeing at sixteen they could, at face value, exchange their names for one of their own choice. They probably will anyhow.

January 1967

Some months ago our nine-year-old daughter, Beth, quoted a friend's school composition which claimed . . . "Spirits, goblins, ghosts, once you've seen one, you've seen them all." I wasn't so sure; I had never seen one. And it was about time. Anyone living in a 121-year-old house, high on a hill and surrounded at night by darkened heights, deserved a ghost. And that's what I wanted . . . not a haunted house but a house with a spirit.

In England, of course, we would be too young for such

carryings-on. There, registered, tax-free ghosts fly in from far earlier centuries. But even here, in our relatively new world, a house such as ours should certainly be able to float a ghost.

There have been times, I'll admit, when I thought there was something in the air. Sometimes the wind wafts through our doors like a soulful harp; *of course* our old pine-board floors creak; and I've often heard wails of an animal that sound like a discontented wolf. (Possibly the nearby Green Spring hounds in their kennels.)

One reason I wanted a ghost was that my husband travels so much. After the children go to bed at night, what I miss is some adult conversation, someone to talk to. . . .

And as much as I enjoy male companionship, I wanted a lady ghost. But no hanky-panky enveloping my ghost. No ghost with a bone to pick, so to speak; or a cause célèbre—like looking for her lover's head. I wanted a ghost who so loved this house, her own 121 years ago, that she just wanted to return.

What an experience to have this vision appear. But I didn't want her around when my husband was home, and if she did, she didn't have to be such a vision.

There was so much to be learned—about this house, about her, her life and times in the 1840s. But first she must have a name; perhaps Deborah Bristol, called Daisy as a child.

I would ask Mistress Bristol where she came from. Did she find her new home very lonely, at least a day's coach ride from the port of Baltimore? Was Polk a good president? (*I* would have voted for Henry Clay, but then I forgot Mistress Bristol couldn't even vote.) Did she plant strawberries and apple trees? How many children did she have?

Did she make her own bonnets? And what about the new-fangled telegraph line from Baltimore to Washington? What did her husband farm? Did he think the novice Naval Academy at Annapolis would ever succeed (much less beat Army)? Did she like Emily or Charlotte Brontë better? But did she even have time to read?

Then one night, when the moon was new, she happened—she appeared. Her long gray dress must have been homespun, but it moved like chiffon; and she had the bluest of eyes. She was, I admit, very pale. But her voice was strong and clear.

"Thou has added on," she said looking beyond the living room.

"We thought we should," said I rather weakly, "what with four children and all."

"Mmmmm, *we* seemed to have managed with our six. But I *am* glad thee kept all the walls white."

"Yes," I answered, not daring to let her know our walls were white only as a background for our paintings.

She moved to the dining room. "That body of water in the side pasture . . . for the cattle? Water was always such a problem on this hill. . . ."

"Well actually, it's a wading pool. . . ."

"A what?" Then she seemed to remember her manners and said, "I do hope thee doesn't mind my speaking out. I've waited so long for this . . . and when the Spirit moves us. . . ."

How did I know I was going to get a Quaker ghost— waiting all these years for her Spirit (with a capital "S") to move here, to preach, as she was doing to me, or to pray?

Actually, she was acting quite human, not *really* liking another woman in her house. And to almost everyone, especially a ghost, there's no place like home.

February 1967

Beth's wardrobe is our own family Community Chest. In fact, almost our own United Appeal. Everyone in the family donates to it.

By "donating" I mean sneaking dresses, too short or too small, from Louise's closet or pinching Tommy's trousers which he won't wear anyhow, but would *never knowingly* will to his younger sister. Beth, age nine, by the way, is the youngest of four.

Beth is delighted by her inherited noncoordinated, nonmatching clothes ensembles. In fact, she was a Mod even before the Mods were Mod, mixing stripes with plaid, plaid with floral designs, dots with a dash.

I certainly never anticipated, not even in my wildest dreams, the combinations she would concoct. Some mornings I objected, not so tactfully, to her selections. She, not so silently, stood firm—if you can call jumping on the bed standing firm. Such a battle, so early in the morning, before the first cup of coffee and while trying to make car pools, was just too much.

I finally admitted defeat. I also told her teacher to try not to notice her rather unusual choices of costumes. And anyhow, what *is* good taste? Especially to a nine-year-old child?

As she once said when she was a very young six, "Everything doesn't *have* to match." Well, that's very hard for a mother to learn.

It's not that Beth hasn't had opportunities to know firsthand clothes firsthand. Oh those lovely, little ladylike, genteel dresses from England! The bodice smocked elaborately, the perfect touches of the *right* colors, the dresses grandmothers love so well. Well, that was Beth's first big rebellion!

No, she would not wear anything that was smocked. No, she would not wear those "baby" dresses. And she had so many, including those of her older sister. Louise's had been treated with royal care; they were for wearing only to birthday parties, on Sunday, and for formal family photographs. But the dresses were not for Beth. No, indeed; she was much more in tune with Todd's button-down shirt and Louise's plaid jumper.

Nor would she wear those neat English red party shoes. The toes were too round, the back of the heels too hard. Beth, unconsciously perhaps, was boycotting Britain's best. She is never too concerned with the current pacesetters—like Caroline's short skirts and John-John's long sideburns. Beth is, I guess, an American primitive.

And she often looks the part. Pants, long and usually of corduroy, always from a brother, are her idea of the perfect costume for almost any occasion. She sees no reason why, if you wear pants to the barn on Saturday, you can't wear pants to a birthday party later that same Saturday. Pants are forever, like from 7:00 in the morning until 9:00 at night. And sometimes under the covers.

Oddly enough, Beth has a strange, puritanical streak when it comes to skirt lengths. Her one edict seems to be that hers are all too short. I like mine high, she likes hers low. Here I am forty going on eighteen when it comes to skirt lengths, and Beth is a little old woman.

This winter we did buy her a beautiful light-blue quilted ski jacket. It matched her eyes. We knew she would be thrilled. A brand new ski jacket, her first, just for Beth. A ski jacket that had never been worn by anyone else.

Well, within three days Louise was wearing it. When I investigated, it seems that Beth, completely on her own, completely behind my back, had bartered, had traded her new jacket for Louise's old red one, purchased two years ago, now slightly limp, slightly soiled, but much more beloved.

Beth, it turns out, likes being a secondhand rose.

Somehow, somewhere, with these early influences, I feel I must be saving my future son-in-law a terrific amount of money.

March 1967

In this day of instant everything, it seems silly to try to save anything longer than tomorrow. Ethel Barrymore never did. She never saved one press clipping, never had a scrapbook, never lovingly flipped the pages of her book of memories. Well . . . if Winston Churchill proposed to me—as he did to her—I guess I could remember that, too, without any scrapbook or faded hearts and flowers.

But as that moment of history was never on his knees to me, I am a collector of the past. Perhaps scavenger would be a better name. Ever since I learned the magic of mixing flour and water I have been pasting scrapbooks.

My first scrapbook was a hodge-podge of pressed leaves from summer camp. I then graduated to a fat volume on Katharine Hepburn, the photographs clipped from every movie magazine available. And believe me, when I was fourteen she was some cover girl!

The habit still persists and I'm still in the paste pot. I have a scrapbook, a single scrapbook mind you, for every child, plus a scrapbook on this house. This must be an indication of something. And I'm afraid to find out what. It does weigh on my conscience— all those heavy books. Imagine fourteen years of Todd Hardie, twelve years of Louise, ten of Tommy and nine of Beth. I guess I could consider them my growth stocks.

But the problem is that I'm always a year behind. And to catch up I must spend at least a week in solitary confinement, invade the local five-and-tens for all their rubber cement, relocate the best scissors in the house (the only scissors) and wonder if we might become addicted to TV dinners.

It's a terrible responsibility.

But, aha—I have discovered new avenues for my memories, a much quicker solution to preserving memorabilia. Now I merely tape *everything* on the inside of our new kitchen cabinet doors.

When I reach for some spices I open the cabinet door and am immediately cheered by Ned's family Christmas card showing them all on a rope hammock. And how about a little boy with a wide smile—that's my godson Patrick!

In fact, I have so many photographs taped to those cabinet doors that it looks like Central Casting. What studio needs five handsome young airmen under a palm tree in the Philippines? Well, you can't have them. That's my memory. That's Tom and his buddies twenty-three years ago.

Not all my records go back that far. These cabinet doors, fake walnut, are only a year old. And so rest assured, I have not taped Todd's first tooth or Tommy's last curl.

I *have* taped, on the left of the canned goods, an elegant purple elephant cut out by Beth, and a breathtaking peacock feather someone gave to Louise. Beauty such as this should be enjoyed— every time you get a can of soup.

The more orderly commitments of life are also inside the cabinet doors . . . those little white stiff cards telling you the next appointment with the orthodontist . . . or scribbled messages which hopefully will help you get to some of those meetings . . . some self-adhesive Green Stamps . . . and torn theater stubs to remind you to get the same wonderful seats for the Ice Follies next year.

The china cabinet also conceals some marvelous modern art. Never will there be more primitive or more sophisticated art than that of a child. As ours get older, unhappily the pictures get calmer. No longer do they bring home the wild forests of Rousseau. Now crayons are kept within the lines.

My friend Alice, another curator of children's art, has *her* gallery extending to the outside of her refrigerator as well. Her children, I might add, are more artistic than ours.

A year ago when we built our new kitchen I had unlimited space, the interior of eight cabinet doors, clean, sterile and quite boring. Now when I open these doors, I have a patchwork quilt of wonderful clutter.

I do have some room left, above the taped menu for Bessie Bogan's stuffed eggplant and green rice ring. But from now on I must be more selective; space is getting tight. Yet, how can one pick or choose? They either do or don't become memories. And you can't tell right away.

The thing about these memories, I can open or close them any time I want.

April 1967

Yesterday, Louise's braids were cut off and her braces put on.

Louise is twelve. And unlike Sampson her strength didn't disappear, but a large part of her childhood certainly did.

We started braiding Louise's hair four years ago. She was rounder, shorter, blonder, and her hair didn't quite know which way to go. So to keep it in line, we put it in braids. And for the first few months those braids weren't really braids; they were short stubs of hair just daring me to get all those loose wisps pulled together at one time.

I had always wanted a little girl in braids, for to me little girls in braids are rather special. They're ageless. And although Louise keeps time with the Beatles and uses Magic Markers instead of quill pens, she could have been from any era, especially in her braids and her blue school tunic. Old-fashioned girls are still the best. Ask any father. . . .

As her braids got longer I had some wonderful ideas—like weaving them with bright plaid ribbons or wrapping them around her ears or twirling them around her head. But Louise always knew exactly where her braids were going to go—straight down, down her back.

Beth, her younger sister by three years, naturally wanted

braids too; wanted to be just like Louise. So at the same age, eight, we started braiding Beth's hair. But some little girls are just born to be flappers, should always have short hair. Beth is that kind of child.

Her hair wouldn't cooperate, wouldn't conform. And when it wasn't in braids it completely concealed her right eye. When Irene Castle first bobbed her hair in 1922, starting the mode for short hair, she must have been thinking of future Beths.

We suggested that Beth have her hair cut. We then threatened. Tom even thought we might cut it in her sleep. We begged. We finally had to bribe. And for a very large sum Beth had her hair cut. Now when I trim it, I not only have to sit on her, I have to tip her.

For Louise there were no such shenanigans. Her hair just got longer and longer. And she had quite a few offers for her braids—one was a whole summer of ice-cream cones. I've also noticed an irresistible tendency for people of all ages to tug affectionately at a little girl's braids.

Her two brothers, however, did more than that. It was their first line of attack. Get the braids, pull hard and don't let go until you see the whites of your mother's eyes. Now we've lost the braids, but maybe she'll win some battles.

Last summer in Europe Louise's braids fooled a lot of people. Beth too still had hers then. Two little girls in braids and blazers were never considered American. Scandinavian? English? German? But then we opened our mouths, and the truth came out. We're as patriotic as the next, putting our flag out on holidays, and our living room is red, white and blue, but it *was* fun to be incognito for a while.

You'll find little girls in braids are patient little girls. They have to be! What with their mothers running around every morning making breakfast, wrapping lunches, looking for lost Latin books, and *finally* getting around to braiding hair.

Louise probably should have braided her own hair, but as agile as she is—she turns a marvelous somersault—she simply could not learn how to braid her own hair, unlike her friends Sarah and Cindy.

Our morning conversations frequently sounded a bit like this: "Louise, please stand still . . . Louise, turn your head . . . all right, Louise, braid your *own* hair!" *Which* of course both of us knew she couldn't do.

Coming up will be a summer of separation as Louise is going to camp in New Hampshire for the first time. And even though Indians once canoed around in braids, a squaw isn't going to be there to braid Louise's hair. Sentiment is overruled—off with the braids!

Over the past four years I've probably braided Louise's hair about 1,450 times (give or take the few mornings I slipped up on Saturdays). No longer will I be brushing her hair, and I'll miss the quick kiss when I've finished. I'll miss the neatness, the freshness of a little girl in braids.

Yesterday I may have lost a little girl in braids, but I gained a daughter in braces. Yes, there'll be many more bridges to cross, many more bridges to cross year by year.

April 1967

Oh, the moments I've had in the theater while doing the dishes! Glorious moments!

Here I am over the kitchen sink removing breakfast leftovers, and Zero Mostel is bellowing forth in *Fiddler on the Roof,* or Rex Harrison is slowly making up his mind about Eliza Doolittle.

And so you now have my only household hint—turn on the record player, loud. Housework, never a favorite habit or hobby of mine, improves immensely if I keep playing records. It becomes more like a game, a stage rather than a labor camp.

It's not really an original idea. I mean it's been done before—for cows and horses. Out here a dairy barn has its ceiling painted light blue and the radio *always* on. And the late Elizabeth Arden piped music into her horses' stalls. And she won a Kentucky Derby!

Well, my track around the house is no horse race, but I move pretty fast, thanks to my musical accompaniments.

Since the only stereo speaker is in the living room, I have to turn it up very high to hear it throughout the house. Anyone chancing by is blasted out by my sound of music. With my husband at work, the children at school, I'm alone on center stage.

Well, not exactly alone. Sometimes I'm in the cast of *Mame,* or I'm one of Herman's Hermits, or I'm doing a twin bill with Barbra Streisand. Sometimes I'm *even* Barbra Streisand.

Choreography, of course, goes with my household "routines." But Jerome Robbins has no need to stomp off any stage. My original choreography is a mixture of a catchy box step, a few twists, a shortened tango and a one-two-three waltz. A limited repertoire, yes, but as exuberant as any chorus girl trying to make good.

And that's how my house gets cleaned!

Once I've left the kitchen and Broadway, I spruce up the living room. And there's nothing like "Everything's Coming Up Roses" for tucking in slipcovers, watering the geraniums, picking up sprawled newspapers and puffing up sofa pillows.

I also need youth that early in the morning. So next I play Les Djinn Singers, sixty *jeunes filles,* ages thirteen to sixteen. They sing only in French, but I still get their message—it's a wonderful, wonderful world, be glad!

For picking up the children's rooms or scrubbing heavy pots and pans—those I left in the kitchen earlier when I wasn't so sprightly—you need a fast, lively beat. I find the Tijuana Brass most inspiring. The things I can get done with "The Spanish Flea" or "Marching Through Madrid." Somehow with their leader, Herb Alpert, playing in the background I don't mind as much when I find Tommy has another hole in his school sweater.

I save my waltzes for mopping. One-two-three, one-two-three, around-the-corner and onward . . . one-two-three, one-two-three. For the very high spots I use revival music. I just raise my arms and wave the dust right away from those cornices. And I really feel noble when I wax our old pine floors to the strains of Barbra singing "My Man."

My husband, on the other hand, does not approve of my musical selections. Maybe that's another reason why I play them during the day. His ears are bent much more favorably toward comfy little numbers like Haydn's Symphony 94 in G or Telemann's Concerto in B Flat Major for three oboes and three violins. (But then he doesn't have to do the housework either.) His only concession to *modern* music is Benny Goodman.

And I can see his point. There *is* a place in my world for his music. I always play his symphonies in the spring on a Saturday morning with the front windows wide open. There is nothing like a rousing symphony to help you attack your garden after its long winter sleep. I dig deeper, I rake with fervor, and my movements are absolutely allegro—or is it andante?

Whatever, maestro, play on!

May 1967

Here on the farm we have hills to climb, crickets to hear and frogs to catch; yet this is the summer our children are going off to camp.

The two boys have been before. And without them that long summer of unnatural quiet and unbelievable peace was especially lonely for those of us left at home.

But when we picked them up at the end of the summer we saw two boys who stood straighter, were even glad to see their sisters, and knew how to flip flapjacks over an open fire (though not necessarily over a stove). They not only made better beds, they were better boys. And so that's why we're again sending our children to camp.

The camps, however, may have other ideas, other hopes. Todd is going to a ranch camp in Arizona where, according to the brochure, "he will develop an appreciation of a number of fundamental relationships including: (1) being right as opposed to the easier route of adjusting to the pressures of a peer group in order to be always popular; (2) comfort in relationship to the capacities for coping with adversity," and, phew, on through four more objectives.

We might not even recognize our own son, much less his peers, at the end of the summer!

Louise's camp in New Hampshire simply states that "it is a place where a girl may develop her special talents at her own pace purely for the pleasure it affords her."

And Tommy's camp, on the same Squam Lake, merely says, "*However,* it must be remembered that healthy, vigorous boys are not apt to be frequent letter writers."

Todd's Arizona camp is the only one with both boy and girl campers. We wondered about this at first. But then Todd, age fourteen, carefully explained to us that the whole world was co-ed. That made it much clearer. Much clearer until I read in the twenty-page brochure that "simple hairdos are preferred for girls, and any makeup which is obvious or in questionable taste, such as eye shadow, is prohibited at all times." The Wild West is *certainly* being tamed in strange ways.

This will obviously be a summer of learning. And in the course of the summer Todd will have a chance to become a Straw-boss or a Buckaroo; Louise is going to be a Rabbit or a Duck; Tommy, a Blue or a Gray, and Beth will be Beth, as she is staying home.

And thinking you know what's going to happen to your children is one thing, but getting them ready for it is paddling a different canoe.

Maybe it's because it's way out there, but Todd is required to take twice as much as the other children. This includes, among other things, six pairs of Levis or other blue jeans, ten T-shirts, twelve handkerchiefs and fourteen pairs of skivvies.

When you go shopping for six pairs of Levis you realize that your older son has suddenly left size 16 trousers forever. He is now involved with the hieroglyphics of young men's measurements—getting a pair of pants that combines the right waist with the right length, at the same time.

Some of his Levis are 29/30, others are 31/30; but maybe

I should have gotten 32/32 as the camp laundry is going to shrink them all anyhow. Fortunately, Tommy is still size 12, good old dependable size 12, as is Louise. And Beth is still at home in assorted sizes.

Now that the trunks are complete, how about the identifications? What every mother does every evening weeks before camp starts, the endless sessions of sewing on name tags. There are some you can iron on, but that seems slightly suspicious. Or you could merely print their names with Magic Markers. But is that cricket? Those little white sewn-on name tags do seem to exert more authority. They are, after all, silent signatures of ownership.

Who says so? Boys might be able to read, but boys will be boys and I wonder who Bobby Wilson might be? I have three of his shirts from two years ago.

Yet name tags, if nothing else, are terrific bargains. What else can you buy these days, custom-made, one hundred for only $1.50? Since name tags *are* so reasonable and since it does get awfully boring sewing on the same familiar names over and over again, I just might consider pseudonyms for the children's camp clothes. At the end of the summer it doesn't seem to matter whose name is on what.

I like to imagine the expression on the face of the camp laundress when she discovers she is soaking the shirt of the GREEN HORNET, or washing the pants of the PRINCE OF WALES, or ironing CARRIE NATION's middy or folding the jumper of URSULA ANDRESS.

They'll probably all end up in the camp Lost-and-Found box anyway, and even a camp Lost-and-Found needs a little class!

June 1967

T he last time I was in New York I had lunch with Nancy Scarsdale. Nancy Scarsdale isn't really her name, of course, maiden or married, but it's the only way my husband Tom can keep my college classmates straight—by their home-towns. So my group includes such geographical beauties as Nancy Scarsdale, Katey South Bend, Barbara New Rochelle, Sally Welles-ley Hills, and Chilly Buffalo.

In our carefree, collegiate past Nancy Scarsdale and I went through a lot together—Dartmouth Winter Carnivals, Eighteenth-Century Literature, German measles, assorted blind dates, scrimpy lunches at Chock Full O' Nuts when we first worked in New York and finally her wedding. Strong ties, indeed.

Then why did it take me fifteen years to call her up? Perhaps I now have more time, more time to think about the good friends I once had. Perhaps I was just curious. Or was it that I thought my hair looked especially nice that day? New York does give me a bravado and buoyancy I don't always have back home on the range in the kitchen.

Nancy was one of the wiser graduates. She had never gone back for reunions. Reunions are fine and dandy for those who keep up, but if you can't remember the name of your sophomore dorm much less the second line of your Alma Mater, what are you going to talk about?

What a silly question! Children, of course! At my fifth

reunion, my first, there was a steady stream of candid, cunning photographs of children who all looked the same. So did their mothers.

We hadn't changed much in five years. We were still in blue jeans, our hair was still a sight and we were still young enough to talk far into the night. And at that point the other man in our lives was Dr. Spock. We were, in a way, majoring in Pablum, minoring in the past.

At our tenth reunion we all looked much better—or at least we thought we did. Our figures were beginning to take shape again, our hair was not only coiffed, it was of different colors, and our children were now the ones in blue jeans.

But reunions still do not ring true if your really good old buddies are not there. You find yourself desperately trying to be a pal to someone you couldn't stand in Freshman Composition. Forced friendships, even for a weekend, are tiring, especially against the background of a whole galaxy of talking women.

And momentary roommates are just as trying. My weekend roommate was a blonde who wore golden charm bracelets, almost up to her humerus (Biology 102). When she turned in bed, so did all her bracelets, all through the night. She also snored. *That* was my last college reunion.

As Nancy Scarsdale had never been part of this after-college search for the fountain of youth and had lived a few years in California as well, I hadn't seen her in a long, long time, and was looking forward to it.

We agreed to meet at Tiffany's in New York. (Amazingly enough she still had a wedding present credit!) And if you get lost at Tiffany's there are lots of detectives to help you out. You can't miss them. The detectives are all those men who keep their hats on inside.

She came, we hugged and then I noticed her cheek was bleeding. It seems in the get-acquainted embrace my pointed earring had pierced her cheek. It wasn't, I admit, the best of beginnings. But the bleeding stopped and the conversation flowed once we arrived at our restaurant—no longer counter chairs at everybody's Chock

Full O' Nuts, but a table reserved by Nancy at A La Fourchette (French 104).

She admitted she had only been there once before, and I admitted I couldn't see. It *was* dark in that intimate little bistro. But perhaps that helped hide the added lines of added years. We both looked, we thought, remarkably well. And after a drink we looked even better.

"You know I usually only drink this at home. . . . I know what you mean. . . . Bob, I'm afraid, has lost some hair. . . . Well Tom has gained some pounds. . . . I'm so happy you called. . . . Aren't you glad you don't understand the New Math. . . . Where are the girls going to camp? . . . I wish they could meet. . . . How do you *ever* get away?"

Within the magic space of one and a half hours we had not only cleaned our plates, we had catalogued each other's past. I knew her children as if they had grown up next door, and she knew mine probably better than I did.

And we learned again the beautiful truth, almost everyone is in the same boat—and it's a marvelous voyage if you can just stop every once in a while in midstream and compare it with someone else. It makes you feel much better, absolutely First Class.

June 1967

W ith our four children last summer in Europe, our behavior pattern of eating was entirely different from the trip we are now taking alone. Although we momentarily removed them from their normal Glyndon environment, their conditioned reflexes were so strong that gastronomically we never left home. But just try to find a hamburger in Spain! However, we did get to know ham sandwiches intimately from the Costa del Sol north to the Costa Brava.

Our children's simple tastes were actually a great help economically. We managed to sleep in some handsome hotels, but often we just couldn't afford to eat. Hotel food in Europe can be much more expensive than the lodgings, especially when multiplied by six. Also, the serving of food is like a stage play with a very large cast. Our children, usually with impatient stomachs, wanted to eat, not watch a three-course extravaganza.

So we started to import. We would shop in the local market place and arrive back at a fine hotel like a caravan of humped camels. Our humps were camping bags filled with delicacies—cold lobster, hard-boiled eggs designed like tiny pigs, sausage, ham of course, artichokes curved into roses, and freshly baked bread. For a few glorious moments "they" even forgot hamburgers.

French bread, however, does make the most circumstantial

crumbs of evidence possible. After eating in our room I would be down on my hands and knees destroying the clues. In a grand hotel with chandeliers shaped like palm trees of diamonds and a telephone by every bathtub you cannot let the three maids who clean your room know you live by bread alone . . . or almost.

This summer we are on different menus. We sit in restaurants. And all of them chosen with much care. Back in Baltimore my husband Tom belongs to a self-styled gourmet luncheon club called Les Fines Gueules which translated loosely means, they think, "the fine palates." Whatever the name, Tom wanted to eat well, for after all you have to have something to tell the boys back home.

Our first adventure was at the L'Oustau de Baumaniere in Les Baux-en-Provence. This three-star restaurant has five crossed forks and knives as well. In all of France there are only nine restaurants that can boast of these precious symbols. Located in a magnificent valley setting, the restaurant consists mostly of a simple terrace. You notice a hushed silence, as if in a cathedral, the moment you enter. Such reverence. Such prices!

We decided on a fish, and one vegetable. The trout, served alone and rather slender, was superb. Then we had the anticipation of the artichokes. We ordered *Mousseline d'artichauts* for the substantial sum, considering it was only a green vegetable, of 9.75 new French francs each.

The great moment arrived and so did our artichokes—for each of us, three plops of artichoke hearts absolutely purée. The taste was slightly reminiscent of artichokes past, but it looked exactly like baby food, particularly like the split-pea mush our children used to spray across the kitchen. For a total of four dollars we had vegetated into our second childhood.

The next day we went back to our necessary budget, and in St. Gilles, a small village near Arles, we found an entire three-course meal for only five francs. I chose snails, Tom decided on chicken. I love snails, strong with garlic, and the usual six served in restaurants never seem enough.

Lucky me, a bonanza. I was presented with a bowl of 41

snails—41, in a slippery tomato sauce. And my only eating implement was something like a rose cutting with a large thorn. Snails are the only known delicacy Tom refuses to eat.

Now we are in Spain and have discovered it is better not to ask what you're eating. Last night we went to Casa Toni with Señor and Señora Paya who wanted very much to provide Tom with serious food for thought. After a tasty tortilla Tom had *Tripa con santaina* and I had a whole plateful of *pulpitos*.

Well, he can call them *pulpitos;* I call them octopi. Baby yes, but octopi nevertheless. Squid may have ten arms (two longer than the others) and octopus only eight, but who would count those ugly little legs? My plate was overflowing with miniature mollusks.

After each bite Señor Paya would glance at me to see my reaction. Now I'm only human. What are you going to do when your host, who looks like a young Rudolph Valentino with long sideburns and the brownest of eyes, turns to you and says eagerly, "You like?"

Like! My heavens, I ate them as if they were peanuts!

August 1967

Most people are born with certain senses. I happen to have limited eyesight, but fine ears. Fine ears that often hear too much. But they don't help me at all when it comes to my sense of direction.

I can't get down on my knees and put my ear to the ground like Daniel Boone to hear a trickle from a tributary of the mighty Mississippi or hear the Indians riding in from the west. *I* have to rely on other tactics.

North, south, east and west don't mean a thing to me; it's the lefts and rights that count. And it doesn't matter what you're born with, if you don't know where you're going.

In addition to a cookbook for two, I think brides moving to a new, strange city like Baltimore should have the benefit of a friendly surveying course from some friendly surveyor to get the lay of the land. But, unfortunately, nothing like this is offered. I'm sure there's a silent honorable code among local men to tell their wives as little as possible about their new city just to keep them where they belong—at home.

I came here pre–Henry Barnes, which doesn't mean a thing except something to talk about with New York cab drivers. Henry's rerouting of Baltimore traffic didn't ruffle my feathers at all. One-way streets *are* more comforting.

My particular end of the world several years ago was the

Johns Hopkins Hospital, where I took assorted children for assorted ailments. I am very grateful indeed for all those clinics, but getting there was another thing. It *is* big, and it's hard to miss, but all those little jigsaw piecemeal streets *are* baffling.

But now I've got it conquered. I go straight until I come to the first hamburger stand, then I turn left, passing the graveyard on the right until I come to the fire house on the corner, quickly to the right, straight to the dome.

Fortunately for me there are other women who don't speak the language of the compass any better than I do. We can communicate. We can, if necessary, find each other.

But I do so admire those women who, when inviting you to their homes for the first time, quick-as-a-flash rattle off, "We live two miles west of the Falls Road on the east side of the Mantua Mill Road, one mile north of Tufton Avenue, and a mile and a half south of Butler Road." Directions such as that are *really* the quickest way to a man's heart!

I should have taken a clue. When I invite people to our house and give directions I still like to include a little lore; makes it more chummy, I think. I toss in a few landmarks, a bit of history, notice that bank of unusual deciduous trees on the left, don't miss the large house on the corner at Shawan, those lovely red bricks were brought over as ballast on English ships, and so on and so on.

But no one ever gets here. Or if they do, they either feel victorious or furious!

Tom has now given me a line of directions to memorize, telling exactly where I live, just like a child going to school on the first day. But in case I fluff a tenth of a mile or so when describing the approximate distance (fractions are another one of my pitfalls), for insurance I now put semaphore signals on our mailbox at the end of our road.

Sometimes it's a white handkerchief, other times a large paper flower or balloons or a warped tennis racquet; it depends on the occasion. It probably would be easier, but not half as much fun, to paint our name on the mailbox. But then that would make it *too* easy.

I know the sun rises in the east and sets in the west, if I put my mind to it. That does take care of one set of directions, but what about the other? If anyone ever asks me if our house has a southern exposure, I pretend I don't hear.

Tommy, our younger boy who knows a lot of boy things, recently told me that moss grows thickest on the north side of trees. Well that's a *big* help when I'm trying to find the Morris Mechanic Theater.

September 1967

E ven though we think they're beautiful, if you looked closely at our four children you would see positive evidence of myopia, flat feet, finger warts and definite protrusions of the upper dental region. . . . Fortunately, each child is only endowed with one or two at a time.

But put them all together, plus yearly school checkups and a journey every six months to the dentist and what do you have? *I'll* tell you what you have—a tremendous lot of time spent in doctors' offices for Mother.

I know that once the orthodontist removes the "railroad tracks" from her teeth Louise may have a winning smile at fifteen, warts *do* disappear another doctor keeps telling me, and as for the flat feet, we just have to rise above that. But oh the time I've spent staring at medical walls!

As a voracious reader of magazines I'm content for just so

long. I've thus become a "critic" of waiting room literature. In fact I'm very picky. Medical degrees are important, yes, but magazine subscriptions are vital. And whenever a new ailment comes our way I'm always hopeful when I call the new doctor's secretary for the first time.

"Good morning, this is Mrs. Hardie. Our son has a queer fungus between his toes, and what magazines do you take?"

"Madam," she replies haughtily, "we cannot help send your son through college, but in two months I might be able to give your son an appointment." And so for two months I wonder what new fields of paperback pleasures are ahead of me.

I could do my needlepoint and I could read that book I should read, but magazines are such immediate amusements. And how else am I going to find out what Candice Bergen thinks about Bobby Kennedy, or how to prepare a floating spaghetti mold for Columbus Day?

Once a child is beckoned into the doctor's office I sidle up, wide-eyed, to the magazine rack. And there is never a more disappointed mother than when faced with a year-old *New Yorker* or a six-month-old *Saturday Evening Post.* Even the elegant, slick magazines become rather grubby after a few days of doctors' offices. And *Look* should really use a better paper.

I must admit that some doctors do try to filter in a little educational reading. Our dentist, who also serves up friendly music as well as pink and blue and yellow dental chairs against decorative wallpaper of daisies, offers me the chance to study *Parents* magazine along with a suggestive title called *Keep Smiling.*

I'm also crazy about our new pediatrician, but as we've only had a shot or two I haven't had time to study his reading list.

Right now, however, the five-star medical general of my personal group plan is our orthodontist. I could luxuriate there all day, and so could you. Here are his magazines, bless his heart—*Horizon, Punch, Venture, The American Rifleman, Paris Match, McCall's, Gourmet, House & Garden, Africana, Reader's Digest, Holiday, Americas,* and to top it all off, three piles of comics! The whole family is happy, even though it hurts.

I realize everyone can't have such a selection, but I do have some other suggestions, depending on the length of your child's visit with doctor. For two cavities or more, how about offering mother an easy chair in a telephone booth so she can make all the calls she didn't make before nine that morning?

For a complete physical examination, how about a resident dietitian to help you plan the week's meals? And if you have to wait for those eye drops to dilate the pupils, how about a handy Swedish masseuse for Mom? I can't think of any better way to fill prescriptions.

September 1967

Although the other members of my family might disagree, I still think my temperament has improved over the past year.

I haven't discovered any special giant tranquilizers, but I have found a new, consuming passion—I've learned how to do needlepoint. And what other soothing sedative, once completed, can you sit on as well?

I'm sloppy when it comes to sewing, and as for knitting, I could never turn the heel of a sock alone. I always needed help. But then I decided I also needed therapy. Something to do while doing nothing. And that is precisely the point of needlepoint. It is also highly recommended for nervous systems, yours or your husband's.

But learning how is another matter. Fortunately I had Mary

Jane. Mary Jane is a clever friend who lives in New York and has been designing and doing needlepoint for years. So far her canvases have captured everything from butterflies to poppies, even facades of houses and backgammon boards. Her current project is a stool cover designed as the skin of a zebra. But not any zebra, a *young* zebra.

So I cheerfully invited Mary Jane and her young zebra down for a needlepoint weekend. And by Sunday our ancient friendship had almost ended. With Mary Jane you don't take needle in hand and meet one hole of the canvas and then the next, horizontally or vertically. No indeed, you work on the diagonal and you put the needle from a side hole to a lower hole. The following row you find a side hole and then go to a higher hole. She kept exclaiming, "Watch it grow, watch it grow!" Well, how could I watch it grow when I couldn't even find the right hole?

Mary Jane hasn't a particularly fiery disposition. In fact I've always admired her cool. But that weekend an army sergeant was teaching me needlepoint. She even brought me a floral piece she had designed of petit point, the very smallest holes, which didn't make it any easier. But by sheer tenacity and almost tears, Mary Jane won and I learned how to do needlepoint.

Once I had conquered the needlepoint technique I had an entirely different feeling about myself—sort of half Mother Earth, half Betsy Ross. Whoopee, I'm creating, all by myself! With my canvas on my knees, a lap full of contentment, I sometimes feel as if I'm making the first flag, or perhaps the last uniforms of General Lee's boys. Sometimes I even feel I'm not in 1967. It's a noble, nice feeling. And sometimes I feel smug. I may be sitting still, I tell myself, but I'm doing Something!

Which is all utterly ridiculous. For what have I made? Four very small frivolous pillows, absolutely useless. But I'm still proud of them. One is copied from a simple stained glass window in the San Juan church where Ponce de Leon was once buried, another is a tiger for Beth because she was a tiger in a school play, and two are bouquets of flowers. (Flowers are the easiest because it doesn't matter if you make a mistake. And my flowers are always wild-flowers anyhow.)

I am now working on my most ambitious canvas—a chair cover. A ram's head is centered on a checkered background. And even though the children say the ram's curved black horn looks like an antique telephone receiver, every stitch still gives me pleasure.

In addition, needlepoint is a lovely wall—"Children, go ask your Father about your homework . . . can't you see I'm trying to finish my needlepoint?" And also I can be sitting in a room and I don't have to talk at all, for you see I'm doing my needlepoint.

Needlepoint has now become a family affair as well. Beth is well into a pink dancing elephant and Louise is creating a large sunburst medallion. But both girls are not as fast as Tommy, although we admit he works a canvas with larger holes, a rug canvas. I thought it was a fine idea ever since I read that a famous heart surgeon was taught to sew as a child. And Tommy wants to be a doctor.

Tommy made his father a French flag for his birthday and has just completed a handsome figure of a Saint Bernard. And if we hadn't all taken up needlepoint I would have missed one of the scenes of the century—Tommy sitting on his bed one lazy afternoon doing needlepoint while listening to an Orioles double header on his radio.

September 1967

A s far as selectivity goes, boys are flops! They collect everything and anything. Including some things which should be preserved in the deep freeze, rather than discovered in a deep pants pocket some five days too late. (Say, like that pungent antler beetle from Arizona.)

We've gone through cycles of saving rocks, birds' nests (one woven from stray sheep's wool), bugs, *Boy's Life,* bottle tops, nails (must be over seven inches), rope and cracked robins' eggs. Except they're not really cycles, they're pyramids—all piled on top of one another, in rooms meant for sleeping.

In a way they *are* treasures, treasures of the countryside. But what's more important? Keeping that solitary cleaning woman happy on Mondays or keeping those boyish caches of explorations?

And so the happiest day of my life came when Todd turned to stamps. Coins had come first, and I thought this was a step in the right direction. Coins, like stamps, are usually small, usually tidy.

But stamps are so beautiful. Japanese stamps are like butterfly screens; French stamps are like Impressionist paintings. You may never travel farther than the pages of your stamp album, but you can't help but feel the pulse of the world's people, the conditions of the land.

We had been waiting for this day a long, long time, though perhaps not fully realizing it. Under Todd's bed, for years, had been a small wicker suitcase filled with my husband's and my old stamp books. Stamp books that show the late King Farouk as a once-slim monarch, or Leopold when he was still King of the Belgians.

And what fun Todd was going to have, we kept telling ourselves, searching for a gray 1923 Calvin Coolidge or that triangular-shaped stamp commemorating the opening of the Suez Canal. These were going to be scavenger hunts, educational as well. Todd was finally launched into the hobby of kings, the king of hobbies.

I'll say he's launched! His small room at the top of the stairs has become the upper branch of the lower Glyndon post office.

He not only receives more mail than anyone else in the house, he also sends out more mail. And having learned typing over the summer his output is even more prolific. His daily incoming mail usually includes stamp magazines, stamp newspapers, constant communications from stamp stores everywhere, official-looking manila envelopes from document departments of the United States Government and small posters explaining what to expect next—in stamps.

When I say to him, "What do you do with these things?" he answers simply, "I look at 'em. I save 'em." He also assures me that as I age so will his stamp collection, and my very senior years might be made more comfortable from the revenue of his very complete collection.

Then I explain, considering myself a former minor philatelist, "You still must concentrate on one field. You must decide exactly what you're going to specialize in."

And he has, so he tells me. He collects American stamps—including old stamps, new stamps, plate blocks and first-day issues. This means an album for old stamps, one for single new stamps, another for plate blocks and two or three for first-day issues.

He has also decided to be the only fourteen-year-old boy on Butler Road to collect postmarks from every day of the year. That means that when I see my mail he has already cut away the stamp and postmark, leaving me a strangely naked envelope that could have come five years ago from almost anywhere. I'm never sure.

But this is his hobby. It is also his money. The beginning

of this past summer he worked hard baling hay, and that is hard work. The minute he got his paycheck he dropped it all with the United States Government at the Butler Post Office.

I personally think what this country needs is a good two-cent postal stamp. An October 16 issue, for example, of Eugene O'Neill costs, believe it or not, one dollar each. That's a lot of hay baling.

Sometimes Todd is so secretive and mysterious about the whole thing I suspect he may be going into counterfeiting. When contemporary stamps cost one dollar each I can hardly blame him.

Last summer when we were in London I bought him some English stamps, not knowing his special American field at the time. When I asked the salesman in the small stamp store if he collected stamps, he said that when he was "young"—at that moment he was hardly nineteen—he did collect coins, followed by stamps. I thought, my; just like Todd! But since then, he explained, he had progressed to archaeology.

I can already see the writing on the wall . . . bones, bones, bones!

October 1967

Homemade ghosts seem to be shadows of bygone, old-fashioned eras, roly-poly clowns are "squares," and where have all the hobos gone? In our house last night it was a hippie Halloween.

Beth and her nine-year-old friends all chose to masquerade as hippies. As a matter of fact if you want to be a hippie you might as well have a one-night stand, like Halloween, and get it out of your system. Some people always want it to be Christmas, and the real hippies look like they always want it to be Halloween. That must be the reason they look so weird.

But I did miss seeing a young witch or two, the witch who wore a black church-steeple hat and carried a kitchen broom. I even think I missed Frankenstein. And I guess all those cute little Dutch girls have gone back to the Zuider Zee.

Actually the hippie costume is awfully easy—any old wig, a few flowers on the forehead, the guitar over the back, a lot of bilious beads, the shortest skirt, the dirtiest shirt, a cowbell around one's left ankle, and perhaps a button saying, "Make Noise, Not War." Haight-Ashbury move over, Butler Road was turned on last night!

In the olden days, like last year, Halloween costumes were a mother's challenge. And the children themselves thought of some dillies. Parades of strange characters have wandered through this house on past Halloweens—a two-headed horse, Abraham Lincoln, child brides, Phyllis Diller, and a magnificent maharajah who became royalty by wearing his mother's paste pearls and paisley bedspread. Then came the Beatles.

There are quite a few clever mothers around here who still make costumes for their younger children. And Halloween is certainly for the young. When else does an ordinary paper bag become a treasure chest? One of these mothers, a mother of five, turned hers all into pumpkins—with the help of curved wires and orange material. Sometimes I'd like to try the same trick with ours, and just leave them there.

Another friend went back a few thousand years. Her son Fletcher, then five, wanted more than anything to be a dinosaur. And so she made him a green saw-toothed tail that was three times as long as he was tall. In the peaks of the tail she stuffed corrugated paper. When this splendid dinosaur walked he went thump . . . thump . . . thump.

In his green suit and spiked tail he thumped off for tricks or treats. But unfortunately that Halloween it rained and the dinosaur's tail got heavier and heavier and the thump got thumpier. Maybe that's why there aren't any dinosaurs any more, even on Halloween. This year Fletcher, too, was a hippie.

Our own Halloween costumes were always quickly assembled and always with a stapler. A needle and thread are just too much of a challenge for this mother. But I do think we got a seventh prize once for a decorated ghost costume. The family ghost also wore his grandfather's collapsible opera hat which I really think clinched the deal.

For years I tried to interest the children in a beautifully brocaded, red Chinese pajama suit. I had actually worn it as an eight-year-old. Although it had been carefully preserved over the years, the children couldn't have cared less for the continuity and always balked at wearing it. Ballerinas are more fun, Mom. . . . Well, maybe grandchildren?

Our twelve-year-old daughter Louise and her classmate

Lydia were preparing their hippie costumes yesterday afternoon. They danced through the house dangling beads, giggling over each new discovery.

But when it was all over they finally decided to go as flappers. Maybe there's some hope after all!

November 1967

Every once in a while my husband really lives it up and takes me to a really elegant restaurant. That's my idea of heaven. I love it. I wear my best dress, an air of abandon, and pretend this happens all the time.

But suddenly it has all changed. I realized this last Saturday night in town when, wearing my best dress and perhaps my last breath of abandon, I ordered for two. Not for one, but for two—for Tuffy and me.

Tuffy is a four-month-old Saint Bernard who recently waddled into our lives. He may be Tommy's dog, but he's my conscience when it comes to leftover steak bones. And in an elegant restaurant how can you elegantly sneak out that steak bone when your small elegant handbag hardly holds your lipstick?

But now I've learned. If I know I'm going to "That Kind of Restaurant" I must pack beforehand. Pack an emergency collapsible carry-out container for leftovers for that dog you left behind.

I'm talking about the restaurants where it's so dark you can't see the prices on the menu, but you can be sure the waiter will see you trotting away with a bone in your mouth. Usually they're French.

You wouldn't think the French waiters in America would mind, knowing their canine heritage. Most restaurants in France, especially in Paris, went to the dogs long ago. Dogs are allowed in almost every restaurant from the smallest bistro to the grandest salon.

But our Tuffy is every bit as important as the fanciest poodle in Paris. He's absolutely fetching. In fact he fetches and then completely finishes off my birthday bedslippers, my newly planted tulip bulbs, almost anything portable. That's why he needs steak bones. Lots of them.

And on this diet how he has grown. When he was five weeks old, a bundle of fluff, and I first saw him amble away to his food I said to his new owner, Tommy, "What an adorable bottom!" Tommy, who had just finished reading a book about Saint Bernards, turned to me and said disdainfully and with great authority, "Those are hindquarters, Mother, hindquarters!"

Mother might not know dog anatomy but now I do know about the feeding of Saint Bernards. Fill the bowl up, constantly. And sneak a steak bone at every given opportunity.

For others who are dog dietitians may I suggest that the emergency canine carry-out should be a plastic bag, freezer size, folded first into a larger handbag. It can then, when opportunity presents itself, be opened wide to catch the juicy tidbits. Some vegetables are allowable. No chicken bones, please. And pork only if it's well done.

There should be no feeling of guilt when you whip out your plastic bag. But for the conservative and the sensitive, emergency bag loading can be done below the horizon of the table. The next step is to plop it into your larger handbag already cleverly lined with aluminum foil.

Bone lifting, however, could lead to other things. But I have always made it a point to collect only perishables. No linen, no silver, no crystal, no tiny, easily concealed cream pitcher with the restaurant name written in French script. No indeed. Just bones.

Just bones . . . except, well, one time I did deviate from the true course of honest restaurant-lifting. I once took a glass ashtray, heavily engraved, from the Ritz Hotel in Paris. I confess. It was a terrible weakness. But I just had to have it.

It was a part of the Twenties I wish I had known. I kept telling myself it wasn't naughty, just nostalgia. But now that the children are older maybe I should return it. Send it back, stick to bones! So back it goes . . . Good-bye Ernest . . . *Au revoir,* Scott and Zelda . . . *Bonne chance,* Paris. . . .

Hello there Tuffy, have a bone.

November 1967

I have been laid low by a common denominator, a common enemy, a common cold. I have lost my voice. Although I thought my timbre was more like Tallulah's, our son Todd says I sound like Donald Duck. It's a low blow when your children tell you you sound fowl when you thought you sounded Broadway.

But mothers aren't meant to be sick. Some people take a dim view of this, especially children who don't like any change from the usual. Mothers are meant to be germ-free Amazons, modern-day Florence Nightingales in skirts and sweaters. But then Florence, poor thing, never had any children. . . . Jump, Mother, jump! Jump out of bed. The children are hungry!

Well, let them eat cake. At times like this, a mother with

a virus should be allowed to collapse. Mothers should be able to recline like Camille, or better still like Greta Garbo playing Camille. What a glamorous way to go, whether by consumption or the common, common cold.

But I don't have a chaise longue, not even a convenient isolation ward. I live in a small family-like hotel. Transients coming and going and our bedroom the main lobby, reception on the left, elevators on the right. Going up?

No, I'm going down, down to the kitchen. Somebody's got to feed me. I can't really understand why the service is so bad, after all these years of taking care of Them. All I really wanted was some sympathy. And all I got was tea and a Tootsie Roll. Beth, the youngest, says Tootsie Rolls can cure anything.

Actually, I like taking care of my family when they are sick. I pamper them and prune their rooms. That's one way of getting a room clean. I puff up their pillows, straighten their blankets, I absolutely smother them with attention. And when I shake that thermometer and take their temperatures I feel as medically important as if I had just discovered penicillin—or at least a cure for diaper rash.

If the patients' temperatures are not too high, I also get a written guarantee that they won't be sick any longer than two days. They sign this willingly. And I do take particular pains with the appearance of the bed tray. Every meal is a movable feast. But my patients don't always agree.

I decorate with colorful place mats, a flower if possible, and I ladle hot soup down their throats whether they like it or not. It is a captive audience. I love it. I may not always feel the pulse of my patients, but I do give a dandy back rub.

However, after two days I'm also ready for a transfer, maybe to Dr. Schweitzer's, and my patients are ready to go back to school or work. And so for a while I put away my starched white cap and the clinic doors are temporarily closed. Such care, such treatment!

That's why it's a little hard to realize my own cold must have a do-it-yourself cure. Maybe they're paying me back. But I must admit my mother-in-law cooked a turkey, which must merit some sort of mother-in-law citation.

A good friend wasn't so solicitous last week when she dropped by innocently. Once in the same room, she sat as far away as possible and I'm sure she would have accepted a white face mask if I had offered one. I suddenly felt great compassion for Typhoid Mary.

But I'm not Typhoid Mary. I'm not even Rudolph the Red-Nosed Reindeer—but that's a closer resemblance. I'm just a mother who feels terribly sorry for herself and would like to give her common cold a very special cold shoulder . . . Gesundheit!

December 1967

Christmas presents for men are almost impossible. And although I'm just as much of a challenge for my husband, he does somehow manage to meet this annual challenge. It's amazing, for shopping to him, any time of the year, is about as entertaining as having a drink with Lucretia Borgia.

He has never, to my knowledge, gone to one of those snappy evening sessions "for husbands only" given by fashionable stores where cute little things tied up in red ribbons help tie up your husband's bankroll by suggesting he buy you ostrich-plumed bed-jackets or sateen jumpsuits. He is, I think, a solitary shopper. He must be.

One year it was snow tires. Now mind you, that *is* seasonal.

But what girl dreaming of diamonds wants protection against that kind of ice?

Another year it was a case, a whole case, of Saint Emilion 1954. There's obviously a great deal of good cheer in that gift. But it also happens to be his favorite wine.

He is concerned about our world. So quite naturally one year I was the lucky recipient of one globe, slightly traveled as it came from a secondhand furniture store. It is more a conversation piece now as it shows a Germany intact and such distant memories as Latvia and Tanganyika.

Somehow he noticed that my face didn't light up like a Christmas tree when I opened his gifts. So the next year he asked me what I would like for Christmas. I said, quite honestly, a flannel nightgown. And a nightgown I got. But it was lacy and lovely and much more Liz Taylor than Ma Hardie. Actually, buying it must have been quite a performance!

However, I certainly don't want him to get discouraged. There's a great gift to giving, especially when it's the right present. And so may I suggest a little list of wifely surprises?

How about:

From September to June, a delivery of fresh-cut flowers about every other week. Preferably deep red carnations and a few pinks.

Or bringing home a chilled bottle of champagne for absolutely no reason at all.

And maybe taking over all my January bills without comment!

But if that's expecting too much I'll settle for a big box of chocolate-covered nuts.

For a while I was also playing his Christmas game. See that Queen Anne armchair over there? I thought it would be just fine for his evening reading, plus the fact I've always wanted a Queen Anne armchair. Well, he can't read in it at night, nor can he read in it during the day. He just isn't a Queen Anne shape. I may have gained an elegant chair but I almost lost a comfortable husband.

If I put my mind to it, I think I could quite simply give

Tom a contented Christmas. But it would have strings attached, winding around the entire next year. I would give four promissory notes wrapped with a mistletoe sprig.

The first would promise that all those little buttons on his shirts would always be there. Another would state that a different dinner once a week was to be his. Highly seasoned haute cuisine, designed for his palate, not for the children. The third, a promise to let him sleep Saturday mornings. That's a hard one. And the last, a little of Disraeli, I'd try to "Never Complain, Never Explain."

I'm not so sure I can do all that. I'm not even sure Mrs. Bob Cratchit could do it. And you know she was pretty noble about everything. But I think I just might give it a try. After all, didn't Tiny Tim?

December 1967

When our children were younger, much younger, it was almost easier going to Jerusalem than getting them dressed for church.

It was more than just finding or matching the right clothes. It was getting them to wear them once we had unearthed their finery. Many's the morning I almost gave up church for want of one left red shoe, size 1. Or how could I ever forget the Battle of the Gray Flannels—short pants versus long?

I often wondered if this was really the way to celebrate the Sabbath—tugging at stubborn braids, insisting on a second hand-wash. There was even, I must confess, a great deal of high-pitched urging, wrestling, call it what you may. It just wasn't what you'd call Christian. And then, when they were finally dressed, they didn't look at all like angels. They looked a little lower than angels. They looked like their human dignity had been nudged a bit. But somehow we got them to the church on time.

Of course, we could have gone to bed three hours earlier the night before to prepare for those morning gymnastics. We could have left that Saturday night dinner party a little earlier. But somehow Saturdays don't have the same conscience as Sundays.

Now that they're older it's so much easier. The beds even manage to get made. The only clothes problems seem to be Tom hunting in his sons' closets for his favorite tie, and Louise or Beth deciding not even a halo would be the right hat to wear that particular Sunday.

Still, there isn't always complete harmony in our pew. A member of our family, who shall remain nameless but his voice probably changed thirty years ago, not only lends his voice to every hymn, he gives his all. I stand next to him. And I know where I stand—a little off key, but at least we're together.

We're together in our church, Saint John's in the Worthington Valley. Rebuilt in 1927, it is quite small, Gothic, stone and, we think, very beautiful. When you approach Saint John's on a late fall day it arises from bordering fields of corn, of course on a much smaller scale but with the same moving simplicity that Chartres Cathedral in France arises from fields of wheat. With snow on the ground nothing seems quite so peaceful.

The very first Saint John's was built of limestone in 1814. And there have been others in between, one burning down exactly a hundred years ago on Christmas Eve. The ministers have been many and as varied as the styles of architecture. One, a Virginian, left the parish before the Civil War, eventually enlisting and rising to brigadier general of artillery. They say that, before discharging his orders, he would cry, "Lord have mercy on their souls! Fire!"

Our new minister is a Southerner and we're so glad he ventured north. Every Sunday we come away with a little more faith, a little more hope. And only once have I caught myself planning the girls' weddings when I should have been singing the third verse of the second hymn.

One summer when we were all together in Europe I wanted to show our children the churches of Paris. I trudged and tugged them all along the Seine. First the majestic Notre Dame. Then we went to that jewel, Sainte Chapelle, and then up to Sacré Coeur. By the time we arrived at the fourth church, the chapel of the American Pro-Cathedral, they were so tired they could not have cared less. But they do care about this church. We all do.

This Christmas Eve, at 5:30 P.M., we're having community carol singing around the Christmas tree on the church lawn. Do come, Butler Road and Belmont Avenue, Baltimore County.

O come all ye faithful, and those not so faithful. Christmas is the best time to sing together, even off key.

December 1967

Tommy and I walked into the hardware store and I said, "I'd like some gray paint, please."

The man asked, "House paint?"

"No," I said, "castle paint."

And that brief dialogue was the beginning of the latest school project at Thornhill Farm. Tommy, our eleven-year-old son, is building a castle. And when else can you build a castle these days? Except when you're eleven.

Other school projects, over the years, have come and gone and even collapsed. When Todd was the same age, and in the sixth grade, he heroically erected Nelson's Column in our bathroom. The original still stands in Trafalgar Square in London.

It was then I knew the age of innocence was not dead. It couldn't be. Can you imagine constructing the Washington Monument, a shape similar to Nelson's Column, out of plaster of paris as high as your knee bone? Well, Todd did. And for months afterward flakes of plaster of paris were in our lungs, our carpets, embedded in our brains. Hail Britannia, but down with sixth-grade columns!

The boys' school is truly a builder of men. But they expect their men to build as well. Fortunately, the girls aren't meant to be so manually dexterous. Louise's last project was on the tropical rain forest of the Congo.

Much to everyone's delight she and her partner in rain, Barbara, discovered an animal named the okapi. The okapi, I was informed, looks like a short giraffe and has a fourteen-inch tongue used to clean ears and face, and to flick flies. The habits of the okapi, I'm sure, will remain with Louise far longer than any other facet of Congo lore. Nevertheless, school projects are here to stay.

Tommy's castle wasn't his first plunge into construction work. He and his father had just finished, rather miraculously, a dog house for Tuffy the Saint Bernard. This clapboard cube, this very basic Hardie concept of dog architecture, was completely acceptable to Tuffy. This encouraged Tommy and gave him some big ideas. First a dog house, next a castle.

Actually, he originally planned to do Agincourt. I was thrilled thinking of all those stirring, colorful banners and striped tents. But Tommy's teacher wisely thought Agincourt was perhaps a little too ambitious.

So Tommy had other choices from his history book. Would you believe? . . . Caesar lands in Britain, Birth of Christ, The Black Death, Magna Carta, Wars of the Roses, The Third Crusade, Hundred Years' War and Vasco da Gama sails to India. I personally thought Wars of the Roses had some marvelous decorative possibilities. But of course I didn't tell Tommy. And since his friend Jimmy took the Battle of Hastings and friend Chris took Hadrian's Wall, Tommy took a castle.

Or perhaps I should say the castle took him. He's been back in the Dark Ages for days. He has enclosed himself in what he now calls a *donjon,* previously known as his bedroom. And from all those various-sized tin cans, popsicle sticks, corrugated cardboard and gobs of gray paint a castle is emerging. Arthur may have pulled a sword out of a rock, but Tommy is making a castle out of soup cans. A noble feat indeed!

I must admit my trigger finger has gotten a little itchy. I love school projects. Way back when I was in the sixth grade my lumpy mountains were made from flour and water and my shrubbery, cut from green sponges, was almost topiary. And I'd still much rather do school projects than grownup projects. You know, grownup projects like cooking and laundry and other glorious tasks of homedom. But Tommy won't let me near his kingdom. He keeps saying, "Ninety-nine percent of this is meant to be me! Ninety-nine percent of this is meant to be me!"

Well, one percent of that project is I. And Mr. Menzies, Sir, I dare you to guess my one percent share!

January 1968

Some short ten years ago, when we brought our fourth baby, Beth, home from the hospital, our oldest child was age four. "Phew," said Daddy Bear, "Wow," said Mamma Bear, and the rest of the family just had to grin and bear it.

Close quarters, yes. Togetherness, yes. But absolutely overwhelming! Although our diapered world may have been padded, there was certainly a lot of noise around.

But I never pushed the panic button; I just dialed the pediatrician. A pediatrician who was wise and patient and always prescribed aspirin—mostly for me. When *his* line was busy I took Dr. Spock in hand—and Dr. Spock took me in hand—and somehow *we* all managed to grow up. These days I'm not so sure about Dr. Spock, but in the olden days his book was my best friend.

Now we all seem to have survived the measles and mumps and chicken pox and roseola—remember roseola? And endless legions of runny noses. I think of those days whenever I pass the humidifier, now put out to pasture in the basement. That bulbous green glass container Tom was sure might explode, but instead gave out magiclike fumes that kept our children from coughing all the night and let us sleep, at least until five.

I sort of miss it all, say I smugly without a baby in sight. We've moved on to another plateau. Yet I still have the remnants, the reminders of all that postnatal care. And there is still a long journey, I would say, until grandchildren pass this way.

But what to do with all that paraphernalia of early parent-hood? The props. In this old house with limited closet space almost a privilege, nothing is kept just for the memory.

With everyone getting bigger—including, unfortunately, the parents—more space seems to be needed. And so, before any-thing goes into a closet for storage it has to pass an entrance exam . . . will we ever really need that bottle warmer again? Maybe for Colt games? Could that highchair possibly be made into a standing lamp? Would this cradle be happier having a second childhood with another child, or should it grow up and be a magazine rack? And finally—can I, the Mother, bear to part with these touches of our past?

Some flunked long ago—like the bathinet with the canvas top that always folded up at the wrong time. But the bassinet, recently rejuvenated, is a blooming success. The legs have been cut off, the basket repainted "jonquil yellow" and it is now filled with pot after pot of pale pink winter geraniums. On the other hand, I have yet to find any practical, adult application for potties.

Baby bottles have really come into their own. I now use them for making drinks as well as feeding motherless lambs. Never much of a mathematician, I have found I am able to mix a passable drink by using the measure of cubic centimeters on the side of the bot-tle. It may not be the "in" way, but after all Eliza Doolittle did say she thought gin was mother's milk.

Diapers too have second lives. Piles of them sit on the top shelf of our linen closet waiting for an emergency. And more than once they have wrapped bloody heads and bleeding fingers before going off to be patched up by professionals.

A friend, however, uses them for other heads—heads of lettuce. She dampens the lettuce, wraps it in a diaper and into the refrigerator it goes, always moist. And somehow, somewhere, I feel wrapping lettuce in diapers rather than finding babies in a cabbage patch makes a lot more sense.

February 1968

T he other day ten-year-old Beth told me when she grew up she was either going to be a librarian or a go-go girl. She couldn't decide which. I told her that was fine, but when I grew up I was going to be a grandmother.

Secretly I hope the books win over the bumps. But on the other hand, it might be rather appealing for a man to know a go-go girl who reads.

Whatever route Beth takes, I'm still ninety-nine percent guaranteed with my line of work. From a family of four children our tribe should increase, wouldn't you think? There is just one hitch. Before one becomes a grandmother, one must be a mother-in-law. And that I would think would be the most difficult of all.

How do you really, truly, easily, with grace, warmth and dignity accept the man who has stolen away your baby? That stranger, that invader, that interloper, that good-looking young man with the terrific personality. Of course there is one vital requisite: he has to like me—a lot.

Actually, I've done away with that awkward preliminary step. I have chosen Beth's husband. She doesn't know him, and he doesn't know her . . . yet. But they will. Believe me, he's adorable. When the proper time comes I shall put into effect Emergency Snow Plan No. 1, and after that all I'll have to do is contact the caterers.

I wouldn't dare choose Louise's husband. I don't even dare

choose her sandwich spread. And I'm going to let those boys of ours fend for themselves . . . to a certain extent.

I've always heard about Jewish mothers, and they sound mighty good. So I plan to be a Jewish/Catholic/Protestant/Greek Orthodox mother-in-law. A maternal ecumenical mother-in-law. I don't see how I can lose.

I wonder how matzoh balls will taste in mulligan stew? I plan to cook for them, you see, once a week. Whether they like it or not. I shall put on my little red hood and cape and carry them a basket of goodies. That way our dear, darling daughter won't have to slave over a hot stove. She'll have more time to practice her go–go routine.

And it doesn't matter where they live because by that time I may have gotten over my fear of flying. I'll be grown up by then. The Flying Mum, perhaps better known as The Witch.

By then I'll be a grandmother. Grandmothers are very important. But unfortunately I'm not very good at knitting mittens, or writing checks, or sewing pinafores. Instead I shall make needlepoint slippers for all our grandchildren and embroider our telephone number on the toe. That way they can call us up collect when their parents aren't around and tell us all those things their mother and father won't tell.

We have two grandmothers, Nanie and Mamoo, or perhaps you prefer Florence and Agnes. They say they now have quite enough grandchildren, thank you, but they are certainly grand to the ones they have. And the wonderful thing about grandmothers is, if you're especially lucky, there are also grandfathers. And everybody knows about grandfathers. They're cool, man, cool!

March 1968

T he other day our second son took a giant step—he graduated from the sixth to the seventh grade, or, in his particular
school, from the lower school to the upper school. Ar-
chitecturally speaking, he's only going from one red brick
building to another red brick building, but emotionally he's entering
the world of men, assuming the ties of early manhood.

And that's exactly where my husband's ties have gone—to
the upper school. In the upper school tie, the jacket and the shirt are
de rigueur; and Todd, our older son, has been borrowing his father's
foulards for years. Now Tommy will tap the tie rack.

Emotionally I was prepared for Tommy's graduation. I
wore my sunglasses, for although these graduations are always indoors, you can never tell when you might want to shield a tear.

Perhaps tears will come when you see those forty-seven
young boys walking into the auditorium to "Pomp and Circum-
stance"; or when you look at that sea of twelve-year-old gleaming,
freckled faces on the stage; or when you think of all those grass-
stained trouser knees you scrubbed; or when you remember that
broken front "lacrosse" tooth, or realize that your little boy is going
to wear a tie five days a week for a long, long time.

During the actual graduation these boys sang two songs—
"America the Beautiful" and "No Man Is an Island." It gets you
right there, even though you've heard almost the same songs for the
last six years.

These young cubs then walked in as manly a way as possible, out of the auditorium, to the tune of The Triumphal March from *Aïda*. If that's not a lofty exit for a group of twelve-year-old boys, I don't know what is.

And what about those they left behind? What about those mothers and fathers who have just finished struggling through those last six formative years? The only awards given at graduation are for good citizenship and the honor roll, and I'm not sure the parents could win either of those. And so may I suggest a few gratuities for the parents:

The Prize for Proficiency in Mathematics: For the parent, male or female, who at least *tried* to understand the New Math when it first exploded on the scene.

The Mr. Chips Award, also known as the Debating Cup: For the father who best qualified, when the chips were down, to discuss his son with his teacher.

The Polkadot Medallion: For the mother who rendered the highest possible service to the school by keeping her son in bed when he had red spots everywhere.

The Wrestling Award: To the mother or father who managed to get their son to school on time, make sure his hair was cut, pants belted, sweater neat, and nails clean—all at the same time.

Thinking it all over, it was our privilege. Sometimes our despair, sometimes our joy, but always our privilege! As for our grandchildren, I hope their spelling lists won't be quite as long. And as for our sons, thank you, lower school, very much, and *"In Tuo Lumine Lumen."*

June 1968

S̶o far this summer vacation (?) we seem to have spent a great
deal of time in the pursuit of how-to: how to play tennis,
how to drive a car, how to keep your head when all about
you are losing theirs. All these recreational programs for the
children turn out to be constant motor tours for the mothers. And
the question is, do our four children want a bus driver or a mother?

Before being a mother I should have been in somebody's
tank corps instead of Eighteenth-Century English Literature. What
can Clarissa Harlowe do for me as a mother when she had such a
hard time as a maiden? I should have studied about transportation
rather than communication.

In all fairness, though, I'm the one who asked for all this
driving; I'm the one who signed the children up for these lessons.
The three younger ones are on the courts, and our eldest is learning
how to drive so he won't ever get *in* the courts. Actually he's taking
a thirty-hour driver's training course. And he's learned a lot.

The other morning at 6:30 A.M. he told me that when you
have an automobile accident, your eyeballs often "bounce out" and
it's very hard to get them back in again. It was a delicious conversation while I was trying to make breakfast, sunny side up. His
instructor certainly knows how to hold the attention of his class.

But I'm getting a little weary of this motorized summer life.
I'd much rather stay home. Maybe it's the scheduling that gets to
me. How can Louise play in that tournament while Tommy gets his

tooth bleached while Beth is home alone and Todd has to be picked up at a neighbor's farm where he's working? To remember what we're doing today, not what we'll forget tomorrow, I walk around with a wall calendar in my hand. I roll it up and it looks like a diploma, but it's simply time marching on.

Next summer I've decided we'll have a different curriculum. We're going to major in Home Studies 104. I'll be head of the department, and the four children won't even need an accumulative C to transfer to my summer school. They *are* my summer school. They are my student body. Anything to rest my own body. . . .

The boys already know about the care and cutting of lawns, but they have yet to experience the joys of spotting vagrant or vagabond weeds. The weed is a versatile, rugged, indecent growth with an inherent desire to defy man and thrive under conditions some might consider exceedingly unfavorable. Horticulture 102, therefore, will analyze the problems of when to weed and when to seed. The entire summer might be spent in a splendid weeding seminar. Imagine the satisfaction those boys will have with their intellectual pursuit of digging in the dirt while I sit in the sun.

For the honor students there will be additional courses in clover versus crab grass, in hardy bulbs versus sissy seeds, and in when to snip those petunias and when to put Myrtle back in her place. Myrtle does get out of hand.

The girls' classes will be held indoors. And I can think of no more pressing issue than undone ironing. Called Arts and Crafts 103, it will deal with the art of ironing a short sleeve on a wide board, and the craft of pressing pleats while watching TV soap operas. No ten-year-old girl should ever turn eleven without knowing how to iron a man's shirt. Beth makes beautiful brownies, but you can't live by brownies alone. Or can you?

If I find they have any open periods in their curriculums, I might suggest, as their friendly faculty advisor, a nifty new gut course called Underwater Explorations—as in washing the car. I may schedule so well that I won't know what to do with all that free time. I might just read a book!

July 1968

Beth is a ten-year-old philanthropist, although, of course, she doesn't even know what the word means. And it all started with more than ten little Indians.

About three months ago, addressed directly to her, came a plea from a large Indian school far out on the plains of Montana. With it came a softening gift of a barometer, encased splendidly in a plastic tepee. When the tepee turned blue, it was supposed to rain, and if pink, the forecast was for rosy weather. Naturally, Beth was thrilled.

Off she scooted to her bank vault located in her second drawer, left back corner under her petticoats and undershirts. Never worn, I might add. On her bed quilt she spread her fortune. Albeit a small one to the world, it was an Indian ransom to the young eyes of Beth. This fortune had been carefully amassed through lost baby teeth, loose change from father, returned coke bottles, and small grants from grandparents.

Beth quickly separated some of her copper and silver fortune from the bed, Scotch-taped it to a letter, and sent it off to Montana. She never once analyzed her gift. She didn't say, even to herself, "Can I afford it? Do they really need it? Could I spend that money otherwise?" She just gave.

Next came the startling news that the Indian school had burned down. Fortunately, no casualties. This time the letter arrived with a thermometer sitting on the plastic profile of a once-valiant chief. By return mail Beth rushed back her contribution which, in all fairness to Beth, might buy a pencil and a half. But her concern was real for these Native Americans; and then there was that pink tepee and a chieftain with a temperature, for remembrance.

Suddenly an avalanche of letters descended upon Beth. Somehow the word had gone around that a big spender lived on Butler Road. She became like a medieval church, also supporting schools and hospitals and, most recently, a leper colony.

To this day she has never refused a plea. I say to her, "Beth, you can't give to everyone indiscriminately." And she replies, "How would you like it if I was a homeless boy?" "Were," I say. "What?" she asks. And there and then I decide perhaps it's better to be a philanthropist than a grammarian.

Maybe this is the answer. Maybe all these charitable organizations should start with the young. The young who are pure in heart and piggy-bank safe. Rockefeller Foundation, move over; there's a Hardie Fund circulating from a second drawer, left back corner under the petticoats and undershirts. Never worn, I might add.

Beth now leaps for her daily mail. But her Scrooge-like mother keeps telling her she has to stop giving sometime. She merely smiles and says, "I like mail."

Her till is now getting lower, and she hasn't many baby teeth left. But fortunately for the Indians, and those homeless boys, and that hospital in Costa Rica and the leper colony, Beth has her grandparents, who don't realize that when they give a few coins to Beth, they are contributing worldwide.

July 1968

U ntil I was fourteen, my greatest personal tragedy was that I didn't look at all like Katharine Hepburn. But then no one looked like Katharine Hepburn. And no one ever has.

I would suck in my cheeks, hoping for her magnificent high cheekbones; I would use "golly" whenever possible because she always did, and I felt positively underprivileged because we never had any calla lilies in bloom. "Hello, Mather. Hello, Father."

Maybe it was the way she came through a door. When *she* came through a door, she would shut it behind her and then lean against it, oh so languidly, yet impishly. And of course she was wearing long, white, flowing crepe. She had class when it came to closing doors.

Kate Hepburn could close doors and open eyes . . . especially small, spectacled, fourteen-year-old eyes. How can you read *Little Women* and not have known her as Jo? What a Jo she was! As for Tracy Lord in *The Philadelphia Story,* it's a wonder one of our daughters isn't named Tracy. (Actually, I thought about it but didn't think I'd get away with it. I didn't.)

Kate Hepburn could have played any of my literary heroines. Easily Jane Eyre. Beautifully Tess. But never, no, never, Scarlett O'Hara. One thing Katharine Hepburn was not; she was not Southern.

Now, after all these years, there is a Kate Hepburn renaissance. And I'm happy as a clam. After reading a recent magazine article about her, I have the strangest sensation I'm fourteen years old.

I can hardly wait to see her as Eleanor of Aquitaine, as Coco Chanel, as the Madwoman of Chaillot, roles I never knew when I was fourteen. I'll even be able to take the children. Well, maybe not. Coco Chanel had definitely a fancy past! *Zut alors!*

But at fourteen-going-on-forty-two I feel much closer to Katharine Hepburn than I did at fourteen-going-on-fifteen. I don't think I'll quite go back to pasting up her scrapbook, but now I, too, know how to play tennis—although that's stretching a point or two. This may not be headline news, but, since I read that she plays tennis every morning, I have rescheduled our breakfast hour. It may help my cheekbones, to say nothing of my waistline. She never did have a waistline.

I also read that she likes old wood. Well, to know old wood is to love old wood; and that, precisely, is our house. She, too, enjoys her privacy. It may sound paradoxical to like privacy and yet try to write a weekly column, but to me this isn't an exposure of privacy; it's a privileged way of airing a cloudy mind. It's the secrets I don't write about that would make smashing copy.

And so, as the happy clamdigger digs, I have found more identification with Kate now than I ever did before. And, golly, it's great! It's a gift, a souvenir from your youth which you thought you had lost. Only she turns out to be more understandable now than she was.

Maybe that's it. Sometimes what you remember as good and true really is good and true . . . like Kate Hepburn, old wood, the first garden tomato of the season, the grace of cool ferns. They don't seem to change, do they? And I must say it's marvelous being fourteen when you're really forty-one!

August 1968

For years Emily Post wisely dictated the last word on social rulings, but today any modern mother realizes that the real queen is—the baby-sitter. Otherwise how do you get out of the house to be social? Baby-sitters, as we all well know, come in all shapes—but the important thing is that they come!

Some even come in their own cars. This situation is called Utopia. This is also the best possible use of C.O.D.

When one lives in the country, the world of baby-sitters is very limited. Usually there's no girl-next-door who can skip over and joyfully tend your flock while you skip out joyfully to enjoy your freedom. Sometimes I think getting into college was easier than getting an evening out. It's like planning an invasion.

First you phone weeks in advance; then you fabricate a few credit reports—"Four children, quiet, good eaters, sound sleepers—you hardly even know they're in the house." Once victory is assured and a sitter is secured, you start threatening on the side to the resident inhabitants—"Don't you dare raise your voices; eat everything on the plate, and, if you don't behave, it's the dungeon." Every home should have a dungeon.

If you're lucky enough to have a list of baby-sitters, you protect it as a family heirloom. And, believe me, some of these baby-sitters are heirlooms—ancient and priceless.

Of course, once the evening is over there is still the hurdle of mathematics. And mathematics do get rather hazy late at night.

"Now let me see . . . that's five and one-fourth hours, right—or was it five and two-third hours? Well, let's just say six, it's easier, isn't it? Now let me see, carry the decimal point and remove four children, at so much an hour, hmmm, there, I hope that's right, and thank you very much." Never, no never, unless under duress, ask how the children were.

After all the accounting, seldom do we have the right change; so I just go to the nearest, roundest number. Once or twice a baby-sitter has ended up owing us money. I should never be the night finance officer as money embarrasses me, especially after midnight.

Fortunately I'm about to retire as a banker. Recently our children started telling us the kind of baby-sitters they wanted— young, fun, blond, one who drives a car. At that point Tom and I decided the girls were too old and the boys too young for blond baby-sitters. It is the end of an era. No more baby-sitters! We're now on our own.

At first everyone wanted to be in charge. But then we explained it was a nonpaying obligation. The volunteers fell back. But how could you expect to be paid for sitting with yourself? we asked them. Easy, they say. Whatever else they say, it's freedom. Or is it?

Now I'm the one who has to feed them before I leap into the tub. Now I'm the one who worries about them between the dusk and the twilight when we're meant to be out on the town. This is emancipation?

We always seem to come home the minute after Tommy, wrapped in a fur rug and stretched before the Late Late Show, has fallen asleep. But there it is—our babe lying in a bunting, our on-guard baby-sitter, and, praise be, a house that is still standing.

August 1968

On September 10 a school close to our hearts opens its doors for its seventy-second fall semester. Then, on September 18, two more hallowed halls of higher learning follow the same pattern. And so, alas, after the long, hot summer, our own personalized, monogrammed summer guests return to school.

And what will we miss most? The crescendo of a boy and girl mixed-voiced choral raised in a lyrical duet, or rather a debate about who swiped the last piece of gum? The clever witticisms of a young man trying on itchy school tweeds while the temperature is still subtropical? Or his sister who at last turns from the funnies and Molly Mayfield to her required reading list, and finds the library depleted because her classmates, too, have decided to become instant educated women?

Yes, it's time to return to school.

You can swim so much, and your nose can peel so much, but there comes a time for other voices from other rooms. Voices of authority, voices of teachers!

Then there is that old melody, always a favorite reprise about "What can I do now?" which seems to be louder, more frequent toward the end of summer. And it seems to be sung by all ages. Yes, it's time to go back to school.

While August is a Father's month, maybe because the grass

is too dry to need much cutting, September, beautiful ninth month of the year, is the month for Mothers.

All varieties of queens were born in September—Queen Liliuokalani of Hawaii, as well as Elizabeth the First of England—and the *Mayflower* sailed from Plymouth. And for any mother September, every September, is a rebirth. The apples of our eyes are going back to polishing the apples. Hallelujah, September has come!

But what will it be like to have four empty beds at eight in the morning? Or just one breakfast hour instead of three different seatings? Or what about those staggered snack times, the first one starting soon after the first button has been pushed on the dish-washer?

What in the world will we do with all that free time? What in the world will we do when all those molars have been checked, all those physical examinations, now printed statistics, sent off to the various schools?

Lest we forget, there are always car pools.

And how can we forget car pools?

Then there is a hockey varsity game on the fourth of October, a football game on the tenth, some badminton on the twenty-second, and it's still only October.

In November perhaps we'll write a letter, paint that wall, paste last year in the scrapbook, maybe even have the girls in for lunch. And on the sixth it's Lower School Parents' Day. Followed by some more badminton, a touch of hockey and a guest speaker!

Now it's Thanksgiving and what have we missed? Mostly, quite frankly, we've missed the children. But the peace, the interim peace, isn't it heaven?

August 1968

T he last addition constructed here on Thornhill Farm was a semidetached Colonial sandbox. We made it for the children from old shutters found in the barn. And it was probably the only paneled sandbox in all of Baltimore County. Now, after many years, the sandbox has folded; but we are continuing our sand castles—we are putting on a new room. And for us it is a giant step.

We've learned over the summer that when one makes a simple addition, one should simply learn how to add. It would also help to know how to multiply and if, by chance, you knew the higher mathematics of square feet, it would be pennies from heaven. But we are growing, we hope, foot by foot—or rather two-by-fours.

Building anew is always an exciting time, although as the old creaking shingles are pulled away they seem to moan the passing of years. But constantly there is the hammering, the staccato, the announcing of a new dimension.

And it's hard just to sit around and wait. I keep seeing the new house as a whole. But it's like dominoes. Once the wall is torn down between the old and the new, the room falls, in my eyes, into disrepair. The question is how to keep your husband and your bank both happy while tidying up the old house to live with the new?

And that's exactly what I've been trying to do—trying to get estimates on future inner beautifications. But all I've really learned is why pioneer women had to do everything for themselves. No one would go that far into the country to give them an "estimate." Or rather a "guesstimate"—as it now seems to be called by those high on ladders, such as painters and paperhangers.

One artisan, whose middle name has to be "guesstimate," not only made me feel as if we lived on the outer fringes of civilization but also as if the road would have to be cleared before he could get his paint truck anywhere near the front door.

"My, my! You live a long way out," he said, and then outlined his route which seemed half Wells Fargo, half Orient-Express. Fortunately I had hidden the Saint Bernard before he arrived.

Then he saw the house . . . which is exactly why he was here in the first place. What a disappointment, as I'm sure all the walls he had met before had been perfectly straight. There has to be a challenge, even in walls. But perhaps we overdid it. After a small tour of our old house, and a glance at the new, with my hope and his despair, he gave me his computations, which floored me.

"Well," he said, "there'll be a big loss of time." (That meant getting here.) "Then it will take about an hour to set up the ladders and buckets. . . . No, you can't help set up the ladders—union, ya know. Then there'll be a loss of wallpaper." (That meant our crooked walls.)

By the time he figured up his losses, I figured we hadn't much to gain. But we parted friends and I gave him a few flares in case he needed them on the long trek home.

It's really all my fault. I'm trying to put the cart before the horse, or rather the frills before the frame. The roof is barely up and I have to know how much it would cost to trellis the bathroom completely. There are no walls, yet I have to know if I can put thirty-six-inch fabric on the south side.

It's too much to ask—even a guesstimate—but you can't stop a girl from trying.

September 1968

Cars should be seen and not heard. But that's seldom the case unless you've graduated to one of those luxury liners that purrrrr. . . . Then there are some secondhand automobiles that are cheerfully advertised as "one-man cars." Ours, alas, would best be known as a one-man band.

But we've grown accustomed to the noise. What can you expect from a station wagon and/or picnic table, cargo ship, school bus, sheep van—a pair of wheels? Every day we should say a little prayer when it moves, and this one even talks to us.

Our very first car was French, but it didn't say much. But then it didn't move much, either. It was a secondhand Citroën, a convertible with a *speed-aire,* which means rumble seat, so you can see how old it was. It was meant to be the model used by French gangsters for their getaways. But this car couldn't have gotten away from the Keystone Cops. And it could only go one way on the Champs-Elysées—down. Oh, the romantic moments we spent in Paris in the spring pushing the car while all around us volatile French taxi drivers urged us on in their own adorable way.

But of course you can't go against traffic whether on the Champs-Elysées or Charles Street; and ever since we left that slightly slow but spicy convertible, we've been in wagons.

I recently drove a friend's car that was neither a station wagon nor noisy. It was quite a subtle sensation. I felt vaguely as if I were unmarried and had never known a car pool. It was rather refreshing for a while but awfully unreal.

No, it's better for me to be back to the old grind and screech of the family chariot. We never name our car because we don't want to get too much attached to it. We know it's hard to see a friend collapse. And our cars do have a way of falling apart. Nor do they have decoration of any kind—no flags, no flowers, no name. It's better, in some cases, to remain incognito.

Sometimes it's better just to get lost. That's what I would have preferred a few nights ago. There we were, way out on a country road, with a carload of teenagers going to a dance. "Oh, I'd love to drive the children to the Thomases' in Phoenix. Tom's away and I have nothing else to do. Hop in, kids." Then six hills, ten miles and twenty-four curves later the car stopped absolutely dead.

It's not that it didn't try to announce its imminent departure date to me. But what's one more knock in a cacophony of rattles? "Knock, knock," it would go, and I never asked, "What's there?" That was the trouble. There just wasn't any oil there!

And now we have a new family chariot. It's a whole new world. This new car is as sterile as a hospital room—and almost as boring. There are no lost, month-old bills under the front seat, no wrinkled road maps in the glove compartment—maps that refused to be folded properly—no right tennis shoe or leftover coke bottle nestled alongside the spare tire. Yes, we even have a spare tire. And the slightest scrap of vagrant paper sentences the offender to bread and water for a week.

But there's still hope. It just might become human yet. There is a tiny scratch under the left door handle that no one else has seen so far. And it's my secret. I'm not going to tell a soul—especially not General Motors or General Hardie.

September 1968

T he other evening we went to our first dance. Our first dance, that is, with our children. By a bold, beautiful, generous gesture we were all invited to the same buoyant party. We were thrilled. But the two children we've known longest weren't too pleased about the company they were going to keep—their senior-citizen parents.

Our hostess, who had organized a party of mixed ages before, told us it was incredible how much better behaved the adults were when their own children were around. You can see why. You're afraid to move a toe.

Driving in, we told our children not to forget to dance with their friends, the junior host and hostess, and they in turn told us not to dance. Period. Those were not their exact words but what they meant was please don't do anything startling—say like a fox-trot.

I wonder why children have to grow up and weather the world a bit before they realize that their parents are the splendid human beings that we really are!

The music was power. The musicians wore sunglasses, bright-green tuxedo jackets, and brought their mothers. The bass looked like a young Oscar Wilde, while the others merely looked wild. And we parents were quieter than usual. It was either that or lose your voice for a week.

It was all a smashing success. The rafters rang and the fuses blew. There was so much electricity sparking on the bandstand that the house lights didn't have a chance. But that was quickly fixed and the tribal dances beat on.

The whipped cream topping on this psychedelic cake was the ingenious presence of a go-go girl with the celestial name of Angel Blue. Angel was very quick on her feet as well as other parts of her anatomy. Her silver shiftlike dress was as short as her dark hair was long, and at her neck was a dainty ruffled lace jabot. And although her dress was sleeveless, she also wore lacy cuffs. When I asked someone why they thought she wore cuffs, they merely said, "She waves her arms." That dismissed that silly question. She also wore high white boots, but I decided not to ask anyone why they thought she wore boots.

No matter what age you were Angel was a vision, and she had zing. But then the whole party had zing. Larger than life was a handsome aqua-colored tent underlined in yellow and white stripes and everywhere yellow tables. Once you took your eyes off Angel, the tent and the decor you tried desperately not to look at your children, while at the same time desperately trying to find them.

What actually happened was that the children acted very adult, behaving beautifully while we were rather childish—ducking behind poles, acting terribly timid as if at our first dance. We wanted to join in, but at the same time we didn't want to get in the way. It was quite a revelation.

But revelations seem to be happening more frequently these days. Earlier in the week our older children went to their first dinner dance alone. Their costumes were strictly lend-lease. Louise wore my shoes, and our elder son borrowed a tuxedo from a friend's father. The trousers were held up by his own father's suspenders and the network in the back resembled a complicated spider web. But somehow it all worked.

Next time we'll probably have to rent a tuxedo. But we can never rent the look on our son's face when all by himself he tied his first black bow tie. It was a wonderful look of boyish victory, and a marvelous moment in our time. We are all growing up, and isn't life sweet.

September 1968

Weddings are the nicest pockets of joy I know. Especially when they are young pockets of joy.

And when the pretty daughter of friends marries the handsome Marine son of other friends, it's almost too much. It hardly happens anymore, even in books. It's bliss, it's the bloom on the rose, the blush on the cheek and all those shiny medals on his dress blues.

It's also a jolt. But the day does come when your contemporaries, your very own contemporaries, have children who are about to marry. No! No! They're much too young . . . the parents I mean.

But time and Lohengrin do march on and there you are. But what side of the aisle do you sit on? Should Tom sit on the bridegroom's side and I on the bride's? No, we must stick together. At weddings you especially want to sit next to your husband, don't you? How else can you compare him to the father of the bride? And you can't hopscotch over to the other side once you've crawled over that sea of knees, the ones who managed to get there before you.

Those knees don't usually move over and I don't blame them. We all know aisle seats are even more important at a wedding than at a play. We all know the bride, the lovely bride, will only pass this way once. And everyone wants to see and remember why brides are beautiful.

Once you've hurdled the knees and the decision of where to sit, you think. At least organ music makes me think. It's either that or blow my nose. It gets me right here. You watch all the hats and husbands coming into the church and you realize suddenly the bride is only six years older than your own daughter, and your own daughter is even too young to wear lipstick. But in six years she might be wearing white rose-point peau de soie.

I wonder if Tom and I should go on Metrecal now. I wonder how I'd look in gray lace, no, better pink. Louise did throw a book at Beth last night. I wonder if she'll ever throw her younger sister a bouquet? I wonder if Tommy Hardie will have his shirttail showing as usual? No, a morning suit will cover that. I wonder if Beth's teeth will be straightened by then? I've never yet seen a bridesmaid in braces. But the orthodontist says she's too young. He doesn't realize she might have to straighten a train of tulle in a few years, so on with the teeth.

Then you don't know if you're crying for this bride or your bride or the orthodontist's bill. I wonder if there's rain insurance for mothers?

Suddenly life's best moments seem to accordion into a very small space. Suddenly you've got all your children married. And you wonder why in the world you give such a wide screen to so many trivial chores. Why, for instance, were you so excited about taking down the screen doors that very morning? Let those screen doors bang for attention one more week . . . for here, here today, here comes the bride. . . .

Are there forty steps down the aisle? Probably more. They are the most important steps she's ever taken since the day she learned how to walk. And my, she walks beautifully. So did her mother, so did his . . . each on the arms of their sons. Where, Tom, is your handkerchief!

After the ceremony the church bells ring out, the organ peals. To get out of the church all I have to do is float.

Once you've floated, you start swinging at the reception. Bouquets of daisies on the stairway, snappy music the minute you enter the tent, and the bridesmaids' garnish pink and perky and pretty.

Will we be doing all this in six years? Who knows? But I do hope I get the screen doors fixed before the reception.

October 1968

I am really in the soup! The other night I was talking as if I had been born with a mixing spoon in my mouth and my diapers tied with a cordon bleu. I was talking big. When in truth I have no taste or talent for cooking, and cooking feels the same way about me. That way no one's hurt.

I try to take the shortest routes in cooking. The other day I bought some "nonskid" spaghetti from Genoa. Even though it might take away some of the romance of the dish, I thought it would also take away some of the sound effects. This spaghetti is shaped like rickrack braid used as trim on little girls' dresses. Have you ever eaten any rickrack braid? I think it must taste like nonskid spaghetti. *Arrivederci* nonskid spaghetti!

But that's not the reason I'm in the soup. I'm in the *potage* because I served a clam bisque at a dinner party, and one of the guests now wants the recipe! This beautiful blend is from a book written by a good friend, Elly Elliott, who lives in New York and serves fancy fare. And as far as shortcuts go in cooking, she is a wizard.

That evening the clam bisque was the star! It was even toasted with raised glass by one of the male guests. As he toasted the bisque, a small child hiding in the rafters was actually heard to whisper loudly, "Awwwww it comes from cans!"

Puffed up by my soupy success, I was heard to say immodestly, "Oh, no, it took me days!"

In a way it did take me days. We had decided to have the dinner party in our unfinished bedroom, a room still highlighted by hanging asbestos, wooden obstacles of all shapes, devious nails and plaster dust the likes of a Sahara windstorm.

Several days before the party we started sweeping. Later, the big day, we repeated the exercise, took apart the scaffolding, lugged in tables and chairs and set candles on sawhorses. There really wasn't much time for the actual cooking.

I also started wondering why in the world we were ignoring a perfectly good, clean, established dining room. A dining room that has served us for years, and never once upset soup on my lap. But no . . . we had to open up new frontiers, unexplored regions, and eat in a bedroom dust bowl.

Yet everything went off beautifully . . . I think. But what am I going to do about this requested recipe? I must send her something. I secretly like the mirage of my bending over a hot stove for days. Now after all my big talk I'm frankly embarrassed. This new friend, who just happens to be the wife of our daughter's new headmaster, thinks I'm a cook, and I'm really a fraud. I'll probably be banned by the food and drug people. Do I make up a recipe—one that sounds courageous?

Find the most succulent clams in the market. Stand over them for hours while they steam with thyme from your garden. . . . Save juice. Pick mushrooms from your pasture, avoiding those known as "death cup." Cook them, then mash for hours the mushrooms, clams, boiled onions and potatoes. Mash only with a wooden spoon. Add clam juice, heat, then strain. Finally, after days, add the heaviest of your cow's cream, and depending on taste, the leaves of a late-summer verbena.

Or should I tell the truth, lose face, and copy out my friend's delicious recipe for Clam Bisque?*

*From *The Glamour Magazine Party Book* by Eleanor Elliott, Doubleday & Co., 1965. Reprinted with permission of *Glamour* magazine.

3 cans condensed clam chowder
1½ tablespoons thyme
1 bottle clam juice
3 cans mushroom soup
1 cup heavy cream

Mix the undiluted clam chowder and thyme with the clam juice. Mix the mushroom soup, also undiluted, with the cream and stir both mixtures together over low heat until thoroughly blended. Strain to remove vegetables and chill in refrigerator. A day-before dish, it is equally good served hot.

This serves twelve and if you get your child to open the cans the mixing time is only about fifteen minutes.

Good-bye face . . . good-bye face.

November 1968

What you wear when you visit your children's teachers could mean the difference between a plus and a minus. Of course, it also depends on why you're there in the first place! Were you invited en masse for an open house, or were you summoned for a solitary conference behind closed doors?

These are the times parents need every little bit of help they can get—including tips on what to wear. And so the following is offered as an extracurricular public service from one parent to another.

It goes without saying that teachers *are* human, and so your school uniform could be gauged by:

a. Is the teacher male or female?

b. Is your child flying high or failing miserably?

c. The temperature—yours and the teacher's.

Now, gray is a good color—institutional, correct and slightly vague. It is also the color of battleships. Gray is smart as well. But you don't want to look *too* smart. You don't want that teacher to think . . . "Hrumpff . . . here I am trying to teach their child algebra, English, mythology, general science, geography, as well as some manners, and look at her . . . she's off to the races, or at least a matinee." No, perhaps it's better to look dowdy. This, however, pertains only to audiences with female teachers.

Nor are we suggesting the latest transparent fashions of Yves Saint Laurent. Heavens no! No peekaboo, please. It's easy enough to see through parents, anyhow.

It has been found that fathers are the best family representatives for failing marks given by female teachers. This situation need not be defined too clearly. Fathers have a certain *je ne sais quoi.* Yet it always helps to wear what we like to call The Cary Granted Pinstripe Suit.

Black for women goes on the blacklist. Rather unwisely I once wore a black suit to school one day and another mother asked me if I was going to a funeral. She had me in the wrong pew, but that particular time was gloomy enough. Brave colors boost morale in teacher-parent confrontations. Colors like apple red, lemon yellow, greenback green, shocking pink, parent blue and that old favorite battleship gray. But remember you don't want to win the battle and lose the war.

If you live in the country and your child goes to a small school as some we know there is a certain gamesmanship in arriving in corduroy pants. This suggests . . . "Well, I've just gotten off the horse and here I am . . . so?" If the teacher is not overcome by the aroma of the barnyard and/or horse stall you just might be able to talk turkey. If she or he is overcome, whip off your stock and/or cowboy hat and start fanning.

Perhaps a smarter move would be to settle for a sweater and skirt, suggesting you've never really left school yourself. If the teacher also happens to be in athletics, you could wear your husband's letter if your husband has a letter. This shows you're one of the boys even though they think you're a mother.

And do try to remember to change from your nightgown and bathrobe. Yes, car pools have been known to be driven in such attire. And it does show a rather harassed way of life and might just evoke sympathy. But it is indeed a chancy maneuver.

Above all you must remember not to be too studied, too frivolous or too careful. Ulterior motives are the last things we want our teachers to attribute to us.

November 1968

To go to a cocktail party without your husband you need a lot of Francis Chichester and a little of Belle Watling. Remember Belle? She was that woman of questionable talents who was a real pal to Rhett Butler and/or Clark Gable. She had heart.

But you need more than heart for solo cocktail party flights. So . . . Sir Francis. As we all well know, Sir Francis can chart almost anything—including cocktail parties, which I suspect he doesn't attend. (Who would with all that free rum on board?)

But first, on this side of the ocean, we must examine the problem closely. Where is your husband? Oh . . . he's duck shooting. Well then you might just as well get out and have a little fun. The next question is, "Why do you want to have a little fun?"

Why, when there's still a demi of chilled champagne left from the holidays; why, when those wonderful children are now back at school, a steak is waiting to be à *point* right in your own kitchen, and the latest English mystery is by the bed to be read in the warmest of eiderdowns, why? Oh, I see. You can hardly wait to get out. Then, go!

It is a strange commentary on social customs to realize that when you do go to a cocktail party with your husband, you hardly see him, much less converse. But when you are alone, all you do is talk about him. It's much safer that way. He's your silent partner. It's like other aspects of marriage. He may not be in sight, but he's there.

Now on the other hand if you really don't care where he is, your whole approach to a cocktail party single could be much more carefree, rather Holly Golightly. But do remember, please, to eat lots of hors d'oeuvres. Don't nibble, eat. Every time the tray is passed. You can also offer sustenance to others from the buffet table. This way you can get the best roast beef for yourself and make new friends at the same time. You can always tell by looking at a man whether he's grated cucumbers or Smithfield ham.

Vitally important is to keep moving. Keep circulating. And don't talk too long to any one man. Pretend you're talking to London and it's twelve dollars for every three minutes. That should cut short any lengthy discussions. But those three minutes should be meaty, witty or devastating. That takes a little bit of research.

But since you're only going to talk three minutes to each man, you don't really have to know much. For a potpourri of ideas that will get you absolutely nowhere, try discussing your idea of Don Shula's last game plan, or Jean-Jacques Servan-Schreiber or *Women's Wear Daily*'s philosophy on Daddy O. Then move on . . . quickly. . . .

The size of the party should influence your choice of costumes. Red is always good at large gatherings except bullfights. Black is smart at small gatherings against white walls. Never, however, wear the same dress as your hostess or Belle Watling. You want to be noticed but you don't want to be disturbed.

So eat, drink and remember, after all, you're married. As for me, I'm staying home. But you-all have a good time, y'hear.

January 1969

T hat Oriental interloper has finally invaded our domestic domain. Finally, Flu Manchu . . . the Hong Kong.

Over the holidays the fear of catching it hung over us like the Dragon Lady's eyebrows. We'd been waiting for it, but it was still a terrible surprise. Now it has struck, and our dogs, yes, our dogs, have the flu.

Tuffy, the Saint Bernard with the red eyes, is in Ward A, which means on our bed; and Horatio, the cocker spaniel with the red nose, is in Ward B, drooping more languidly than his own long ears, on the sofa.

For weeks I thought it would be the children who would catch it, and then we would all fall like dominoes. They skated in the rain, and skied in the rain; the sun hardly set on their wet britches. But for once we fooled the virus.

But the flu is no fool; it did enough damage. And we count our blessings, including collapsed canines.

It was Tommy who first diagnosed the malady of Tuffy,

who is floppy enough even when he's one hundred percent healthy. Of course, Tommy had a clue when he read in the newspaper that three whales had the flu. I wonder how whales react when they're having chills. Small tidal waves?

When Horatio also started dragging around, something was obviously wrong. He didn't even want to bite anyone. And everyone knows the usual touchy temperament of a cocker spaniel.

The vet verified what we had suspected once he hoisted Tuffy up onto the table. Fever, sore throat, lung congestion—yes, definitely, the flu. And Tuffy looked sad as only a Saint Bernard can look sad.

Horatio rallied momentarily as he tried to chew the vet's hand off at the wrist. But vets are smarter than dogs and Horatio got the needle after all. However, he didn't get the same thorough examination as Tuffy did, for, as the vet said, "It isn't worth it to upset the dog. . . ."

Now both patients are convalescing at home and are having absolute bed rest. Our bed. But I'm the one that should be in bed. It's the first time I've ever taken two dogs, albeit sick dogs, to the vet's alone. One sweet but mammoth, the other small but nasty! I felt quite agile, yet desperate, as I hustled Tuffy in and out, then Horatio in and out. I hadn't counted on that large police dog in the waiting room.

But we're all doing as well as can be expected. In fact, it's quite peaceful. I'm hoping the fleas get the flu, too. Four times a day I raise Tuffy's tired head to offer him a yellow pill rolled in raw hamburger. He looks at me with those large drooping red eyes and I think he knows I'm trying to help. Horatio gets the same yellow pill three times a day and even he's too weak to object.

We haven't gone in for any hot mustard foot baths or lemonade. I think the pills are a more compact remedy. There's no doubt about it—the dogs are depressed and tired.

Now that I think about it, I'm rather depressed and tired, too; but I'm not about to take yellow pills. . . . Tuffy, do you hear me? Tuffy . . . move over!

January 1969

At last my new friend has arrived. My desk. My "antique distressed" desk, as they call it in the trade. It's Italian and it's fern green and has very bowed legs. But that's not why it's distressed. It was anguished on purpose. Someone had a big time bumping it around, hammering it up, giving the desk some patina, some instant age. And to think I actually paid for it!

It must be far cheaper, I'm sure, to find an antique distressed wife. All you need is a sudden surprise snowstorm with a husband on business in Ghent, Belgium, and no snow tires here in Glyndon, Maryland. Or try a flooded kitchen in the middle of the night. Flooded because the electricity came on again unexpectedly after twelve hours, but you had forgotten to turn off the faucets.

No, it has to be more fun to distress a desk. Although this desk was made in Italy it was tortured in New York. I wonder if the artisan-in-charge called his friends. . . . "Come on over, we're having a distressing party. Don't protest tonight. March over here instead. And bring your rocks. First one to hit the desk without spilling his *vino* gets another peace button."

Frankly, I had my desk distressed so it would match our other furniture. You know . . . tricycle scars, vacuum-cleaning bumps, heel kicks and the other sturdy marks of life. Now we're all one big happy distressed family. The furniture that is.

I wonder if I'll begin to look like my desk—the way people

sometimes look like their dogs. I feel I'm going to get that attached. I am rather green, often distressed, antique in the children's eyes, but only not bowlegged, as yet. I *have* seen some roll-top desk type people. And there are plenty of upright desk type people. It takes all kinds of desks to make all kinds of people. . . . Thank you, Edgar Guest.

Actually I'm looking forward to living with this desk. It took me long enough to make the decision. Six months to decide to buy it, then six months to get it here from New York. Once it was lost in a warehouse. Then I was also distressed. What, I wondered, was an Italian desk doing in a warehouse in Virginia?

But now it is home, and I'm very happy. A desk is certainly a personal piece of property. In a way it is my first adult desk. Good-bye kitchen table.

As we have just met, we're still rather shy. At this point, for instance, a kitchen table does seem friendlier. You write faster in a kitchen. Who wants to look at a stove when you can look at a sky. . . .

This desk is going to share about every emotion. And I'm going to spend a lot of time leaning on it. It's going to be a very good friend, often probably an enemy. Is it going to beckon, or inhibit, or inspire? Is it going to be a conscience, or a pal? Sit down at that desk, Dee, and pay those bills!

Think of the letters I may never write sitting at this desk looking out the window. The desk stands in front of floor-length French windows looking out on a primitive red bank barn. I see the Saint Bernard majestic in the snow, the line of sheep wandering down hopefully to find a patch of green pasture, the Oriental grace of tree limbs laced with white. . . .

Maybe I'd better get back to the kitchen and keep this desk just for thinking. A thinking desk. How nice. Not a distressed desk, but a thinking desk for happy thoughts.

January 1969

I t's all so easy, says Louise, who at fourteen has decided ears are for earrings rather than for listening to mothers. "Let's get my ears pierced, please! Look at Becca. When she was eight, she pierced her own ears with a pin!" . . . This has to be called doing your own thing. (Becca is now ten and miraculously still has ears.)

Louise not only has ears, but has somehow accumulated seven pairs of earrings and even saved a Christmas check, earmarked for you know what. There seemed to be no way out of it. As if I didn't know enough about pierced ears. . . .

In days gone by, ears were usually pierced after inheriting dangling diamonds from a great-grandmother, or simply if you were a pirate. I was in neither category. No diamonds were around, nor any treasure chest of any kind. It was merely that I didn't have any identifiable lobes on my ears and was tired of constantly losing one earring, paste or otherwise.

In Paris, where my ears were pierced, most females get the job done quickly and casually in their own kitchen or at the corner drugstore. And it's done when they're very young. Spanish and Italian babies as well seem to have solid-gold earrings even before they're on solid foods.

But I was certainly no baby, and so there I was in the American Hospital in Paris with my ears being scrutinized by the chief surgeon who, it turned out, had never pierced ears before. He was undoubtedly as surprised as I was over this rather ridiculous position in which I had involved him. But how did I know I was going to get the chief surgeon? You miss a lot in translation even in the American Hospital. Anyhow, he was already washed up; and my position wasn't much better.

I had a sheet up to my neck and a ball-point pen marking my ears for this surgeon's scalpel. All his years of medical school . . . for this!

The first ear he did with a scalpel, and a determined grunt. Then he summoned his nurses, changed his instruments and did the second ear with a large needle. And it was then I wondered if diamonds really were a girl's best friend after all. I'm still wondering.

Some eighteen years later there are still no diamonds but there are daughters. . . .

Daughter Louise and I spend one afternoon in Baltimore finding the right earrings—with fourteen-carat posts. "And make sure her hair is shampooed the night before," warns our doctor's office in Cockeysville. The next morning, Saturday, we sit in the waiting room and sit and we sit. It has to be a Saturday because I can't in my heart of hearts get her excused from school to get her ears pierced.

In about an hour and a half we see a secretary. She quizzes us and makes checks against a long list . . . "Did Louise have a normal birth? . . . How about her eating habits? her sleeping habits? At what age did she walk? talk? Has she hypertension?" We remind the secretary we are there to have Louise's ears pierced, only her ears.

In another hour we see the doctor and he promptly tells us we have the wrong earrings. I run across the street to a small jewelry store and buy the right earrings—fourteen-carat posts with fourteen-carat balls for what I now feel are Louise's million-dollar ears. Deftly he pierces the first ear and Louise almost faints. I almost faint. Then it is over. We now have a daughter with holes in her head.

And she has changed. Her hair is tucked neatly behind her ears "so they won't get infected," whereas before I often didn't see her right eye for a week. Her head is more erect, although she won't admit it. She obviously cares.

Maybe Louise will get those diamonds.

February 1969

W hen you travel you always feel you're going to bring home some new and exciting ideas. Recently when we were in Mexico we had a tasty dish for lunch called Cabrito Asado Al Horno. Loosely translated, very loosely, that means "old goat." And it, too, has given me some ideas.

We just happen to have an old goat in the garden, very much on the hoof. He hoofs into our bushes, he horns into our trees. Of course he should be tethered properly; he should be secured more securely. But he is the Houdini of the herd. Nothing keeps him in his proper place. And anyhow a goatscape is a new scene for us.

In the first place we've got someone else's goat. He's not ours. We found him in our front field, not our cabbage patch. He was, to put it bluntly, unloaded on us by the light of the moon. (Unwanted goats always seem to get unloaded when the moon is full.)

And he has been granted asylum for only two reasons. First, our children have grown very fond of him, and secondly, he has a certain style. When Oscar, as he is now called, holds his head high, which isn't too often, he looks like the gallant Navy goat. Sometimes he even looks slightly Oriental; the ancient mandarin of the barnyard with long beard and horns which curve rather than spiral as those of the ram.

He is handsome, there's no doubt about it. Until you turn

around. Somehow the golden rule of goats seems to be "do unto others . . . the minute they turn their backs. . . ."

Our own Hampshire ram has finally accepted him after considerable loss of body wool, the Saint Bernard thinks he's another Saint Bernard with horns, and the Springer spaniel just bounces along with the group. In fact it is rather refreshing to drive up to the house after a long day of car pools and be met enthusiastically by such a trio, all in a row, the goat, the Saint Bernard and the tiny spaniel.

And I've got to admit it is fun to look the goat straight in his beady yellow eyes and say, "Get out of my way you old goat, you old goat, you really old goat. . . ." It helps because you can't just say that to anyone . . . even though sometimes you feel like it.

And although we now know where he came from, his origin, Oscar now seems to be part of this picture on Thornhill Farm. In many old French and English sheep prints you often see a goat mingling with the flock. Even his scent hasn't gotten to me yet. And the March winds did blow.

But spring is coming and I hope he doesn't go on a high floral diet. Right now as I look out my window he is nibbling on a lilac limb, and for a *digestif* he's trying a bit of early forsythia. Things are looking down. Especially Oscar's head.

A friend was here the other day from Kenya, far away in East Africa "near the borders of Abyssinia" as he put it. He has goats too. But he has other goat problems. The leopards get his.

Maybe a leprechaun will have to get ours. The first tulip Oscar shreds, the first daffodil he enjoys, the first grape hyacinth he savors will be, in effect, his walking papers. It's either the garden or the goat. And a full moon is soon here. In fact it is this Thursday. I just might take Oscar for a walk and do unto others as they have done unto us.

April 1969

L acrosse to me is the game in which there are sticks in every corner of our kitchen and what they do most is fall down. And that, I suppose, is Treason!

~~~   But I might add that whenever I am away from Maryland and the word "lacrosse" is mentioned, I immediately get to my feet, stand very straight, and put my hand over my heart. This shows (1) that we have sons, and (2) that I have probably spent a lot of time looking for lacrosse balls in the bushes in the spring. I'm very good at looking for lacrosse balls, but other than that I still don't understand the game at all.

Where I grew up, boys were boys and played baseball. It was all so easy, so clear-cut, so apple pie. Then I married, moved to Maryland and had to learn an entirely new way of life. It's been hard. But I do like the costumes.

Yet here I live in the midfield of the lacrosse belt and I'm still not sure where the crease is. Oh, sure, I know it's down at the end; but I don't know who is where when. Or even how or why. Sometimes it's like a swarm of bees down there. And everybody looks the same. Other mothers probably won't agree; but I've often seen little lacrosse players in serious play and they all look the same, all slightly undernourished in oversized uniforms.

I do favor lacrosse over wrestling since I have now seen one wrestling match. I found the face-to-floor combat entirely too much for my emotions. And who in their right minds would walk around with their weight sewn on their sleeves? I wouldn't do that for the world. My heart maybe, yes, but never my weight. (I noticed there didn't happen to be a weight class for me.)

I also took in the last basketball game of Louise's season. Darks versus Lights. It wasn't exactly Bullet speed, but it was awfully polite. Yet even that was too exciting for me. The evil, too, comes out. Sometimes I even think about tripping the other team. Lacrosse is better, since I can't tell one player from the next.

However, I am particularly aware of the equipment for the older boys. Cleated shoes made out of kangaroo hides, King Kong–sized padded gloves, and the stick itself made by the Mohawk Indians. Since it takes the Indians almost a year to make a stick, I think they should include a ready-made pocket. That way my iron would not be put out of commission as a pocket maker. Boys will be boys in Baltimore and play lacrosse, but remember it's those squaws who do the stringing.

It hasn't all been in vain, though, my education in the sport of the wild Indian. I've learned that lacrosse is a game in which a boy will "cradle" a ball ever so gently one minute, then bop another player with the stick the next. I've also learned lacrosse is a sport of braves to every male in this family—and the best possible reason for spring. Would you believe a home game of lacrosse yesterday at 7:15 A.M.?

In the spring a barn door isn't just a barn door, but a backboard for lacrosse as well. And spring isn't really the time of the tulip; it's the time it takes to try to fit five lacrosse sticks and five boys into one car pool at the end of a busy day.

April 1969

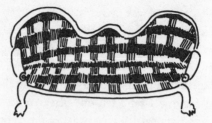

I have an old sofa that is aging me rapidly. It is shaped like Queen Victoria lying down. Victoria, as we all know, was around a long time and this sofa has been around a long time, too.

About six feet in length, the sofa's back goes up and down, rather curvy for a staid Victoria, more like a roller coaster. But this sofa doesn't give you any funny feelings in the pit of your stomach. Only when you sit down.

But my husband likes it. It is a link with the past, for it was his grandmother's. And when it came up from New Orleans, it was covered in grandmother-colored velvet. Gentle, faded rose.

If it had only come by river boat, I might have felt differently about it, have more of a feeling of the romance of the South. Lift that bale, tote that sofa. But it came by a big, blustering van that managed to carry away some lower limbs of trees on our narrow country road.

As soon as possible, I put a red-and-white toile de Jouy on the sofa, and for a moment it seemed French. Its character completely changed and then it seemed all right to be so curvy. But that moment has turned into thirteen years and it is time for a change. In fact, it's almost a necessity. Behind my back, long-haired dogs found it very comfortable and short-haired children used it as a jumping-off spot.

Actually, they only jumped off the sofa when they were the Fratellini Brothers, and how are you going to be trapeze artists without some sort of an elevated platform? All children go through jumping periods. It's either that or you might jump out of your own skin. I hope I remember this when I have grandchildren.

Nevertheless, all this activity weakened the backbone of this Victorian. And it took me three months, at least, to find someone to take on the reconstruction of the South, this Southern sofa. I talked to one man who claimed to have done work for the White House and another who had rejuvenated chairs for the Edgar Allan Poe house, or so he said.

They boasted, but they didn't produce. They were all too busy. Why is everyone so busy? Why does it take so much longer to get anything done these days?

Finally, one man took pity and told me about another man, but told me not to tell who told. And so in this devious manner I found someone who cares. I have a new hero, a restorer of sofas, as well as my spirits. To me, his measuring stick is a magic wand. Of course, I have not seen the sofa yet and it's been months, but I'm keeping the faith.

The delay is not his fault, though. I'm to blame. I had to pick out the material on my own. Not that he liked my choice. Nor did another upholsterer who called it a "half-breed fabric." It is bold, bright, honest blue-and-white squares. The fact that it is only forty-nine inches wide rather than the conventional fifty-two or fifty-four is what upsets them. And that it is loomed in India didn't help much, either.

It sure didn't. The material arrived from India all right, but there it sat on the New York dock for three months during the strike. When it did arrive here, we discovered I hadn't ordered enough. And to add to my discouragement, the loom must have had grease on it that day, or else the weaver spilled his curry. The material was not only checked, it was spotted.

So we had to start all over again and we're still sitting on the floor. Maybe we should just stay on the floor and contemplate.

You begin to wonder if it's all worth it. The time, the energy, the worry about a few yards of material. But we'll soon find out.

The finished sofa is promised for this week. To think that the odyssey of this piece of furniture started in 1845, its date as we have now discovered. And to think of all that has happened to it in those 124 years . . . and to me in these last six months! Now all may see a very young sofa and a very old woman.

April 1969

Completely unprepared for this role, in fact, never suspecting four children could happen to *me,* I used to worry about our children all the time, especially about my own motherhooding. I wanted desperately to be Mother Earth, and I can hardly make Brownie Class.

I don't know how to darn, and I would rather dig in the garden than dig in a closet for a lost left sneaker. No matter how I try I can't keep the girls' navy-blue school socks straight, or even in twin sets. Nor can I stop the soles of Tommy's socks from resembling graying Swiss cheese.

I never seem to stock enough snacks in the cupboards. ("What!" they say, "no more peanut butter for the celery?") And I never never get the right undershirts in the right drawers or the proper clean trousers on the right boy. It's been tough. It's been the survival of the fittest, or as Tommy says, "the call of the wild."

But I no longer worry about all my shortcomings. I have

just read an article on Outward Bound and I'm saved! Outward Bound is a worldwide group of schools, including five in the United States, where young men and recently women, for less than a month, go through the most terrible trials, the hardest of knocks, the most difficult of situations—all on purpose, to shape up for life, to help find their "potential." And now I realize my failings may just be the foothills of future successes for the Hardie four. If they can stand life with Mother, they can probably stand almost anything. . . .

As an Outward Bound instructor explained in a recent article, "Our method is to confront them with a series of anxieties and even panic-creating situations unlike anything they have ever faced before." Well . . . welcome to Thornhill Farm, an unconscious annex of Outward Bound!

The article continues . . . "Outward Bound wants its youth exposed as much as possible to real-life emergencies." That, in a nutshell, is the story of our lives.

"At Outward Bound at 5:30 an atrocious horn blasts the boys loose from sleep." Well, I give them until 6:30; then the atrocious horn and/or Mother's voice starts the day rolling. And for years I've been trying to introduce them to water, any water . . . clean water, bathwater. They don't even have to jump off a cliff into the 41-degree ocean, as at one of the Outward Bound schools in Maine. Maybe I'm too easy on them.

But the real trial comes when we have weekend guests. Then, as we call it here at Outward Bound, the children go "solo." Almost like the real Outward Bound where each student is dropped off alone in empty country to spend three or four days living off the land, sea and streams.

Here the chosen one has to find another bed since the guest has to sleep somewhere, doesn't she? Guests usually come in the springtime, because then it doesn't matter if our children don't have anything to wear. It's usually warmer. Eat? Of course our children eat. I find leftover crackers in desk drawers where they have obviously hidden provisions; there are a few wild strawberries on the hill if one only puts one's nose to the ground; garlic grass is amazingly tasty, although green teeth aren't too attractive; and how about the parsley in the fridge that I forgot to put around the roast leg of lamb?

The main thing is to keep the children hidden from the guests. The guests wouldn't understand. They wouldn't realize what we are doing for the children—that this hardship tour of duty is for their own good, that makeshift beds under half-collapsed tents, faces stained with wild berries, and torn T-shirts are not only fun, but that we're working on their potential.

I knew there must be some reason I felt so close to Outward Bound. Josh Miner, one of my husband's college classmates, helped found the first American Outward Bound in Colorado, in 1962. Josh visited us years ago in Paris, and one big evening we "did" our own personal tour of Paris by Night. That, I'm almost sure, is one of the reasons Josh started Outward Bound. After all, Paris by Night, is no easy obstacle course.

May 1969

The other morning we had a two-level conversation. Beth was upstairs and we were downstairs.

"I want an animal!" said eleven-year-old Beth.

"You've got two nice parents," answered her father in a what-more-do-you-want voice.

"I want an animal! You're a man, she's a woman, and I'm a girl, a good girl who needs an animal," she hollered down the stairs.

Cagey Beth knew that very morning she was going to the Valley School Fair. She knew at the fair they always had cages of animals for sale . . . kittens, gerbils, guinea pigs and other assorted animals I try not to see. She knew the time was to attack.

"Tommy had the chickens and now he has Tuffy (a Saint Bernard), Todd had Colonel (a horse now in greener pastures), Louise has those cats, and before she had the pigs. And I don't have anybody. . . ." (She forgets there are thirty sheep in the fields, but that doesn't count. To have an animal, the animal must be given directly to you.)

"What about Horatio?" asked her father.

"Horatio is everybody's," she moaned. (Horatio is a cinnamon-colored spaniel who is usually in a bad mood.)

She's quite right, though. When you live in the country you need a friend, a furry friend of your very own whom you can talk to by the barn, or have sleep by your bed. A friend who doesn't talk back—like brothers and sisters and mothers.

You can't say we haven't tried. Todd's horse was around until one day he slumped against a barn post and died of old age. The barn post has never been replaced and neither has Colonel. Louise's pigs, two white hogs named The Dolly Sisters, eventually went the way of all pigs, thank heavens, and now she has cats. Legions of cats. And they're all black.

At least this year they're black and when you try to count them, you think you're repeating yourself. Only unfortunately you're not. She also had a lovebird, but it died of flu which it caught from the dogs.

Last year at the Valley School Fair, Beth did get a guinea pig. Nice guinea pig. We put it in a cage which once held rabbits. Before that it may have been inhabited by very small ducks. This guinea pig was extremely adroit.

From his cage, he could toss wood shavings at least a foot. Pretty good for a guinea pig who never had any training. Never had much of a chance. Then one day he disappeared. He honestly disappeared. Or should we say he disappeared honestly? Without any help from adult outsiders.

Beth was very sad and somehow we had to fill the vacuum. Fortunately about that time Beth's friend Kate was going away. And so Kate's gerbils came to visit. Gerbils, as I understand it, often eat their young. That might be their idea of planned parenthood, but it's not my idea of animal husbandry.

I never went near Beth's room, the gerbil guest room. She took complete charge and luckily just as many went home as had arrived.

And now Beth has accomplished her mission. She came home from the fair with an animal. At least she had something. And lo and behold, it was a turtle in a tank complete with a miniature plastic palm tree. Turtles can't give you any trouble, can they?

One problem has arisen already, however. Beth thinks he's lonely. That sounds like Phase Number 2. That sounds suspicious. What's next? Anyone know of a loose llama? Or a friendly kangaroo?

June 1969

When you marry and promise to love, honor and obey, I wonder if you could also insert a travel clause for husbands only: Love, honor, obey—and promise not to travel when the snow is high on the hill or the grass is deep in the fields.

But it's business, m'dear, business, he invariably says eighteen years later. And business is business, we agree. But it just so happens we have a leader, husband and father who travels to France every six months—on business, he says. Dangerous place, La Belle France. *N'est-ce pas,* General?

The thing to do when your husband travels is to make sure he's kept very busy. This takes a bit of research, but it is well worth the effort, no matter if he's going to Paris or Kenosha, Wisconsin.

It's not that you're really so interested in the material objects you're asking him to search for, it's more of a spiritual togetherness, although miles apart. In other words, you're sending him on a gigantic scavenger hunt so he won't have any free time on his hands.

Most husbands hate to shop, but they often feel a tinge of guilt, or at least they say they do, when they realize they're leaving you home with the children, the sheep and the snow tires still on in June. They are usually so busy and harassed trying to get away that they'll agree to almost anything, even whale's teeth. . . .

In Iceland, where the females are especially attractive, the best buys are whale's teeth. Don't bother to give him the address, for this assignment will take him at least half a day. No one in Iceland speaks hardly anything except Icelandic and whale's teeth are an impossible charade. Now . . . don't you feel better already?

The moment you know he's going on a business trip, rush to your local library and take out all the available travel books on his itinerary. You must know his countries better than he does.

It won't take long, because you're only going to read the chapters on shopping in France, shopping in Portugal, shopping in Italy, shopping in Spain and best buy in Kenosha (underwear).

It must be admitted that there are some compensations when he first departs. You can eat early and then stay up very late watching the latest television and you don't have to go around picking up wet towels.

But it stops right there. There is nothing quite like a man around the house, especially if you've seen his face for some eighteen years. . . . But now don't soften. Our plan to Keep Husbands Occupied at All Times and at All Costs (to him) continues.

If he has five hours in Milan before flying on to France, there is no reason why he can't, between his five business appointments and his Fettucine Alfredo, just troop over to Ken Scott at 37 Via Corridoni and pick up one of those nifty little dresses that cost only one-half as much as here. After all, you're saving him money.

Don't forget to state size, color, fabric, design and short or long sleeves. If, in desperation, he asks you what kind of collar, be big about it and tell him it's completely up to him. This gives him a feeling of fashion maturity.

When he is in France, never let him buy you perfume. This is too easy. No, instead have him find a pair of very long white kid gloves with ten pearl buttons. Don't give him your glove size, no, just a drawing of your left hand.

And give him the length of your arm from your elbow to your wrist in inches, not centimeters. This makes it more of a challenge.

As for Portugal and Spain, handmade rugs take much longer

to find than, say, tiles. Picking out a rug can be a horrendous decision. This may be the finest hour of the obstacle course.

When it is the day of his arrival home, you must meet him at the airport in a new dress, a new scent, and if you are especially bold, a new color hair. He will either turn around à la Mr. Corrigan, or wonder why he ever left home. He may also decide it's easier, after all, just to take you with him—which is really our ultimate aim.

Bon voyage, ladies!

June 1969

A long time ago I had an English friend who told me quite seriously, "Always travel heavy." She always did. Included among her traveling accessories were her favorite collapsible chair, a slender vase, one small lace pillow, a china tea cup and, I suppose, her wearing apparel. But then she did spend a lot of time writing about the nomads, and I guess she learned which way to fold her tent.

Another good friend did just the opposite. Longing for freedom after World War II, he traveled around the United States and Europe with a toothbrush, a typewriter and one change of clothes—or so he says. Then he met and married me, and came home with two trunks, five suitcases and one wife. I don't know which of my friends was the wiser wanderer—the nomad or the new husband. But I do know, when he married me, he also married a trunk.

I've always been a trunk fancier. But I expect so much from trunks. The minute one lifts the lid, the adventure should start. What I wanted most as a child was a grandmother's trunk filled with surprises, like a Pandora's box. Oh, how I dreamed of a trunk filled with dresses from the youth of the old—and maybe, at the very bottom, a parasol. But my grandmother was not a trunk type and I never dug deep into her memories.

I did have a Swedish grandfather who arrived in Massachusetts with a large wooden trunk which I now own. But by the time I got to the trunk, he being Swedish, it was clean and neat and empty. Not even a false lining to spur the imagination of a child.

But in my later years I seem to have made up for all the trunks I didn't have in my youth. Important moments always seem to have been locked up in these trunks. The first was an immense secondhand steamer trunk purchased before I left to work in Europe. It was entirely too big; but when you leave home for the first time and cross an ocean, doesn't everyone feel a little bit like Marco Polo? Now *there* was a man who really traveled heavy!

Anyhow, the drawers stuck and the hangers fell and I practically had to climb inside to find the right clothes to dress for the day. But we, the trunk and I, managed to make it to London, where we were met by our editor, a gentle woman who has since been decorated by her Queen. And she well deserved the honor, even then. Since my steamer trunk wouldn't fit on top of any English taxi, Miss Withers promptly rose to the occasion by escorting my trunk in a fish van—the only available vehicle big enough.

The next trunk that got me into trouble was the one I sent home from Paris after living for a year with a husband who still says he likes to travel light. This trunk, a product of a Saturday shopping trip to the flea market, was covered in mellow beige canvas, with rounded lid and black locks. It took me all of a week to pack it. That's rather good, seeing as I was crowding one year of Paris into one trunk. It did get tiresome, though; and so, to make light of a heavy trunk, I painted THE DANCING HARDIES on every side.

So innocent, or so I thought. This trunk was being brought home by another innocent friend who, it turned out, had a miserable time getting through United States Customs. They were sure she was smuggling something evil into the country . . . The Dancing Hardies, ho ho. This has to be a front! Grass from Indochina? . . . The lead dancer at the Folies-Bergère? . . . Fortunately Elly and I are still friends, but we still never dance together.

The only traveling trunk now in our lives is Louise's camp trunk, which we pack every year about this time. I can never remember what goes inside, but we have a lot of fun with the outsides. This year we plastered it with colorful circus posters. I wonder if it will get to Squam Lake, New Hampshire, or go to Sarasota, Florida.

We do have two other comfortable trunks, but they are relatively reserved, peaceful and stationary in our bedroom. One is a wide wicker trunk from Paris, which now holds our linen and blankets. The other is newer, again wicker, but from Hong Kong.

It's the Hong Kong one that I'm counting on for my old age. After all, how do you give away those tartan pants that a four-year-old boy once wore, or that smocked dress that looked so beguiling on that small blond girl? It also contains a box of funny rings and serious bangles that hang to the knee.

How about that large black hat with pink cloth cabbage roses trellised down the side (Longchamps, circa 1950), or the clown suit, the real straw boater, or the khaki flying suit (Philippines, definitely 1945)? A pile of children's books . . . even a parasol. . . .

This, as we see it, will be grandmother's trunk, a Pandora's box. But I wonder, I wonder if they'll giggle when they poke their noses in and say, "Boy . . . was Granny camp!"

July 1969

W ear a dress!" said Beth, incredulously.

"What's wrong with these shorts?" asked the older son who shall remain nameless by request.

And all I asked them to do was get ready to have their photograph taken. All we had to do that lazy Sunday afternoon was to smile. Just smile. All right, don't smile, just stand still. After all, if Mathew Brady could record the Civil War, we could at least capture in print our family jewels . . . our diamonds in the rough.

Actually nothing was wrong with the older son's shorts except the lacrosse season has been over for months. And by the look of the shorts, their last lacrosse game could have been with the Algonquin Indians. However, they were better than the blue jeans which probably could have stood up alone, anyhow.

Over the years, our children have been photographed and shuttered hundreds of times by their father. And when they look back on their scrapbooks, they laugh uproariously, smile coyly and on the whole seem rather pleased by their youthful visages.

But comes the plateau of ages eleven to sixteen and they suddenly would rather go underground than have their photographs taken. We had the negatives even before the picture was taken.

Tommy didn't care one way or the other, since there was no Orioles game on radio or TV. And unfortunately, Louise wasn't even here. She's up singing camp songs on Lake Squam. We weren't really our true six-person family. Our leader has a theory that if you're going to do something, do it. Shoot!

But if the situation ever arises again, it might be easier just to go out on the street and hire four more reasonable facsimiles.

It really wasn't that bad. Not really. It's just that the three younger subjects couldn't decide whether to be the Three Stooges or John Barrymore. They compromised. They became unidentifiable movable objects.

And how can you take a photograph of a family, they asked, if you don't include the Saint Bernard, which actually is very photogenic if he can just remember to face the camera, an extremely affectionate two-month-old Springer spaniel, and the other spaniel which suddenly eats photographers?

Fortunately, the giant rabbit didn't arrive until the following week. And barns don't move.

And so there we were, the zoo story, sitting under the graceful cascades of the willow tree with the barn in the background. Again we thought of old Mat Brady. Ask David, our friend who photographed us. Our friendly photographer. Our brave photographer. There he was catching us on Plus X film, twenty times. Each time a new hope.

The photographs have since been returned and after a few nights of animated debate around the piano, we have decided on The Family Portrait. Five people . . . twenty shots . . . and guess if anyone ever agreed with anyone else! I was probably the biggest offender. And why not? I thought I looked the biggest.

Suddenly my ego became as large as my shape. Out with those four photos. Then why did that one child make devil horns on the head of another? Eliminate that one. Oh, we had such a good time.

Finally, I took care of everything. I cut out one good head and pasted it on a good body, and presto five people, three dogs and one barn all looking fairly respectable at the same time. What a nice family group, so relaxed.

Shoot, if you must, this old gray head, but no photos please.

August 1969

T omorrow we have friends coming in from New York and
London and I have spent the entire day trying to grow a
vegetable garden. But our local supermarkets haven't
helped me a bit. No one has any garden lettuce that I could
call my own. . . .

When you have old friends from big cities on hand, the
country has to look more beautiful and the food taste more delicious. As a matter of fact it does, but it takes a bit of doing.
Especially since a week of rain has flattened our garden and washed
away the glories of a country summer feast.

After all, half the fun of the game is telling guests, "Everything is off the place." Fraudulent, perhaps, but fun. Especially since
your guests think Jack and the Beanstalk were small potatoes compared to what's grown right here on the farm.

But today, yes, we have no bananas or garden lettuce or
anything. The rains came. The rains blew over the cornstalks and
smothered the tomato plants. Now we have hollyhocks interwoven
with the bowed heads of corn and roaming morning glories have
volunteered to grow in the tangle of tomatoes. It's a lovely country
patchwork, but it's a poor garden. Our crops have gone.

But Les Gals are coming . . . Mary Jane from New York
and Bettina from London, and where are the trophies of a country
garden? Our garden is bare.

The same thing happened the weekend before when two

Italian businessmen from Milan quickly said *si* when my husband invited them for dinner before I had time to say "No!" I had half an hour to prepare an American feast. That was the beginning of my counterfeit kitchen life!

Superbo they said as they ate the fried chicken purchased hastily from Reisterstown Road. *Deliziosissimo,* as they ate their fifth croissant prepared from manufactured dough in a can that I had shaped into crescents. (In truth, the apple pie was the only honest, homemade dish of the evening.)

But they thought I had done everything with my own little lily-white hands. I knew I could get away with it because their next stop was Las Vegas and nobody was going to give me away in Las Vegas. And it is rather nice having a young Italian count of twenty-four and an older Carlo Ponti type think you're the American Queen of the Kitchen, at least for a night.

I felt I was on trial that evening for all the women of America. You know very well that Sophia Loren or any other Italian signora worth her weight in pasta can whip up a wild dish of spaghetti.

I haven't always been such a fake. When we first moved to the country, some fourteen years ago, we had a vast agricultural spread from rutabaga to melons. But every year our vegetable garden seems to get smaller. And now it is only our late, tidy patch of lettuce, corn and tomatoes. But hooray, we still have two surviving melons waiting for our call.

Those melons will be the girls' breakfast. And then the menus will be the same as we had for the Italians. It's getting to be a habit, this noncooking-under-false-pretenses. But what is a girl to do if she has no garden lettuce and the last Hardie leg of lamb went two weeks ago?

I hope I can get it all out of my system by Thanksgiving. A thing can go too far. I can hear myself telling a French visitor that I went down to the barnyard and shot the turkey myself. Living off the land is one thing, but lying off the land is another dish.

August 1969

For easy, relaxed summer reading, give me a good English mystery. For more suspense, give me newspaper wedding announcements. I love them.

And I don't read them only in the summer. I read them summer, winter, fall and June. But things do pick up in the summer. More garden weddings—trim and green and pink-tented, more daisy-decorated pavilions, more garlands under the old apple tree. More details. I love them!

There's a lot of intrigue as well. For instance, the young woman who was on the 1968 Olympic Equestrian Team is about to marry a man who is a "huntsman to the Tewkesbury Foot Bassets, a group that hunts on foot for hares." It worries me. Will it work?

Every newspaper, every Sunday, gives you an aisle seat on weddings of the week, but for a daily reference the best source for this daydream reading is *The New York Times.* Every day of the year photographs of brides and brides-to-be smile forth with hope and the whitest of teeth from the pages of this daily journal, this fortress of fact. And the details are exquisite.

Of course, Sundays are the big feast days telling of the fashions and flowers and families. But it's the weekday announcements that often tell the unusual type of intimate trivia that makes my day complete . . . such as "her maternal grandmother was Susan B. Anthony's second cousin once removed," or, "his father invented gin rummy."

It's not that I'm nosy. It's just that I have an insatiable curiosity about people I don't know and probably will never meet. I read every line, every limb of the family tree, every school attended, as closely as men study the stock quotations on the following pages.

At times, this New York paper takes extraordinary liberties with their future brides. A few months ago a girl's engagement was announced, but it was her fiancé's photograph they printed. Just because he would someday be head of General Motors. I call that going a bit too far.

This wedding announcement analyst can certainly see the writing on the wall. It doesn't take much to see who's going to be in that family's driver's seat.

Then there was the lovely Oriental who married the young man from Omaha. He, an artist, thought they should wear Oriental ceremonial gowns for their New York wedding. She did not.

They compromised and both wore her native garb only at the reception. A reception filled with red and yellow balloons (red and yellow being the Chinese wedding colors). On each balloon was written in gold, "Thanks for coming . . . Lin and Charlie, August 6, 1969." And to think I wouldn't have known any of this if I hadn't read the paper that particular Sunday.

And I wonder how many people know Edward S. Lowe was the creator of Bingo? Helga Hensing married Mr. Lowe, a toy manufacturer, last July 14, and she, by the way, was in charge of American investment funds in Europe for the Deutsche Bank of Frankfurt, Germany. You see how everything works itself out in these wedding announcements. Bingo!

Another young lady whose father was once chairman of the Securities and Exchange Commission is about to marry Walter. Walter is "a portfolio manager in hedge funds." Since I'm a gardener, not a gambler, it doesn't sound too romantic to me, but from the bride's background, you can see she can handle this hedging. And so you feel better.

A simpler announcement recently revealed that a groom's father, a Frenchman, was a "landowner." What a noble statement, and only a Frenchman would include it in his son's wedding announcement. Somehow I feel all this extraneous information I'm gathering is bound to be of value someday. . . .

However, things are a little different down in Texas. When we were in Houston in the marital month of June, the newspapers announced that from that day forward, wedding announcements would cost cold cash. That changes the whole complexion of the details of the bridal bouquet. Does a bride suddenly become a legal announcement? Or a classified ad?

In Texas, I'm sure, all the hearts and flowers are soon going to fade from nuptial newsprint, and I'm very, very sad.

August 1969

O ur second son, Aga Khan Hardie, hopes to be financially independent next year by the time he reaches fourteen—and he just may do it. However, we told him we absolutely could not weigh him on his birthday in March and give him his weight in Kennedy half-dollars.

If he realizes his goal he plans to motorcycle across the country and then spend the rest of his life surfing in Hawaii. Now, if a boy is that serious about his future, you really should try to help him. And try we do.

I try to explain to him there's easy money, really easy money to be made if he would only get his hair cut (especially during the academic semesters) and keep his nails as neat as the columns in his bankbook.

But he's a good boy, and he wants "honest work" as he calls it. He wants to sell me things. Things like the negative of that photo he took of me in a bathing suit where I look like "Before."

He's now painting a wall and a bookcase white in the basement hall, the wall that wasn't quite finished by the last painter here in residence. He offered to do it for five dollars. "For anyone else it would be three dollars, but you're my mother."

And I jumped at the chance to get all the painting finally done. He has now been in the turpentine two days and we'll never have to worry about his hair turning white again. In fact, he may be the only barefoot, white-haired boy of fourteen at Waikiki Beach.

Nor will we ever see again that nice pair of blue jeans, only half-a-summer-old, or that yellow shirt he could have worn to school, or for that matter any of his right toes. (He's using a right-handed lower roller). What price one white wall?

After the first day at work, he announced that since he was now a professional painter, "Call me Mr. Thomas," he wouldn't be back the second day. Maybe the third or fourth, but sorry not the second. I didn't think he was half as funny as he did.

In addition, I'm still waiting for someone to get sick. His last bargain sale is still dormant in my desk drawer—six boxes of "get well" cards which almost entitled him to the back wheel of a bicycle. It's funny he never got into the Christmas-card trade and thank heavens he's too young to sell magazines door to door. We have lots of doors.

His nest egg is steadily gathering because he always sits on his Christmas checks as if he were a mother hen. Maybe that's where he got the idea for eggs, for two years ago we were also in chickens.

At first we didn't have any penned area and every morning it was like an Easter egg hunt . . . one egg in the hollow of a tree, whoopee, another by the barn, that makes two, and so on.

Finally, at considerable expense to his financial backers, alias

Ma and Pa Kettle, Tommy constructed a chicken work-and-play area. Wire, water trough, food tray, oyster shells—deluxe quarters for thirteen layers.

Suddenly we reached our peak—four eggs daily. It shows—money makes money. And to think, Tommy never, never asked us to pay for the eggs. He soon learned, however.

Now Tommy's older brother, J. Paul Getty Hardie, is getting into the act. They have decided to educate musically—for a price. When we are all together in a car, they turn the radio on, always way down at the lower end. If, and when, I identify a record successfully—say Booker T. and the MG's or Gladys Knight and the Pips or Donovan, I'm meant to give them carfare.

They're never going to get to Hawaii that way, but it gives them a lot of laughs. I wonder if they've ever heard of Glenn Miller? "String of Pearls"? "Tuxedo Junction"?

Anyhow, it's the end of the summer and I'm absolutely broke. It's time for everyone to go back to school. . . . I hope to be financially independent before I'm forty-three.

September 1969

I could live without the telephone, gladly, but never, no never remove my telephone book.

Take away my pink Princess, disconnect me if you want, but please don't take away my sloppy, wrinkled, torn, decorated, dear five-pound bundle of joy, my telephone book. It's just one great big scratch pad and I love it.

A telephone book is to sit on when you're small.

A telephone book is an old friend in a new city.

A telephone book is to show you how to spell "barbecue" when you don't have a dictionary nearby, trying to keep it a secret that you can't spell.

And a telephone book is for pressing wild flowers in the summer.

Sometimes it's a handy place to hide bills.

Now the Paris telephone book has an entirely different personality. Very split. Very French. The split personality of the French telephone book is that it is divided into four different volumes. A–G, H–M, and so on. They are easier to hold, perhaps, but who reads telephone books in bed?

Mystery books, yes, but not telephone books. On the other hand, the telephone system is so impossible, so mysterious that you might just read the books in bed. It's much easier than getting a call through.

The only thing a French telephone has that we don't have

is an additional earpiece which might get you in trouble. In this way, two people can listen at the same time to a third person's conversation. (The little earpiece hooks onto the side of the big papa or mama telephone.) The French go in big for this three-way living, only they call it something else.

As a public service, may we suggest, only use a French phone in the most desperate of situations—such as mixing up your irregular verbs, getting pinched, or losing your *Paris on $5 a Day* in the Tuileries.

Our fourteen-year-old daughter, Louise, uses our telephone in the most desperate of situations—doing her homework. And for her, our telephone book offers a wide canvas. She is our artist-in-residence by the telephone.

Butterflies, flowers, calligraphy, dress designs, Latin verbs, French nouns, all in living color, decorate the covers and the inside pages of the telephone book. It's quite pretty, but she has completely obliterated by purple daisies the number of the FBI. And you just can't tell when you might want to call the FBI.

Of course, I could simplify all this by putting our important telephone numbers in a small book. Think of the time I would save. Oh, but the fun I would miss.

I wouldn't have the romance of getting lost in those four-columned lanes of the mighty volume. Those pages and pages of names of people I'll never meet.

And so this closes my ode to my telephone book. Ode . . . O . . . now let me see . . . where is it? . . . M, N, ah, O . . . Oden . . . Odenheimer . . . Odensos . . . Odenton . . . Odinga . . . five new names, five new worlds I've entered lightly and they don't even know it. Oh, the magic of my faithful, five-pound telephone book.

September 1969

L ast summer when we built an addition, the profile of our house on the hill changed considerably. It wasn't exactly a facelift; it was more of a landslide.

And because of the steep lay of the land, part of that new profile—down around the chin, as a matter of fact—had to be subterranean.

And now that double chin is Tom's office.

This is his office, his peace, his private world where he has diplomatic immunity—freedom from regulations and the police. It's where he likes to be all by himself. He doesn't even like to have it cleaned. If you put one piece of paper on top of another, he thinks you've changed the whole room around.

Frogs also like the office, almost as much as Tom does. The wall which is smack against the earth has one deep window. The base of this window, the earth held back by a curve of corrugated aluminum, is now the home of a large family of frogs.

Father, mother and many slimy siblings sit and stare with bulbous eyes. And you can stare right back through the window, feeling exactly as if you were looking at some amphibian exhibit in some museum of natural science.

I do wish the museum would change the exhibit though. Every night croaking lullabies float up to our window high above.

The opposite wall of the office, with wide glass doors, looks out on a hill rising to a leafy horizon. This slope, in fact, is the sheep's favorite and they often graze there during the day. And this is Tom's view from his desk.

Tranquility, Incorporated. That is, until last Monday morning at approximately 9:51 A.M.

"Eeeeeeeeeekkkkkkkkkkkk!" screamed Myrtle as she sailed up from Tom's office. "Mrs. Hardie, there's a snake . . . down there."

To introduce Myrtle, may I say she is my good friend, our cleaning woman—the extraordinary one who has the intestinal fortitude to reorganize our house once a week. She's very down to earth. However, she's not sure the astronauts landed on the moon.

"Mrs. Hardie, do you really think they landed on the moon? If He had wanted men on the moon, He would have put men on the moon. . . ."

I had convinced her, yes, man *had* landed on the moon, but now the snake was a different cup of logic.

Myrtle had discovered this "python" curled behind Thomas Wolfe while dusting Tom's bookshelf. When we returned in force, and armed, the snake had disappeared. But where? It's not that we are afraid of snakes, it's just that we'd like to know "where he's at," in the vernacular of today.

While I stood on the desk and "covered" her with a broom and a hammer, Myrtle put gasoline-soaked rags around the amplifier of the music box. The last five feet of the snake were seen disappearing in that direction. The fumes, of course, would make the snake come out with his hands up.

But no snake. Now I've got to buy sulfur candles. We'll close up the room, light the candles, and soon the sulfur will make the snake drowsy and the reptile shall be ours. Or so we hope.

When Tom came home from his other office, I told him what had happened. He didn't seem to mind much. In fact he smiled. "That snake has done more for my office in one day than I have been able to do in one year." And he's right. No one, absolutely no one, will again venture near his office. Or as we affectionately call it when he isn't near, the snake pit.

September 1969

Picture postcards are like the crumbs left behind by Hansel and Gretel. They lead you on but they don't exactly get you there, and they certainly make you hungry.

~~~~~ Postcards are colorful birds that fly in between the bleakness of bills and the absence of letters. Postcards tease and they flaunt and flirt. They also make me sick.

Now, is that nice? What have postcards ever done to me—except make me dream a little? But I have finally realized, bitterly, that I cannot uphold my side of the postcard.

I can't write them.

I've failed the postcard test.

I cannot truthfully pen "Having a wonderful time wish you were here" when, after all, escape was my first objective. Nor can I write in twenty-five words or less a bubbling cablese log of my trip so far. I look at the bare, white back of that postcard and delirium tremens sets in.

After all these years of twirling tall card racks and sitting at café tables trying to compose gay messages to the folks back home, I'm finally facing my inadequacy. It's doubly sad because I love to receive them.

My case has been quite similar along the years. In a rush of dishonest enthusiasm, I buy loads of postcards on the first day and if by chance I haven't lost them or fed them to a seagull, I write them all on the very last day of my holiday. This could be a hopeless case.

Jumbo postcards don't count. Jumbo postcards aren't fair play. Never send a jumbo postcard unless you're desperate. I'm desperate.

I must somehow overcome my deficiency. If one is to travel, one must know the art of postcard prattle. But it is an art perhaps too late in life to learn. I admire so those who in seventy-five words (the most words you can legibly get on the card) can tell you the lore of the country, their own itinerary, before and after, the weather report, the names of temples you will never see, plus what they had to eat last night. Perhaps, when in doubt, mention food. I merely write big.

I think the answer for me is just to write bigger. If I ever leave the house again, that is, travel, I'll go MacArthurian and write on my postcards "I SHALL RETURN." In capital letters, because I think it was said in capital letters.

And I rather like "Today the museums; tomorrow the Pyramids!" regardless of where I am.

If all else fails, I can always copy old Western Union birthday messages. They did give you a choice. Maybe they still do. But I can't go into telegrams when I still haven't mastered postcards.

A choice is not such a bad idea. Before leaving on a trip, you might work up a package postcard portfolio . . . a message for parents, notes for friends and lines for people you forgot to ask back.

Postcard writing, of course, is schooling for those biographies and backgrounds you write yearly on Christmas cards. And it's never too soon to think about Christmas greetings and joy. Here again I'm in the wrong pew. I never know what to say.

It's the same thing for class notes written for your school alumni bulletin. "Everything is just hunkey-dory on the farm! Tommy, thirteen, is a senior at Duke, Louise, fourteen, received her driver's license in Georgia yesterday and Beth, eleven, has eloped. And we are now twenty-three sheep, a goat, three dogs, seven cats, a turtle and lots of things under rocks. Hi to everybody in the class of '48!"

We shall return . . . does anyone really care? . . . Museums today; tomorrow the Pyramids.

September 1969

A duck hunter, a waterfowler is a rare bird *(rara avis)*. He lives off blistering cold weather and good companionship, wet boots and a keen eye, the freedom of an unshaven face and the boundaries of a stilted blind, the beauties of a sunrise. His plummage is assorted.

A duck hunter is part hedonist, part pioneer, and all man. He also has a one-track mind. And those tracks are always high in the sky—a lofty embroidery of game—the V formation of geese; black cross-stitches of an aerial sampler, or the straight, direct threads of duck after duck after duck. Unlike the game he shoots, the hunter's enthusiasm and dedication are unlimited.

Why? It's primeval, of course, but it's also a modern-day escape hatch. And I'm sure there's many a day when there's more hatching going on than hunting. It's a mystique. It's when a man is perfectly reasonable, quite normal in July, and by late October has started honking, or at least quacking. It's a man who has finally decided to have his disk operation now so he'll be able to hunt when the season opens here October 31.

It is, as in another emotion, such as love, probably unexplainable. Or maybe it's to be again a boy, but to shoot like a man.

Whatever, it's too big to overlook—especially if you've lived on the Atlantic Flyway for years and never even known it. And most doctors, one of my favorite species, duck shoot so it can't be all that bad. In fact I've never met an unhappy duck hunter, even with an empty bag. That must mean something.

I bear no arms. Once was enough. A few years back my

husband took me duck shooting. I was dressed for Siberia and I should have thought Palm Beach. It was, as we say in the blind, a bluebird day. Not a duck in the sun-filled sky. It was tremendous toil and trouble and yet we came home with not one treasure.

But now I'm more mature, stronger, I know where I live; the Atlantic Flyway, and who knows when I may be called on to honk or to quack? Of course I will probably never be invited again to honk or to quack because one reason men duck shoot is women. But one must be prepared.

And I'm trying, I'm studying. I'm also exhausted. The Department of the Interior has got to get a new copywriter. Their pamphlet has become my Waterloo on waterfowl. For example: Section 10.53, our 10.53, because we're the Atlantic Flyway, is titled "Seasons and Limits on Waterfowl, Coots, Gallinule, and Wilson's Snipe."

We are then footnoted all over the place and I finally find that in Maryland our "basic daily bag limit is 3 and the possession limit is 6, and may not include more of the following species than: (a) 2 wood ducks; (b) 1 canvasback or 1 redhead; and (c) 1 black duck; and the possession limit on ducks may not include more than: (a) 4 wood ducks; (b) 1 canvasback or 1 redhead; and (c) 2 black ducks." . . . You don't need a gun, you need a slide rule.

And I still don't know what time it is. But the Maryland Department of Game and Inland Fish tell all. Their little pamphlet tells you the daily hours of sunrises and sunsets in Baltimore. Under that table is another table that tells you that on October 31, opening day, you must subtract four minutes from Baltimore sunrise to get the rise of the sun at Salisbury.

Baltimore sunrise is at 6:33, so I subtract four minutes and we have 6:29. I know, thanks to the Department of the Interior, that I can start shooting thirty minutes before sunrise. So thirty minutes before 6:29 is five something or other. I give up.

I give up. The ducks win. And now I know that duck hunters are more than hunters of waterfowl. They are translators extraordinary of double talk, and mathematicians beyond belief. Happy hunting, gentlemen.

October 1969

L ast Saturday we went to an auction up the road a piece. Grant Wood was there. And so was Andrew Wyeth. Grant Wood's people, the faces of *American Gothic,* and Andrew Wyeth's stark farm wagons, and wheels and angles of barns. It was an especially clear, blue and green and golden day in Maryland.

We came for a manure spreader. Others came for other reasons. For some, it was a social gathering. The fare for the day— bean soup in paper cups and hot dogs rolled in sandwich bread. When that gave out—corn soup.

But it must have been sad for the ones who lived in that neat, white shingled house. This was obviously the end of their family's life on the farm, Sprawled about the lawn, for anyone to see, to examine, were the furnishings from their once world, the miscellany of years . . . the big brass bed, the apple-green kitchen chairs, the scrub board, bushels of potatoes and jar after jar for canning the past summer's treasures, the "putting-up" for winter.

On the side of the porch was the farm equipment, and the corn was sold still in the fields, as if this hadn't quite been expected. "Eleven and a half acres," said the auctioneer, "we'll say eleven even."

After scrutinizing the manure spreader, which gave evidence and aroma that it had been doing a good job for many years, we followed the crowd, listened to the spiel of the auctioneer, his speedy delivery, his hypnotizing tones.

But even more compelling, I thought, were the faces of the men in the crowd. There were many men there . . . old, middle-aged and also young farmers. And most of all, it was the old that caught the eye. Those craggy, handsome faces of men who had worked the soil, honestly and long, all their lives. Some were doubled over and bent, but their eyes were bright and the only things faded were their blue shirts.

They knew a lot more about manure spreaders than we did, and they got it. We thought it was too expensive, but they knew better. Brand-new manure spreaders are exorbitantly high.

Although I longed to bid on the brass bed with all its turrets and steeples, we left because our grandparents were coming out to the country that Saturday afternoon. And with them came a pearl, a pearl about the size of a medium baroque pea.

This pearl had been sitting in a safe-deposit box for years, and Agnes thought it was about time to give it to the younger generation. The pearl was discovered seventy years ago in a shell bank on a bayou in Louisiana by two small children. Since it had a crack—the children had whacked away at the shell—a jeweler in New Orleans had offered only fifty dollars for it. No, said the great-grandfather, I'm on my way to New York anyhow, let's see what Tiffany says.

Tiffany said the same fifty dollars. But the great-grandfather was a gambler. "Peel away the first layer and I'll be back in two weeks." In two weeks, Tiffany peeled away the first layer, and fortunately only that had been damaged. Tiffany then offered the great-grandfather a vastly different sum of money, which he turned down. Instead, he had the pearl mounted with very small diamonds, and he gave it to his mother.

The minute the story was told to us, Tom, straight from the auction, said, "We'll sell it and get a manure spreader." And why not? Why should a pearl sit alone in a safe-deposit box? We're going to New York in a few weeks and we're going to see if Tiffany really meant what they said seventy years ago.

In the meantime, I've been wearing the pearl on a small gold chain and I've become very attached to it. I know we should have a manure spreader, just as there had to be that auction. But I wonder . . . whenever I look at our manure spreader, will I see a pearl?

October 1969

U pon viewing your very first gray hair for the very first time . . . sit down. You'll have to sit down because a strong negative reaction will probably follow. "No! No! It can't be. Why, me? Never!" How can one so young, you wonder, have premature gray hair when you haven't even grown up yet?

Gray hairs could come as even more of a shock if you haven't seen your real hair in years. (Will my real hair please stand up. . . .) Years ago you told yourself there's no excuse for mouse-brown hair. And so every six months the mouse-brown hair is pulled through a rubber sieve by the friendly high executioner in white.

The beautician pulls each hair with a crochet needle, bleaches it, heats it and stirs everything around. Hours later you emerge beaten, quite pink, much poorer and too platinum. Your children tell you you look ten years older and your husband asks, "Why are you wearing a crash helmet for dinner?"

Gray hair *must* be more honest.

But if you do tint your tresses, those gray hairs are apt to be a bit retarded. Until the day you see one or two strands not as dull as the other dyed ones, the ones that sparkle, sparkle gray. Not exactly like tinsel on the tree, but they do stand out. Rationalization won't get you anywhere. Madame, you have gray hair.

Helen Hayes, a few weeks back, said words to the effect that she wouldn't trade any of her wrinkles for anything in the world because every wrinkle meant something vital, and true. Helen Hayes is a brave woman. She's also an actress.

I suppose I should treat my new gray hair the way she treats her new wrinkles—thanks for the memories—silver threads among the gold. Phooey.

Since my gray hairs are rather new accessories, I wonder when they first decided they wanted to live with me. . . . I think I've finally narrowed it down to a recent momentous weekend.

We have a good friend, a very good friend, who loves music. He just turned sixteen. We asked this friend if he would like to spend his birthday in the quiet countryside, say Glyndon, Maryland, pastoral, easy, lazy, home, or a weekend in New York City. Noisy, dirty, polluted.

Hello New York City! He also asked to see the rock, undraped musical *Hair*. Well, after all sixteen *is* a big one. And you don't have to tell the grandparents everything. Lady Godiva did start the whole act centuries ago. (Bet she's having a laugh now.)

We saw *Hair*, so to speak. However, we were so high in the balcony it could have been *Oklahoma!* But it's also what went on before, the alien idea of this new kind of theater with a sixteen-year-old boy, a good friend. Generations trying to unite.

Well, that's exactly how you get gray hair!

Next week is *my* birthday and I'm going to New York with my best friend, and someone has given us tickets to the undressed version of *Oh! Calcutta*. Why not? I'm grownup now; I've already got my gray hairs. *Hair* gave me those. Now I want to see if *Oh! Calcutta* turns them beet red!

October 1969

About this time every year, the grammar books come home from school to shake the security of parents and to prove again that silence is golden. I'm in double trouble, because I happened to be an English major in college. That was my first mistake. I should have kept it a secret from the children.

But because I was an English major, our children think I know all about grammar. That's the second mistake. Being an English major has absolutely nothing to do with grammar. All you need is a good editor.

But when Tommy comes to me with grammar book in hand, I can't say "Go ask your father," because his father was an economics major. Economics seems to me to be a very safe major. Your children won't ask you any questions about that subject until they are in college and by then, you're not under the same roof.

I had one reader, bless her heart, who frequently wrote, praising me a little, then plowing through what I thought were some of my more innocent sentences. She even diagrammed those sentences, which made it rather painful. She was taking out my stitches.

But my dear friend the reader knew what she was dissecting. She had taught English in high schools after graduation from Smith College the year I was born. Alas! (that's an interjection) I was eventually exonerated. After reading some early Noel Coward, she discovered he made the same mistakes. Hallelujah, the first Noel is my cup of tea.

But Noel isn't around to help me with subversive subordinate clauses or a gerund. Who was that gerund I saw you with last night? That was no gerund, that was a noun acting up. . . . A gerund, it seems, is a word ending in "-ing," which acts as both verb and noun—as in "Screaming is my bag."

When a child does come home with a grammatical problem, I have to borrow his textbook, lock myself in a room and quickly bone up. And it is very exciting to study the mysteries of the English language after all these years. Everything fits in so neatly. Every clue means something.

This has absolutely nothing to do with the beauty of a word, the beat of a sentence, the rhythm. This is the why and the wherefore, the how, when, where and what that makes sense. But there are always the villains.

For instance, the case of *Who* v. *Whom*. Breathes there a man with soul so dead who to himself has never said, "who" when he should have said "whom"? It's the whoms of this world that may someday end communication.

If we ever have twins, I'm going to name one Who and the other Whom. Then if I make a mistake in grammar, I can say I'm talking about the children. "Whom is going to bed . . . but Who is not."

Lovable are the predicate nominatives and the predicate adjectives, so definite, no beating around the bush. I'm crazy about predicate nominatives, as in "My husband is the boss," and predicate adjectives, "My nose is red." I didn't have half this fun when I was fourteen. Maybe grammar should only be taught to people over forty with red noses who are married to bosses.

Interjections are probably among my favorites in English usage, because an interjection is a word which "expresses emotion and has no grammatical relation to other words in the sentence." You can just throw them in the soup for flavor, like an onion. *Alas!*

and *Ha!* have already been used here, but don't ever forget *Oh! My goodness! Hurray! Ah! Ouch! Bravo!* (page 16 of the textbook). And I would like to add *No!*

No! I cannot explain the verbs *lie, lay, sit, set, rise* and *raise*. Ask your teacher (the "You" is understood). Misplaced modifiers, such as parents, really don't know what they're talking about.

October 1969

I have never been in on one of those Think sessions, those brain-storming meetings on Madison Avenue where those slick ad men think of smooth names for oven cleaners. I imagine the conference room must be filled with wit and worry and words, all at a machine-gun staccato.

The other night, however, I felt as if I were in the same kind of company. I wasn't on Madison Avenue though. I was driving home from Glen Rock, Pennsylvania, on the Harrisburg Expressway. In the backseat were two young ladies, ages eleven and twelve, who have never been on Madison Avenue and if so would probably insist it was the street where our fourth president lived.

These two young ladies, who are extremely companionable, extremely volatile and extremely loquacious, especially when together, were at their highest pitch. Not a sales pitch. A pitch of joy and of excitement. Beth, our twelve-year-old daughter, had just picked out a dog for Christmas. And Beth and friend Kate were tossing names back and forth, nonstop, for the new dog.

The dog in question is an eight-week-old Basset hound of tan and white. Not the usual tricolors of black, tan and white that I had expected Beth would choose. Not that the dog isn't colorful enough. She has one eye as blue as the sky, the other brown as a Basset. Beth succumbed immediately. And little wonder.

If the dog was held on a small chest she managed to sneak up and punctuate each move with a lick of newfound love. Then mother succumbed. Even though the untrained mother had been told repeatedly you don't buy an untrained dog in the middle of winter.

Kate, the eleven-year-old, had come along as a friend and as a Basset hound expert as well. Kate is the mistress of a Basset named Tut, after Thutmose III, an Egyptian pharaoh, 1504–1450 B.C. (You learn a lot of history these days, it seems, by knowing a few dogs.)

Kate knows the right level of a Basset's eye, which looks mighty low to me, and the right length of the ears, which is even lower. I was more concerned with the legs. Those Basset legs look just short enough not to want to chase our sheep. Rabbits I'm not too concerned about.

The minute we left the basement bassinet of our new Basset hound (who won't arrive until Christmas Eve) squeals of happiness filled the car, followed rapidly by a barrage of name-dropping.

"Vanilla, that's it, I'll call her Vanilla," said Beth breathlessly.

"No, Ginger is better," offered Kate.

"Oh," ventured the mother, "there are so many Gingers in the world already."

"Ginger happens to be the name of my gerbil," said Kate rather indignantly. She is also a gerbil expert.

"Then why not Ginger Rogers?" asked the mother, trying to make amends.

"Ginger who?" they both asked. "No, it's going to be Blueberry," said Beth. "Or maybe Paul McCartney!"

"He's a boy, silly," said Kate. "Why not Wish because you wanted her so, or there's always Turpentine, Miracle Whip or Robin Hood?"

"Ugh," was the verdict from Beth. "Now Butterscotch (the dog is actually that color) isn't bad, or how about Sagittarius?" (Beth's sign) wondered the new owner.

"Then she might be called Saggy," volunteered Kate wisely, "and that's all right when she's little, but you've got to think of how she'll feel when she's big."

"Well, what about Hannibal or Hammurabi?" tried Beth.

"Boys' names again. How about Girdle? Now there's a girl's name!" (gales of giggles).

"Or Kimono because she wraps around you, or Christmas because she's coming now?"

"Peace is nice. Here Peace, here peace."

They then decided that to name the dog after themselves was the best idea of all.

"Why not Kate?" said Kate.

"Why not Kate Hardie?" said Beth.

Tommy, Beth's thirteen-year-old brother who came along to help us find our way, spoke for the first time. (After all, how was I going to find the second exit off the Beltway after the Maryland line, turn left at the first stop sign, go one hundred yards, right at the second stop sign and find the third house after the water tower?)

"What's wrong with Spots?" said Tommy.

"Gross!" shrieked the girls. "Dogs just aren't named Spots anymore. . . ."

I'm personally, silently bucking for Butterscotch, but who knows? And although I'd love a white Christmas, I'm almost sure this one is going to be an especially wet one. And so a Merry, Merry Christmas from Beth, Kate and What's Her Name.

December 1969

When Tom and I saw the comedy *Plaza Suite,* I laughed and laughed. That funny fifty-two-year-old husband. He was patting himself on the back because he was so proud of his firm physique.

Actually, he was patting his stomach. Have you ever noticed that when a man brags about how little he weighs, he always pats his stomach at the same time?

The husband in *Plaza Suite* also put drops in his eyes, even went so far as to have his teeth capped to stay young. And I laughed and laughed. Then I looked over at Tom, but he wasn't laughing at all. I poked him in the ribs, which I actually found, and all that came out was a moanful groan.

And then he revealed that he had started an exercise class at the YMCA in Towson that very day. And he was so stiff he could hardly move. Tom is not fifty, nor will he be for some time, but he'll not strain his eyesight looking for it. (I married a much older man, I keep telling him.)

We've passed the so-called seven-year itch, but perhaps I should start preparing for the fifty-year stretch. Obviously Tom already has. Every Monday, Wednesday and Friday for forty minutes, Tom is doing calisthenics. I can hardly get him to pick up a chair at home and now he's going to push down his body forty minutes three times a week on some alien floor.

I would think there would be so many interesting, challenging exercises one could find around the house. How about the Snow Shovel Shuffle—fifteen times with the right hand over the left shoulder, fifteen times with the left hand over the right shoulder? Or the Storm Window Push-Ups—you just keep pushing until the storm windows stay up?

Then there is the Log-Cutting Contest—just between you and yourself. Pretend you're Abraham Lincoln for five minutes and that alone should give you strength. Let the older son bring in the logs.

But I'm really very happy Tom is going to bend his knees and who knows what else forty minutes, three times a week. I think it's wonderful, simply wonderful. And the men in his class were so nice to him, knowing it was his first time.

Of course he was out of uniform. He was in a brown sweater inside-out, or so he tells me, and old gray flannels. They were in white. And I have now collected a proper uniform for him. It's the least a wife can do.

And they do it all to music which I think must be fun. Tom couldn't quite tell me the name of the tune, but this isn't surprising because he is a Beethoven man and I'm sure he didn't twist his torso to Ludwig. Maybe John Philip Sousa? I learned to type to "Stars and Stripes Forever" and never quite got over it. Think what martial music could do for your figure if it can teach you to type.

Tom has actually joined T.Y.A.C., which means Towson YMCA Athletic Club, and they have sauna baths, the works. I'm very proud of him for taking the step, being in step, keeping in shape. Then I asked him about his physical instructor, his leader. . . .

"The boys call her Sugar."

"The boys call her What!?" said I in hopeful disbelief.

"Oh, she's this cute little thing," he said simply.

"And I suppose she wears a black leotard," said I trying to keep my voice from breaking.

"Oh no, it's pink," said he and smiled as men do when they're bleep age.

Well, I think the time has come for the YMCA, or rather the T.Y.A.C., to have a Parents' Visiting Day, I mean a Wives'

Visiting Day. Other schools do, don't they? And I think Tom might be learning quite a lot besides knee bends. But I'm not too worried yet.

He was so stiff yesterday morning that he could hardly get out of bed. Nevertheless, today I'm beginning to start saving my money. And on his fiftieth birthday, I'm going to take him away for two weeks so he can forget about the whole thing, relax and age gracefully—with me.

March 1970

Some women prefer lawyers or merchants or Indian chiefs. I'm wild about doctors. So isn't it lucky I moved to one of the great medical centers of the world some sixteen years ago?

I don't know what came first . . . Baltimore, then my penchant for doctors, or my penchant for doctors, then Baltimore. Well, what does it matter? Here I am . . . there they are . . . yum yum yum.

I guess it's about time to say my husband is not a doctor. For years I've been trying to get him to go to medical school, but he can't stand the sight of blood.

I thought he could be the doctor and I could learn how to test blood and we could go off together as a medical team to Africa where they might need us more than in Baltimore. But we're still here, and if he's taken the Hippocratic Oath, he hasn't told me.

To keep me quiet, he has given me a knee-length starched-white doctor's coat to wear while I'm working. And when I wear it, I feel much better. I wear it with the stethoscope he gave me for Christmas.

It's not that I want to be a doctor I just like being with doctors. Put me in a room full of people and within minutes, I'll probably be standing next to a surgeon. To sound doctors out, I have a built-in stethoscope (not the one I got for Christmas, for I never wear that one out of the house). It's not that I'm seeking free medical advice, never. And it's not that we discuss my medical problems, we simply discuss medicine.

Before our son Tommy's operation this summer, I was very big in vascular and arterial surgery. But now that his aorta has been corrected, I'm in bones.

The reason I don't seek free medical aid is because I usually diagnose my ailments myself. And I pride myself on my work. For instance, I'm quite sure I have bursitis in my left shoulder, but my orthopedic surgeon assures me I have only a chronic shoulder ailment. One which appears about once a year around stress time, over the spring holidays.

He's absolutely right, of course, and to keep me quiet, he now has me in a cervical collar. (I have a doctor for about every part of my body except my head, where I probably need one most.)

This cervical collar is an inch thick, almost two feet long and was made in Warsaw, Indiana, which doesn't sound too medical to me. The collar is meant to relax me or at least keep my head still when I'm talking, or something, but what it does best is keep my chin warm when I stick it down deep on a cold day.

It's a rather horrifying sight when you first look at yourself in it. But when shopping last week, it didn't scare the salesgirls at all. I thought maybe I'd get some first-rate attention, a little sympathy.

But it didn't work. And when I told my husband I thought a large jewel in the center might soften the effect, he laughed. He thinks I'm funny at the funniest times.

Then I decided I looked like the White Queen from *Alice in Wonderland,* which I rather liked, but no one agreed. Instead, they said, I was much more Elizabeth I. Well, have you seen Elizabeth I lately in any old history book? She never married, you know. And her collar was ruffled. . . .

This cervical collar has to be redesigned, or at least camouflaged. Looking like Elizabeth I is not going to get me anywhere.

For Christmas, my friend Sydney was given the most glorious eight-foot feminine feathered black boa by her husband, while I was given a stethoscope. That boa would not only camouflage my collar; my diagnosis is that it would also cure my shoulder ailment completely.

I wonder if Sydney would want to trade . . . just for a week . . . her boa for my stethoscope?

March 1970

W hen our son Todd was in the fifth grade, his big project was in science and he decided to go into trees. We do have a lot of trees around the farm and behind the barn are ten acres of lovely woodlands.

Somehow by hook and by crook and by mother, he collected sixty different leaves. And I learned a lot. For instance, do you realize George Washington took command of the Continental Army in Cambridge, Massachusetts, under an elm tree?

Todd glued every leaf to a page as only an eleven-year-old boy can glue and once he got the glue off his fingers, he wrote some vital information about each leaf. I suggested, quite quietly I thought, that he might title this epic piece "Leaves from Family Trees."

And I must admit I was rather pleased with my suggestion. But mothers should know better. Boys believe in brevity. Final title: "Leaves," or maybe it was "Trees."

It doesn't really matter now as many of our family trees seem to be leaving us. A few years back, Hurricane Doria took away a quarter of our chestnut trees on the front lawn. That was sad enough. That's where the children when very young had their treehouse, very split-level.

That's where they shined the treasure of chestnuts as if they were pearls. That chestnut tree, as a matter of fact, was their baby-sitter. And for hours they would be sitting there . . . shining, carving, collecting. And then Doria carelessly came and took away part of their childhood.

Now the elm trees are leaving us! I don't know why it took us so long to realize our elm trees were not long for this world. Whatever it is about not seeing trees for the forest is quite true. But I don't think we could have saved them, anyhow.

These enormous elm trees guide the road up to our house and suddenly this fall, they started dropping hints—like limbs. And once the leaves left, it was obvious we had some sick trees on our hands, much less on the road. Once shorn of their greenery, they looked like the big, bad, wicked trees from *Hansel and Gretel*. Their long, scrawny limbs hovered precariously over the road.

The other mothers mentioned it first. The mothers who drive car pools up this long, tortuous road. And so for the first time, I looked up, rather than straight ahead. The next thing I did was to call in a tree man. He probably calls himself a tree removal expert, but I thought he looked like a lumberjack.

He was as sturdy as an oak, straight as a pine, immaculate as good, healthy trees are immaculate, and he had on a red plaid shirt.

Originally from Black Mountain, North Carolina, he looked the type Daniel Boone would have chosen to cross the country with him.

I would have trusted him with my own limbs, to say nothing of the limbs of the trees. And he knew our problem immediately . . . Dutch elm disease. There was nothing we could do except cut them down. One of the elms was the largest he had ever seen, and it was gigantic. If five people stood in a circle hand to hand, they wouldn't reach around the trunk. And it could easily be two hundred years old, said Mr. Lumberjack.

Can you imagine cutting down two hundred years of tree! Think of what that tree had seen. I thought that I would never see a tree that had seen two hundred years of Thornhill Farm. Then when he told me it would cost $850 to remove the trees, I took command under the elm tree like General Washington and decided we couldn't cut down two hundred years of history. We merely amputated. And now we have a lumber camp at the lower turn of our road.

On the first Sunday after the operation, Todd got into trees again, along with our friend Rowland, and electric-sawed all day. We now have firewood stacked against the house, not as tall as the elm, but mighty high. And every night we have a roaring fire. Elm burns and burns.

Some old friends, it seems, stay around longer than others even though they've fallen.

April 1970

The other morning, Tommy was already eating his breakfast when I made my way into the kitchen.

"I don't feel too well," he said as he finished his third raw carrot.

"Then don't go to school," I suggested, thinking of course of the health of his classmates.

"No, I have to go," said he as he ate an orange and then drank a chocolate milkshake. "I'm giving a speech in history on Thomas Edison."

"But I thought you were studying ancient Greece," I said.

"I am," he replied and then proceeded to finish off three pancakes, two pieces of bacon and a glass of milk.

His health improved, I suspect, after Thomas Edison was unloaded on his peers and Mr. Scroggs.

Tommy's breakfast menus, however, are often as puzzling as what Thomas Edison was doing in ancient Greece. His favorite breakfast is a roast beef sandwich topped off with a bowl of hot oatmeal and perhaps a slice of pound cake.

He also likes bacon, lettuce and tomato on white. But that takes a little more time. He eats P.M. food in the A.M., but his stomach doesn't seem to know what end of the clock is up. He does, however, have pea soup only at night.

Beth is more conservative in the early morning. At least compared to Tommy. She likes grits and bacon or cinnamon toast and tea. And Todd eats everything. Each morning, it is as if he hadn't seen food for days. He is a delightful bottomless pit. I glory in his appetite.

After all, breakfast is your most important meal of the day. That's what I've been hearing for years, the only food maxim I remember from childhood. But not everyone around here believes me.

Louise, for instance, floats into the kitchen after everyone is well into their oatmeal or grits. And I think she lives only on orange juice and apple sauce. I'm afraid to look. Strangely enough, she looks in perfectly fine shape.

The other morning after they had left for school and I had finished my breakfast (four-minute egg, bacon, toast and artichoke hearts), I started reading about ancient Greece just to see how Thomas Edison could possibly fit into the toga scene. I didn't learn too much about Thomas Edison, but I discovered Louise would have been a perfect ancient Greek. They didn't eat breakfast, either.

Most ancient Greeks only ate two meals a day . . . The midmorning meal, or *ariston,* often consisting only of a dish of beans or peas and a raw onion or roasted turnip. Even Louise does better than that. Then about sunset, they would eat their main meal, the *deipnon* . . . bread, cheese, olives and sometimes a little fish or meat.

Suddenly Louise seemed quite Greek, Louise the Greek, and I stopped worrying. If they could build the Parthenon on a diet like that, Louise can get through school on apple sauce.

As for Thomas Edison, I never did find out what he ate for breakfast. I did discover he had two wives and they both complained bitterly that he spent most of his time in the laboratory. So maybe he didn't eat breakfast, either. Just like the ancient Greeks. Maybe Tommy has an angle, after all.

April 1970

If all my cookbooks were laid end to end, I still wouldn't know which end was up.

I have enough cookbooks, gifts of well-meaning friends, and a husband, to feed our family from the French Quarter of New Orleans to San Francisco's Chinatown, across Alaskan fish dishes, through a Swedish smorgasbord and back to New York's finest Armenian cuisine.

But what good is a cookbook if you can't cook?

However, at Thornhill Farm, there are no starving Armenian Hardies. Thanks to Rita. Since Rita has come into our lives, I don't have to do as much translating of food from the book to the table. Rita is one of the great natural cooks of the Western world and she and I cook together on certain days—the ones with "R" in them.

Back in October, an unknown voice called me on the telephone and said, "Mrs. Hardie, I hear you might need help." I always need help. And from that day forward, the kitchen took on different dimensions; no longer a scullery, it is a triumphant scene—Rita's scene. And when I say we cook together, I really mean Rita cooks and I scurry.

Imagine, when the days have "R" in them, a young woman who looks like a Toulouse-Lautrec lithograph with the spirit of Annie Oakley. And you can see how lucky I am. Her hair is a swoop of golden auburn, very Belle Epoque, and she wears a pink turtleneck jersey and blue jeans.

When I mentioned Annie Oakley, I wasn't just dropping names. On occasion, Rita has shot a pistol into the air over the heads of dogs when they chased our sheep and she was the first to realize our Saint Bernard was a bird dog.

Late one afternoon, she saw Tuffy, the Saint Bernard, cross the terrain with a mysterious object in his mouth. She retrieved, she plucked, she soaked in salt, and the next day, much to my surprise, we had Quail à la Rita.

But right now we specialize in bread. In fact, we are up to our elbows in dough. First we thought we would use the recipe from one of our many cookbooks, *Mrs. Putnam's Receipt Book and Young Housekeeper's Assistant,* published in Boston in 1858. It belonged to Louise Cutter Carter, a great-great-grandmother, and I had never looked at it before Rita came around.

The yellowed pages told us to "bake the bread in a tolerably hot oven about three-quarters of an hour." That was simple enough, but then we were warned, "All kinds of raised bread rises much quicker in a kitchen in the daytime, when the kitchen is warm, than at night, when the fire is out. Therefore, 5 or 6 hours in the day are equal to 12 at night."

Rita, being a quick cook, decided that this recipe was all right for 1858, but not for her. She devised her own recipe, and we are all pounds heavier, but deliciously so.

> 2 cups milk
> 1 tablespoon salt
> 3 tablespoons sugar
> ½ cup light honey
> 2 tablespoons shortening
> ¼ cup water
> 2 cakes yeast or
> 2 packages dry yeast
> 5 cups sifted flour

Place milk, salt, sugar, honey, shortening and water in a saucepan and heat gently until melted. Pour mixture into a large bowl and add yeast and stir until yeast is dissolved.

Sift 2 cups of flour into mixture and beat well with a wire beater. Then add 2 more cups. Add last cup of flour and mix by hand. Turn the dough out onto a floured wooden board or counter top. Knead until dough is smooth and sticky. If the dough is too sticky, add a little more flour.

Turn the mixture into a greased mixing bowl and cover with a towel. Let stand in a warm place until double in bulk, about 1½ hours. Divide the mixture into two parts and punch down the parts into two rectangles. Knead dough for about 10 minutes. Then place each rectangle into a lightly greased bread pan. Let the dough stand in a warm place until the dough rises to the top of the pan, about another half hour.

Meanwhile, preheat the oven to 400 degrees.

Bake 25 to 30 minutes. Knock on top of bread after 25 minutes and if bread sounds hollow, it is done. Yield: two loaves.

Now if it doesn't turn out, don't call me, call Rita. But I'm not going to give you her number.

May 1970

I own a chaise longue. I can't pronounce it, but I own it. Now, that's not absolutely true. I can say it, but I have to take a head start when I say it and go as fast as I can. Shayz-long, there, that's my new chair.

It is also the only chair I have ever bought strictly for myself. Mine, mine, mine, all mine. Other chairs in the house have been inherited, grabbed or purchased for rooms, rather than for people. But this chair was bought for one person in mind, myself.

And I didn't sit in it for a year. I didn't know how. It was a new way of life and I wasn't quite ready. It's not that I didn't try it out first. I sat in it very self-consciously right there on the furniture floor under the eyes of that saleswoman. Furniture saleswomen are different from, say, lingerie saleswomen. They stand straighter.

I like chairs. It's one of my idiosyncrasies. I like chairs better than tables just as I like deep red better than light blue, just as I like Bibb lettuce better than iceberg, just as I like men better than boys. (That's not absolutely true, I like boys.) And a one-piece, old-time movie chaise longue is hard to find these days. I wanted it more than any other chair in the world.

I never had space for one before. But last year, when we built on our new bedroom, I finally had the chance. I think I thought a Theda Bara might emerge when I sank into the chaise longue. A new me. Whom was I kidding? What did I think I was going to do in the chair? Collapse? Read? And more important, when?

When my chaise longue and I were first getting acquainted, I often scheduled a "sitting," perhaps between a child's dentist appointment and dinner. It wasn't easy. And after knowing only upright chairs all my life, I found it hard to accordion out onto a lying-down chair. It was a hangup, a lying-down hangup.

A chaise longue, I kept telling myself, should be for reading. But for the last thirty years I have read mainly in bed. I love to read in bed. It started with the complete set of the *The Bobbsey Twins* under the covers by flashlight and now I'm on the second volume of Harold Nicolson, openly. It's a Pavlovian pattern, a conditioned reflex. Give me a book after dinner and I head for bed.

Our son Tommy compared the chaise longue to a psychiatrist's couch, our daughter Beth called it simply a long chair and a little girl who came to visit said it was a caterpillar. (She lost her toy under it and discovered the chaise longue had eight legs.)

It was beginning to look as if I were born too late, as if the chaise and I were not in the same era. But then came summertime and I was a certain age. . . .

Before I decided to be a "certain age," I occasionally mentioned my real age in this column and I discovered it was very un-American. My contemporaries thought I was out of my head, others were suspicious. What a pity, European women ease into it so gracefully. But then they've always had chaise longues.

Now for the rest of my life I'm going to be a certain age, with my chaise longue to back me up. And after a year of testing, I know a chaise is for not doing anything in particular, but a great deal in general.

You know what I do on my chaise longue? I flop, I plot, and when no one is around, I nap. But I still read in bed. A chaise longue is a friend, a good friend, especially in the afternoon, and very appealingly female.

The curious, comfortable fact is our daughters, ages fifteen and twelve, have learned early what has taken me forty-three years, oops, I mean certain years, to learn . . . namely, to relax.

It is here they study, read, I hope dream. It's their new island in the sun.

But on the other hand, move over, Louise and Beth, that's my chaise longue, and I'm coming in.

June 1970

I've decided the only way to get your children to listen to you is to become a dentist. Dentists, of all professions, have the most captive of audiences. It's awfully hard to talk back to a dentist. You may have your mouth open, but you can't say much. How can a mother compete?

Before I decided to go for my D.D.S., my best lecture time used to be at breakfast. They had to listen to me to get fed. The bigger the breakfast, the more points I made. Keep their mouths filled and you get away with murder. And it's especially difficult to protest over your mother's snap, crackle and pop.

If I wanted to bawl them out for keeping the car out until after midnight, I served blueberry pancakes and sausages. If I wanted to persuade them to study auxiliary French verbs the way they studied Bob Dylan, I served grits, bacon and one egg over light. I thought I was pretty crafty, although, *I* didn't get much to eat.

Recently at lunchtime, even though I push submarine sandwiches as a subterfuge, they have started telling me how old they are. "After all, I am seventeen. . . ." or, "After all, I am fifteen. . . ." and so on. As if I didn't know how old they are! After all, I was there.

The time has come, obviously, to go into dentistry and get them in the chair if I intend to make myself heard again. All I have to do is take the piano out of the kitchen and put in a big padded baby-blue chair that tilts. We happen to have an old upholstered chair that does that without being asked. Then I'll run a narrow hose from the sink and I'll be in business. All I need are some of those small cotton sausages that fit so dryly next to your gums.

"Good morning young man, have a seat. Son, I want you to open wide and cut your hair, cut the lawn, clean your room, stop marching on Washington and so what if Princeton gave Bob Dylan an honorary degree. Rinse please."

"Next. . . ."

"Hello, Louise. Lie back and would you please find my earrings, put back my clothes, stop bringing new kittens into the kitchen, start putting away the dishes and would you please stop saying 'Oh Mother never mind!' Don't eat on that side for twenty-four hours."

Now it's time to scrub up before my next patient. And I think I'll look at a few X rays and moan.

"Well, well Tommy Hardie. Let me see your bite and no more TV during the day, don't tell me one more time to 'cool it,' try not to outgrow your trousers for the next three months and why don't you tell me who you danced with in dancing class? Stop biting."

Fortunately Beth is away and so she doesn't get the chair. But then Beth is only twelve years old and she still listens to me. No needling necessary.

July 1970

I n our kitchen cupboard, we have two patterns of glassware, service station and supermarket. Service station is tall, fluted at the lower part of the globe and shaded the color of gasoline. Supermarket is an assorted collection of old jelly glasses and peanut-butter jars.

Plebian, perhaps, but all of them have lofty ideals. The main aim is to see if they are still with us in September. I doubt it. Summertime seems to be the high breaking point in this household. We break glasses as if we were Russians at the Yalta Conference. And we're not even toasting anything.

When Tom and I were first married, thanks to wedding presents we had more glasses than a small-town soda fountain. Monogrammed, Swedish, collegiate, you name it, we could fill it. We were heavy in glasses, light on anything else. But now if we have more than eight people for dinner, I have a hard time finding vessels even vaguely resembling each other. Each place setting has a way of looking as if a prize was to be given for originality.

This American gimmick—the giveaway—has certainly helped a lot. So what if I've driven hundreds of unnecessary miles, I now have a perfectly matched set of twelve glasses the color of gasoline. I'm a lucky, lucky girl.

I sigh when I think of the glasses that have crashed through this house. One time I bought some Finnish ones, extremely sturdy.

You have to be sturdy if you come from Finland. At the last count, we had three left.

Tom once carried twelve enormous, beautiful wineglasses home from Paris. He had purchased them from a shop selling only to restaurants. I wonder what he said to the proprietor? *"Bon jour, j'ai une petite auberge dans la campagne, et nous avons toujours soif."* Somehow, he got the glasses. But at first I thought they were too big, *trop gros,* but now I love them dearly. Especially the four survivors I now use for the hot-pink roses of summer.

Probably before we start using a new set of glasses I should put one aside. Then when the other eleven are just a memory, I could bring it out and set it proudly on the shelf. If I had done this from the very beginning, we would now have a collection I could call the Hardie Glasswork Museum. It might even help present-day social historians. I would show them the ups and downs of one family, how they lived and what they broke.

Over the years, I've learned not to get too emotional over glasses, the curves of crystal. Here today, probably gone tomorrow. At least we haven't lost any fingers. I must admit I do have some glasses I like a lot, Christmas gifts I hide on the shelf of Tom's clothes closet. They're not allowed out except after five in the afternoon and are only handled by slippery adult fingers.

I can't believe all this is complete carelessness. After twenty years of glass watching, I feel that someone is trying to tell us something. Maybe we should go into tin.

But as my optimist husband hastens to say, "I like to think my glass is half filled, rather than half empty." That's one way of looking at it, as long as you still have a glass.

August 1970

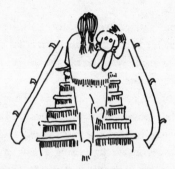

On the second floor of our house there are a series of small bedrooms, characteristically cramped quarters of a simple farmhouse built 125 years ago.

To the left is the "zoo," domain of an older son, and to the right is the "jungle," Louise's bush country with an overgrowth of crepe-paper flowers. Across is Beth's room, best described as the "Smithsonian." After all, if you're the fourth in line, you're bound to inherit valuable cast-offs.

And in the middle is Tommy's "dog house."

It is here that Tuffy the Saint Bernard and Horatio the Springer spaniel both sleep—all on the same bed. And if you look in early in the morning, you have a circular jigsaw puzzle with one boy and two dogs all incredibly fitting together. But Tuffy is getting so big, we thought at first we should give her the guest room.

Now that Rosie, the baby Saint Bernard fluffball of love, has joined our ménage, Beth, her owner, naturally thought Rosie would sleep in her room and then she and Tommy would have adjoining dog houses. (Tuffy, incidentally, is Rosie's aunt.)

There's only one problem, however, Rosie can't go up or down steps. For centuries, since A.D. 1081 to be exact, her ancestors have been climbing the Great Saint Bernard Pass, 8,100 feet high in the Alps, and Rosie can't even make the fifteen steps to our second floor.

What Rosie does best is flop. Her front legs go out straight and her back legs go out backwards and she looks at you with those droopy, doggy bedroom eyes. But she still can't get to Beth's bedroom. That doesn't stop Beth. She picks Rosie up and somehow manages to struggle up those fifteen steps.

And in the morning, she comes down with Rosie in her arms, staggering as if she were a Scot balancing one of those gigantic, tall poles at the Scottish games.

Rosie is also very adept at crumbling, especially if you try to put a leash on her. She'd make a terrible demonstrator. I recently read in a news magazine that "the act of sitting down or going limp is often treated as a separate offense of resisting arrest." I don't want to arrest Rosie, I just thought a leash might teach her who's boss. . . . Meet Boss Rosie.

I'm not too concerned, however, about Rosie's prone view of the world. Her Aunt Tuffy wasn't much different at that age. Tommy and I once took Tuffy to an obedience class at a local armory. The class was conducted by an ex-Marine with the same haircut he had in boot camp twenty-five years ago. And the German shepherds were the stars. They stood at attention, they followed orders, they made me sick.

Not exactly sick, but awfully nervous. I got a terrible hangup because all Tuffy did was sit down. I was terrified at the weekly meetings. I kept thinking how I could beat the racket. I even considered appearing in a Marine uniform. Anything to gain a little sympathy. Finally it got too big for all of us—Tuffy, Tommy, but mostly me. Meet the first drop-outs the ex-Marine probably ever had.

Now we have her niece, Rosie, and she is our furry rose. A rose is a rose is a rose, especially if it's Rosie. She has even made the second floor at last!

Incidentally, Beth's room isn't the "Smithsonian" anymore. We now call it the Great Saint Bernard Pass.

August 1970

W hen our two daughters were much younger, they often dressed alike. Courtesy of the nimble fingers of a grandmother and an aunt and the Women's Exchange. Smocking up to their tiny chins and little red shoes to boot. We thought they looked adorable.

The girls, however, hated it. And when the day finally came when they no longer had to dress as a sister act, they rejoiced.

But now, years later, Louise and I have a mother-daughter coat. One coat. Louise saw it first and immediately wanted it. Then I tried it on and asked why not? It is long and flowing, a taupe brown, belted, upper and lower pockets and hits us both about four inches above the ankles.

We were pleased with ourselves. Louise would be nice and warm with the new length. After all, her school tunic is five inches above the knee when kneeling and I knew I was going to New York. I was sure coats were sweeping the sidewalks of New York.

And when in New York, I was going to have lunch with a fashionable fashion editor and heavens-to-betsy, I didn't want to look as if I had just arrived from the provinces. This new long coat was the answer.

Once we were home parading in our new coat, we knew for sure we weren't from the provinces. The men in the family let us know we were more from the last world war. Tommy came right out with it and said we both looked like Hitler and my husband muttered something about "storm troopers."

It wasn't exactly the reception we had expected.

I must admit that when I wear the coat, I do feel like Irene Castle giving out the last doughnut on the French front. But I like that. It has a warm feeling of nostalgia.

However, I didn't dare wear it to New York after the unkind comments of the male members of the family. But I did have another choice, another "mother-daughter" coat. A red coat with a raccoon collar that I had bought sixteen years ago when Louise was very much with me, but not yet born.

After the natural process of birth and the loss of a huge front, the red coat fell at least eight inches in length. Now it's exactly the right length for the so-called longuette. Belted it looks quite Chanel.

But the men didn't like that, either. Instead, I wore a black-dyed muskrat that hopes everybody thinks it's mink. And it just about covers my knees.

When I arrived in New York and picked up my fashionable editor, Angela, she looked like she was about to read my palm. She was in the latest New York gypsy costume . . . long black skirt, ruby-red satin shirt, baubles and beads, a swooping cape and Ruby Keeler shoes. She was really with it and I tried to slouch lower so my coat would look longer.

Then she took me to La Grenouille restaurant, affectionately called the "frog pond" by *Women's Wear Daily*. There were wall-to-wall Oscar de la Rentas and as a matter of fact, Oscar himself was sitting right behind Angela. My knees and I were miserable.

When we finally left the restaurant, a photographer snapped our photo. The next day, front page, *Women's Wear Daily* showed a photograph of Angela the gypsy and my nose. I had been deleted. My nose had been cut off to spite my costume.

Not that I care, of course, but if I had looked like Hitler, maybe I would have made it. Sieg Heil Fashion.

November 1970

I 've been studying reincarnation seriously these days. We have a new body living in this house, but I feel his soul has been around a long, long time. He's supposedly a cat. He may look like a cat, but I have my suspicions.

When he first arrived two weeks ago, I was slightly sick. So in the afternoons, I would try to take little cat naps, but the cat would stare at me with those wide, wise eyes, sprawled in a nearby chair. I felt strangely guilty.

Where he comes from, people rarely get sick. This isn't just any old cat. This is a large New England cat. And not just any New England cat, but a cat from Nantucket, Massachusetts. Sturdy stuff, those islanders.

For years, I've been giving away cats. We have a kitten factory down in the barn. At last I thought we were free of them. Then my friend Eleanor-the-animal-lover told me about two cats from Nantucket whose mistress had died, how they needed a home, and suddenly I heard myself saying, "I'll take one for Louise." It was my voice, but it certainly wasn't my true self.

The cat is from a part of Nantucket called Sconset, where whaling captains once had summer cottages. He has wide, yellow eyes and a coat of many colors—striped, a white waistcoat, white boots and a buff goatee. There are black stripes that extend upward from the corner of each eye, making him look very dramatic.

In fact, he is pretty much of a ham. Eleanor told me, "He

looks very well on furniture." I must say he does a lot of posing.

He arrived with as much luggage as a movie star—his traveling case, bags of Kitty Litter and boxes of canned food. And he was very partial to one certain kind of tuna. The first week, he walked around with his striped tail as erect and as high as a mainsail. Then one day, I opened my desk drawer and he slept there all afternoon.

He landed here with the ubiquitous name of Peanuts. Since he was born in Nantucket, but was now living in Maryland, I felt we should somehow remember his noble beginnings.

"How about Moby?" I suggested to the children who were involved with this new baptism. "Or Whale? India? Captain Coffin?"

No indeed . . . they have named him Charley.

Charley Whale, as I call him, is more relaxed now. His tail has lowered and it now circles around himself, Louise's pillow, where he likes to sleep, and my heart. It's ridiculous how my affections have been swayed by this cool cat. And he is cool sometimes. Sometimes he sits on the Ouija Board and looks as if he's receiving the First Lord of the Admiralty.

Charley wasn't a cat last time around . . . I'm sure of it. I think he rounded Cape Horn on his own ship. Reincarnation, thar she blows.

He's as tidy as a bow knot and in two weeks has become absolute master of two Saint Bernards, one cocker spaniel and me. His favorite berth during the day is my desk chair. He sprawls on most of the seat in the back while I scrunch up front typing. It isn't very comfortable, but it's probably good for my posture. The chair is from Italy, so I feel he still likes foreign ports.

Sometimes he sits on the desk and looks out the window for a long time, as if he were scanning the horizon. He has one habit I'm not too fond of, however. When we are at meals, he likes to join us and insists on hopping up onto the table.

But maybe we'll get used to it. After all, maybe we're sitting at the captain's table.

November 1970

Our Aunt Alice lives in a hill town surrounded by the Black Mountains of North Carolina. It looks like Europe from different slopes, dotted Swiss with some chalets, such as Aunt Alice's, but for the most part, there are the gingerbread-trim white cottages from another era alongside the more contemporary rectangular houses of today.

She leaves this peaceful hamlet once a year to drive north for the holidays with her only nephew, Tom. This year, I went along for the ride. Down there I discovered the word "Yankee" is still in the working vocabulary, met a lovely old woman who hides the sherry bottle behind her hat box in the closet and saw Billy Graham's mountain right next door. I also learned it's later than I think. . . .

Although Aunt Alice's age circles gracefully around the eighties, after a few minutes in her house, I was the one who was aging rapidly. . . .

As I went from one room to the next, I saw a gallery of photographs of our family from the year 1—or rather since 1950. Sure, we have the same photographs around—the more favorable ones in frames standing at attention, more in scrapbooks, others stuffed in desk drawers.

But Aunt Alice has them all in full view, every single one of them. Obviously, over the years, when in doubt, send Aunt Alice a photograph. Happiness may be a blue blanket, but loyalty is Aunt Alice.

It was touching, but it certainly shook me up. Twenty years of the same family and how it grew. The family wasn't the only thing that grew. How it hurt when I looked at that photograph of a slimmer mother in that black-and-white that was just given away last week—not because of style, but because of seams.

You also tend to forget four teenagers were once toddlers. That is, until you get to Aunt Alice's bedroom. Along the mirror frame were tucked the momentary triumphs of keeping a squirming child still while you captured a grin, a tear, a pocket of a long time ago.

No matter how you snap it or splice it, twenty years have gone by with a wave of a wand. That towheaded baby is now a towering teenager with hair about the same length as his sister's when she was six. That sister, no longer a fat-faced cherub in red-and-white gingham, is now a slim, long-legged young lady of sixteen.

Tommy, fourteen, is still in overalls, but now they are the kind housepainters wear. And Beth, just thirteen, wore more dresses when she was three years old than she's worn in the last two years.

As for the mother, someone should give her cosmetics, lock, stock and barrel, for Christmas. I was deep in despair.

Then Aunt Alice's friend Marie had lunch with us. She had just taken up painting last year and is so busy she hardly has time to write to her children. Marie is eighty-eight years old—just twice my age. And suddenly I felt years younger.

It's not children who keep you young. That's an old wife's tale. It's people like Aunt Alice and "Miss Marie," as they say in the hills of North Carolina.

And I've just loaded my camera again. I have so many photographs to take. Aunt Alice, here they come.

December 1970

L ast month purely by accident I stumbled upon the Happy
Hardie Principle of Christmas Giving. I couldn't write of it
before, of course, because everyone would then have known
what they were getting. Books, books, books.

At first I had no intention of giving away these books. I had
bought them all for myself. Me, me, me. I don't usually go on such
literary sprees, but suddenly all my old friends were on sale . . .
Dorothy Parker, Ogden Nash, Frank Sullivan and Antoine de Saint-
Exupéry, friends I had treasured in my bookcases since college days,
my twenty-one-year-old inspirations.

And books are more than mere pulp these days, they are
vast investments. The life of a man, good or bad, costs at least
ten dollars. Anyhow I settled on the chaise with the lives of
many men (Dorothy Parker had a lot of men in her life) plus the
letters and pieces of Frank Sullivan and the rhymes of Mr. Nash.
I never had a better time. I also didn't get any Christmas shopping done.

Finally, Christmas was upon us and the gift list was long
and my eyes were short-sighted. So out of necessity I gave away
most of my books. I gave Dorothy Parker to my mother-in-law
because they are both five feet tall, and I gave Antoine de Saint-
Exupéry to another dreamer I know.

I did not give away Mr. Sullivan or Mr. Nash. I'm not even
going to lend them. I don't trust book borrowers any more than I

trust people who buy books for themselves, read them, then give them away for Christmas.

I did manage to do most of my Christmas shopping this way, plus have a marvelously restful two weeks before Christmas. Next year I'm going to do it on purpose. Buy books.

It was one of those propitious accidents, the same way we discovered roast pork when the poor man dropped his only pig in the fire. I don't know why it has taken me so long to give books as presents.

I think I was too sensitive before. I felt that if a friend was a collector of the Ming Period, his book present should be on the Ming Period. That's crazy period. Give him a book on macramé (the art of tying threads into knots). Give him something else to think about.

The giving of books eliminates the problem of color choice as well as neck size. It also removes the returning of presents—a national ritual now taking place all over the United States. At least you can't return the books I give.

I write long, flowery inscriptions as if the British Museum, manuscript department, might someday take heed. And of course I never sign my own name. I never say "Merry Christmas, 1970, from the Hardies," or "Affectionately, Mother." No indeed, I always sign the name of the author.

Sometimes I use my left hand, sometimes I use my right hand. After reading their books I usually know whether the authors are left-handed or right-handed. And I write something special. Wouldn't you rather have a book signed Ogden Nash rather than Dee Hardie? I would.

And who knows? Every day you keep reading about the soaring prices paid at book auctions. Maybe in twenty-five years when our daughter needs a new space ship she can auction off the copy we gave her of *Alice in Wonderland*. Signed, of course, "Love and kisses, Lewis Carroll."

December 1970

L ouise is now sixteen. And sixteen is special. Mothers and fathers have tears in their eyes, while daughters have their eyes on the road. Freedom at last, thirty hours of classroom study, seven hours of lessons behind the wheel. Whee, wheels!

But before Ralph Nader got on Louise's trail, I wanted to have a sixteenth-birthday party. A mother's version of a sixteenth-birthday party—old fashioned bouquets and dewy eyes and sweets. I probably would have included a hoop skirt if I could have found one. And I wanted it to be a surprise party.

Just the week before, I read how the Plaza Hotel in New York had celebrated Serge Obolensky's eightieth birthday. Serge Obolensky is a Russian imperial prince turned public relations man. The various rooms of the hotel were transformed into the Winter Palace of Russia for his gala eightieth.

I felt if the Plaza could do that for a press agent, we could blow more than a few balloons for our sixteen-year-old daughter. And we hadn't had a birthday party in a long time. When Louise's older brother became sixteen, he chose to see *Hair*. For a daughter, I thought another production was in order.

When they were younger, we had lots of parties. Of course, they were more for my enjoyment than for theirs. I think I considered myself the Cecil Beaton of the pabulum set.

Just because someone gave Tommy a sailor suit, I once had the entire kitchen looking like the tourist-class dining room of the S.S. *France*. And on Beth's ninth birthday, we had a "Sunday Salon" with the guests dressed in their parents' clothes. All the little boys looked like Charlie Chaplin, while the little girls looked like Sadie Thompson. I was a French maid.

When they are younger, it is easier to set the scene. They take naps. But girls Louise's age are now inquisitive, alert, sensitive, curious and just plain nosy. And I have discovered that to have a surprise birthday party for a sixteen-year-old, I should have been taking night courses at the Kremlin or be a card-carrying member of the CIA.

For years, I had been waiting to make a "sugar bouquet." You buy eighteen inches each of about ten different colors of ribbon. Attach a large sugar cube on the end of each ribbon, hang them together and tie at the top with a big bountiful bow. You then somehow awaken at three A.M., tiptoe up to your daughter's bedroom door and attach the bouquet to a waiting nail.

The next morning, the new sixteen-year-old awakes, sees the beribboned sugar cubes swinging on her bedroom door and then knows she is "sweet sixteen." Violins fade in and out.

Well, Louise not only sleeps late, she found the carefully concealed "sugar bouquet" days before her birthday.

Then our plan "GLOOTH" backfired completely. That meant "Get Louise Out Of The House" while I decorated. A friend who lives in the city invited her for lunch three times and Louise steadily refused. "After all," she said to Ann, "it is my birthday and I know my mother wouldn't want me to leave. My mother is big on birthdays. She's sappy that way."

I was not sappy, I was in agony. The Bay of Pigs failed and I felt I was in the same boat. I had already drawn the game "Pin the Midi on Louise," made the cake with a cat on it and heard her tell her sister she hated surprise parties!

I thought for sure Louise had guessed. She has the quality of knowing where everything is in this house except, of course, her school sweater in the morning when the car pool is already five minutes ago.

But she didn't know! And you know what? . . . We had an old-fashioned birthday party with bouquets and sweets and a charming young lady who is now sixteen. As for her mother . . . she's years older.

January 1971

These young peacocks who stroll around with their plumage of fringed ponchos and tie-dye jumpsuits undoubtedly appeal to the present generation of pea hens, but to me a man is at his most elegant in a black tie and dinner jacket.

Maybe that sounds too Noel Cowardish for this time and place. Too Cole Porterly, perhaps? Well, that's just the way I feel.

I have a gentleman friend in his eighties who feels the same way. His uncle, E. Barry Wall, was the first man to wear a dinner jacket in America, at the Grand Union Hotel in Saratoga Springs at the turn of the century. It caused quite a stir. Before that it had been strictly white tie and tails, according to my friend Harvey.

After introducing what soon became known as the "tuxedo," Mr. Wall stuck by his guns and told his young nephew Harvey never to go anywhere, "not even the North Pole," without his dinner jacket.

As it happens, shortly afterwards Harvey was crossing the Arabian Desert with some Bedouins. The wind was blowing through the tents and Harvey was freezing in his pongee suit in his sleeping bag. He got up, put on his trusty dinner jacket and slept in it every night the rest of the trip.

Tuxedos, it seems, mean many things to many men—and women. Now white tie and tails are a different cut of cloth. Although a man is supersuave in white tie and tails, he is also a primitive animal while getting there.

Fortunately a man is not called upon too often to wear white tie and tails. For a daughter or son's wedding, perhaps, a formal ball, or if he happens to be a French headwaiter. . . .

I have another good friend, a resident, who must get dressed up in white tie and tails about once a year. A week before, I go through an interrogation that would make the Gestapo pale, a veritable inquisition. He asks me if the shirt is ready, plus the white tie, the stiff collar, the studs, the whatever-you-call-it that keeps the shirt together in the back and so on. (The tails are so old they should be able to stand on their own.)

Then, the big night he has to wear the outfit he always cuts his neck shaving, an act which does not help the scene. But at least it isn't my neck. I have only two studs and he needs three; the collar isn't the right size and, besides, it's turning yellow; the vest doesn't seem long enough this year.

A very nice man, normally kind and generous, suddenly turns into a stranger. This sort of episode may have been the inspiration for Dr. Jekyll and Mr. Hyde.

I wash my hands as if I were a surgeon, and become marvelously patient. I pin and I borrow at the last moment, and somehow we manage to get him to the ball on time. Too bad he wasn't born a member of the Forsyte family. They seemed to have done this so easily, every night for dinner.

But actually I love it. It is my supreme moment of the year. When I was younger, it made me nervous; but now I relish it. He is absolutely dependent on me. He absolutely cannot attach his stiff white collar to the back of his shirt.

By the time we're finished he thinks I'm indispensable, and I think he's Fred Astaire.

January 1971

M ice. As if we needed any more. Not that we don't have enough already. This farmhouse is a field mice oasis once the winds blow cold.

We have one house mouse who always spends her winter season with us. Her Biarritz is our bread box, her Palm Beach palms are the straws of our broom and her pâté de fois gras must be the coils of our electric stove. She has eaten them two seasons in a row.

I feel no comradeship with these urchins of the fields. They terrify me. So Beth knew what she was doing. Indeed she did.

Kate merely marched in with the mice—a fait accompli. These new additions to our rodent world are not just mice mice, however. These, according to twelve-year-old Kate, are a fine combination of field mice and domestic mice. The result are white-and-black polkadot mice with pink noses and long, long, long pink tails.

Kate was formerly in gerbils, but now she has gone into the mouse field and her production line is most prolific. About every three or four weeks, she has a new batch. (Her mother, she claims, as a child had baby mice every three weeks on Sunday.)

Beth, knowing her mother, told Kate yes, she would like three female mice, but no, she wouldn't tell her mother. Mothers, according to Beth, need surprises every once in a while to keep them on their toes. There's no question about it. Mice definitely do keep me on my toes.

One sunny Saturday afternoon, Kate and her father came to call, carrying the mice splendidly encased in a glass box with chrome corners. Their field of green was chlorophyll litter, a merry-go-round was in the middle and on the side was a small juice can where the three of them sleep, one on top of the other.

I didn't look at them for five days. Not Kate and her father—I mean the mice. Then I had to. They escaped. Once I controlled my fear, I realized they were fascinating.

I still like to look at them, under glass, of course, but they are suddenly appealing. Sometimes they sleep under the merry-go-round with three pink noses together and their tails spread out as a pink fan. But when they move, they move. Up, up, up they scramble on the merry-go-round—but never quite making Mount Everest. Such determination, such courage, such exercise. You can tell they're female.

We are now about to visit friends for a weekend and I planned on bringing along the mice. After all, they travel with their own mouse house. And I have become very fond of them. Besides, mice-sitters are hard to find. Kate's kingdom of mice has covered the countryside as pets for friends and everyone's minding their own mice.

The Saint Bernards will go to a wonderful kennel, the cocker spaniel stays with his friends Jim and Clara, Charley the cat is coming with us, too, so why not the mice? We're visiting understanding, animal-oriented friends. And they've probably never seen mice like our mice. Talented, outgoing, polkadot mice.

But no indeed. Beth immediately rose up in arms. The mice cannot travel because they get "carsick." They're too fragile, Beth says. Her mice have been the saviors of science for years. Their behavior patterns have solved medical mysteries for centuries. They've told us not to smoke cigarettes and they might even conquer cancer.

But our mice can't go 138 miles because they get carsick. See what happens when you go domestic!

April 1971

I n my youth, I was the peanut queen of Fenway Park. I probably shelled and ate more peanuts than any nine-year-old girl in the Commonwealth of Massachusetts. You see, my father liked baseball and I was in lieu of a son.

Then I grew up and instead of peanuts, I began concentrating on Ted Williams. I was fourteen and he was .406. What a batting average! What an age to fall in love with baseball! Nowadays, fourteen-year-old girls have other things on their minds, but honestly, Ted Williams in left field under the Burma Shave sign was a sight to behold.

Now I live in the land of the Orioles and am married to a football fan. We occasionally go to the games, but I can't say that it's the same as sitting in the left-field bleachers and being fourteen.

Then the other day, I read what Michael Burke, president of the New York Yankees, said about baseball and waves of nostalgia came bouncing back to me, as fast as any fast ball. Said Mr. Burke . . . "A baseball club is part of the chemistry of the city. A game isn't just an athletic contest. It's a picnic, a kind of town meeting."

Isn't that true? If you go to chance baseball games as we do, you sit next to people you have never seen before or probably will never see again. Yet within five minutes, you've probably passed the peanuts. You talk, you admire, you are friends for nine innings because you groan together, cheer together.

Admittedly this happens at football games, too, but baseball is warmer. Baseball is the geometry of that neat, clear-cut diamond, the green green, the white uniforms of the home team, the flags flying, the sun shining.

Last fall, Tommy, our fifteen-year-old son, and I went to our very first World Series game. It was the only game the Orioles lost, but even in defeat, it was glorious.

The Rockettes couldn't have done as well as those majorettes who flung out yards and yards of red, white and blue making a mammoth flag. And that cart with the large Orioles cap as a roof kept delivering celebrities to their box seats while Tommy and I and all our neighbors kept straining our necks identifying everyone to everyone.

Casey Stengel had me practically in tears. Then when I saw Joe Cronin, I was home again.

"Where's Ted Williams?" I asked out loud to anyone who was listening. Two rows in front of me, a new friend explained he was fishing in Florida. Even that didn't diminish the excitement.

You can't win them all and lose we did. But the emotion of seeing a World Series game, the first one after years of shelling peanuts, was overwhelming. Tommy and I both came home exhausted.

A new season has begun, a new ball game and many more picnics. What a terrible world this world would be if there were no more double plays, no more Nureyev leaps against the center-field fence to pocket that ball.

I'm not so sure I like the umpires in blazers and gray flannels. Black seemed more in keeping with their line of work. But you can't have everything the way it was when you were fourteen. But baseball is still the same old wonderful ball game. But never, no never, will there ever be a .406 again.

April 1971

N owadays I can't even remember my grocery list or the years our children were born, but when I was a sophomore in college I could quote verbatim more than thirty-five of Ogden Nash's poems.

He was my idol. I was meant to be majoring in English, but instead of Shakespeare I should have been taking Ogden Nash 203. In a way I guess I was. His books of humorous poetry were always nearby.

I can't tell you the times his poems came to my rescue on college weekends. Whenever the going got too serious I would throw out some of his wonderful lines and titles . . . "Do Sphinxes Think?" Or, "Have you heard 'To a Small Boy Standing on My Shoes While I Am Wearing Them,' or 'A Clean Conscience Never Relaxes'?"

In New Hampshire one summer I actually met Mr. Nash. He didn't even know I was coming. I was visiting a friend nearby. I just parked myself on his front steps and waited. Remember, I was nineteen, he was my hero and I was out to get a story. Girl reporter stuff. I haven't been quite that brave again. Interviews now scare me to death.

Then this gentleman arrived. He talked for more than an hour to this strange, unknown young female. I just reread that interview and it is about the most sophomoric piece of writing I have ever had to read. I tried to imitate him and fell flat on my typewriter. But at the time twenty-five years ago, I thought it was special and so sent him the college literary magazine with the interview. He not only took the time to write me a note, he even encouraged me. The only thing special about that interview was Mr. Nash himself.

I even wanted to write my senior thesis on him, but they, the Establishment, wouldn't let me. Humor wasn't serious enough for a senior thesis, they said. In retaliation I wrote on the fallen women of eighteenth-century literature. I titled it "Ladies-in-Waiting" and somehow I managed to graduate.

Years later we moved to Maryland and were invited to his daughter's and son-in-law's house. I knew Mr. Nash was going to be there. And I must say it took me a long time to get dressed. I went clutching the same favorite book I had clutched all through college. I didn't bring up our meeting many years ago, I didn't want him to remember.

I had given the book to our older son who was having the fun, the joy of reading Ogden Nash for the very first time. At the party I got all my courage together and said, "Please Mr. Nash will you sign this for our son Todd?"

And he did so, acting as if it were the first book he had ever autographed.

The last time I talked to him at length was when I found myself sitting next to him at dinner. I might add I was probably the happiest woman in the world. I thought I was doing pretty well. At last I was acting grownup in front of a hero. I had come of age.

We discussed books, people, and then in a spurt of literary expression, emphasized by a wave of a right hand, I knocked over a glass of wine . . . all over the white pristine dinner shirt of my other dinner partner, probably the most gracious lawyer in town.

I was absolutely horrified. I had fluffed my big moment. But Mr. Nash quickly said something about never crying over spilt Saint

Emilion '64, and the gentleman I had stained with the juice of the grape forgave me, I think.

I'll probably never come of age when in the presence of poets or authors or gentlemen I admire. But at least I had the privilege, the pleasure of trying to grow up during the life and times of the late Ogden Nash. And for that, I am very grateful.

May 1971

Todd has just hung up his tie. The same way the sheriff hangs up his holster when the job is done and the sun is sinking in the west.

We knew it was coming.

"This," he announced triumphantly at his graduation the day before, "is one of the last five times I am ever going to wear a tie!"

"Oh!" we said nervously, and not really wanting to guess the occasions for the other four times, we started taking photograph after photograph lest we forget. And he did look so nice—an eighteen-year-old boy with Sir Galahad hair, blue blazer, white shirt, The Tie and white trousers. In fact there were 120 boys dressed exactly the same way. And I think that I shall never see, a graduation as lovely as thee.

But once graduated there is the 26th Amendment, I was told, the Freedom of Dress. And that's why Todd went to Europe in overalls.

The first time I went to Europe it was with a steamer trunk that looked as if it also held my dog act. But then, I was going to stay six months. (Todd, remember college registration is September 6.) My trunk was so ungainly and awkward a London taxi couldn't carry it, and we had to hire a fish van to haul it to the hotel.

So maybe Todd in his overalls, sleeping bag and his pack on his back is much wiser than all of us put together—his parents, his grandparents and all those others with raised eyebrows when he boarded the Metroliner for New York—dressed as a walking motel.

Peter, his classmate, his cohort, his guide, his translator, his pal, met him in New York and together they climbed the mountains of last-minute details to adventure—the railroad passes, the airline tickets. But there was one formidable obstacle they couldn't pass. A doorman.

In the morning they went to Peter's grandmother's apartment where they were to spend the night before the flight. And the doorman wouldn't let them in.

They were finally rescued and taken out to lunch by grandmother. But only before she checked the restaurant to see if the two boys in blue overalls would be admitted. They were.

Todd always has another change of wardrobe if his overalls get too objectionable, his lacrosse shorts. And by this time Peter and Todd have already done London and are in Scotland. Then Paris, Munich, Vienna, Rome (not exactly overall country), the island of Elba, and who knows where else.

At graduation my mother-in-law told Peter's father she was going to pray for Peter and Todd when they were in Europe. Mr. Ridder quickly said, "Forget Peter and Todd. Pray for Europe. . . ."

June 1971

L ast summer, our telephone number changed three times and for weeks I was Saint Joseph's Hospital.

   We changed first because we were in the wrong zone, second because they turned us into a toll call, even to our children's school, and education is expensive enough. Finally, they gave us a number we thought might like to stay awhile.

   But our friends kept getting one of the various numbers, but hardly ever the last one. Finally a nice man from the telephone company came out with a map showing me where I lived and an offer to have my name printed on two hundred cards with my new telephone number. All I wanted, I told him, was peace.

   He assured me everything would be all right when the new telephone book was published in the fall. He gave me such security we decided to put in another phone. One for the children.

   Four children, ages thirteen to eighteen, become particularly attached to the telephones. In the evening especially, I guess it must be my scintillating, tasty dinners that loosen their tongues. Whatever, the phone is never out of any of their tentacles. There's so much to talk about on the telephone—Latin verbs, girls, boys, French verbs, boys, girls, and so on.

   Occasionally we wanted to use the phone, the minority group, the mother and father, even before I became Saint Joseph's Hospital. So we plunged ahead for another phone.

   The phone, of course, had to have a name. Why? I asked.

That was ignored. Naming dogs is one thing, but why bother to name a phone? Anyhow, we had sort of an interfamily competition. Beth came up with Hardie Pizza Parlor. And Tommy came up with another kind of parlor (he has a macabre sense of humor) and Todd wanted to call it the Red Cloud Reservation after his tribe in North Dakota.

Finally Tom thought of Hardie Casino. Everyone agreed. It had a certain *je ne sais quoi,* a dash of drama, shades of the Riviera. We were all crazy about Hardie Casino.

The next day, I talked to about the sixty-sixth girl I had talked to over the summer at the telephone company to let her know our new telephone, the second one, would be listed under Hardie Casino. She couldn't have been nicer.

She called about four days later to let me know we couldn't use Hardie Casino or Casino Hardie unless it was the name of one of our children. By then I had had enough and without thinking, I think it was without thinking, I told her Casino was the name of our sixteen-year-old daughter. I then let her hear me call, "Oh hello, Casino, home from the *chemin de fer* already?"

But crime never pays. When the phone book came out in the fall, the children's telephone had the wrong number, the absolute wrong number, and I was confused with Saint Joseph's Hospital.

If you want to reach me, try Saint Joseph's Hospital first. I just might be there. Or perhaps the tables at Monte Carlo. Anything is a safer bet than Hardie Casino.

July 1971

Y esterday Todd went off to college with enthusiasm and distinction. The distinction is that it's the first time we have ever sent a Social Security number to college. They (the university) gained our son and all we lost were all those triplicate forms sent all summer long to 218541901.

How shall I write to him?

> Dear 218541901,
> We miss you already but what did you do with the car keys? Did you mean to leave home *Freedom and the Court, Civil Rights & Liberties in the U.S.?* Beth is reading it and getting moody. Why did you leave home all your ties, white shirts, gray flannel trousers and that nice blue blazer we bought you last fall?
> With love from your M-O-T-H-E-R

In June when 218541901 filled out his five forms for desired courses, he was told to do it with a No. 2 pencil. It was hard enough finding a No. 2 pencil, much less filling out the blank, which wasn't a blank at all. It was a maze of spaces and numbers where you penciled in blocks at the proper places. Somehow he did it very easily, but young people today must understand computers' personalities. I find it all very cold.

But they certainly do communicate. Reams of paper arrived this summer and 218541901 is going to live in Butcher Hall which really doesn't make the whole scene that much warmer for a mother. He was also told to donate blood, order linen, order a newspaper, food plans, tuition bills and of course that he was going to be in a co-ed house (that was on the first line) and that No Pets Are Permitted in University Housing (that was on the last line).

I began to think it was just all business, no heart. Then he received a postcard from Russia which read "Greetings from Russia, See you at September Auditions. Penn Glee Club." Now wasn't that nice! I was beginning to feel better, even if 218541901 has no voice, glee-club caliber I mean.

Then came the brochure for the Faculty-Freshmen Day projects. On the first day, 218541901 has a choice of sixty-eight courses he may attend. And he is having a hard time deciding.

Currently, he's vacillating between "Animal Communication—Trip to Philadelphia Zoo to observe communication among baby gorillas and how these signals compare to communication among human children" or "War: Its Control and Avoidance—New approaches to controlling war and a discussion of reality and fantasy in social institutions."

Then there is "Criminally Insane—Judicial process as an instrument of reform: study of a case in which 500 'criminally insane' were released" or the rather sedate subject titled simply "Movie-making."

They do care, after all. And he's not a number anymore. On his registration permit, Todd, alias 218541901, was told his student group code was "Ugnew." Somehow having a son called Ugnew is so much more comforting.

September 1971

Most of our family has Rover fever. It's spreading. Rover fever is when you want a Land Rover more than anything, almost as much as you wanted your first two-wheeler. A Land Rover is a British-made automobile that has the grace of a hippopotamus and looks like a mini Mack truck.

Todd was infected first. This summer, he was meant to be roaming Europe with a pack on his back, but I think he spent most of his time in automobile show rooms.

But he was earnest. And when he came home he found two jobs. During the day he weeded the historic sites of Nantucket and by night he washed dishes. By the end of the summer, he figured he had made enough money to buy two hub caps and one piston.

In between jobs, when he had about an hour's freedom, he would moon over the price list of extra accessories for this car of his heart. "Just think," he would say, "a ladder is only eleven dollars!"

Who ever heard of a car that needs a ladder, I asked myself.

A doctor friend of ours is always stressing athletics, especially for young boys. "It takes their minds off other things," he claims. Land Rovering seems to be our new sport.

"They used a Land Rover in *The Great Train Robbery*," contributes Tommy, as if that was going to influence his father. "And it's the strongest vehicle in the world."

My husband, Tom, is the one member of the family who isn't seduced by this machine. Personally, I think it is a post–World

War II hangup. He won't eat Spam either. And the Land Rover does give you the impression that Rommel might step out at any minute, the dust of the desert flaking off his boots.

Cars have never been one of my favorite companions. But when I first started driving children, I wanted a beach wagon, those old station wagons with bodies of wood, real wood. The wagons I knew in my youth. But not one was to be found.

Then I upped for a combat jeep. And with all my car pools I *should* have had a combat jeep. In a way I *did* have a combat jeep, but it was really a normal American station wagon that became decorated with battle scars.

Now that I am almost out of car pools and into long pants, I want something new, something different. I'm not allowed a sports car. So I'm beginning to think a Land Rover would be a good idea. Safari, anyone?

You can go through water in a Land Rover, over all kinds of bumps, practically scale mountains. I've been doing that all along anyhow. But I've never had an accident. . . . Not while I was in the car anyhow.

One day my car managed, all by itself, to crash into not one car, but two cars, simultaneously. I had left it in a supermarket parking lot and the next thing I knew two men in long white aprons were after me. The butcher and the produce man. It seems my car had rolled back into each of their fronts. The meat man's front and the produce man's front. Quite a trick.

What I need, I keep telling Tom, is a car that knows no obstacles. A car that can handle *me*. And I know there is one on sale right now only twenty minutes from this house.

It's white, though, and I'm not sure I'm right for a white car. But I have figured that out, too. I could paint red crosses on each door to give me a whole new image. I could be Hemingway, I could be crossing the Sahara and those schoolboys I pick up every Tuesday evening could become troops instead of tired tackles. It would certainly give *me* a lift.

And if I get it, I'll give you a lift, too. Look for those two red crosses!

October 1971

Y esterday I put a big sign up in the kitchen . . . "We've Lost Our Lease. Everything Must Go." And I meant it. I'm tired of all the Hansel and Gretel droppings that are dropped all over this house. These assorted cast-offs, the stranded shoelaces, crippled pencils, yesterday's hair ribbons, forgotten Latin assignments, *my* borrowed sweaters, the paraphernalia I have to pass through every morning to find the kitchen. And they don't lead to a house of sugar, they lead to my back problems.

Wiser mothers have "in" and "out" baskets where they put their children's left sneakers and other goodies they find under the sofa cushions. Some mothers even have children who pick up their own clothes. Somehow I obviously never established a pick-up pattern. . . .

When I go to bed early at night, I always know, the next morning, where our children were at 11:00 P.M. How could I miss? There's that line of popsicle sticks. . . .

I've learned never, no never, to go upstairs. That's where they live, sleep and eat more than they seem to eat downstairs at the table. Climbing stairs are meant to be good for your heart. But not in this house.

But they are good children. I'm actually crazy about them. And perhaps this is all hereditary, passed from generation to generation. Their father does rent a box at the Butler Post Office, even though we have mail delivery here because he said he was tired of finding *his* mail under *my* car seat. Why don't you look in the glove compartment, I asked him, or try that last book I read or underneath the bed? It's not that difficult. The mail does get through. . . .

He's no angel either. When he was in college, his mother was so exasperated by seeing all his clothes on the floor during a holiday, she threw them all out the window. Unfortunately they all landed on the telephone wires and the telephone men had to come to retrieve the clothes, not Tom. He's very good about it now though. But we still haven't conquered wet towels.

We are going to have spring cleaning this weekend, even though it's October. Spring isn't the time of year to clean anyhow. Spring is the time to lie on the grass and look at the clouds.

Maybe I should start on my own closet. Why do I have a Chinese jacket that I wore when I was ten, why that basket of shells from the seashore in Maine or that pair of tartan shorts Todd wore, then Tommy? There's not a thing I can do with that linen scarf from Marrakech and whom am I kidding when I look at that French suit circa 1950, circa 118 pounds?

Hetty Green, a miser from Rhode Island and once reported to be one of the richest women in the world when she died in the Twenties, always saved everything. Especially black bonnets. But then Hetty never married, never had any children to leave their stray rubber bands for their braces in the breadbox or confuse their mother with their pyramids of old magazines and baseball newspapers.

But even though we've lost our lease and everything must go, I think I'm still the richer.

October 1971

Just about this time last year, I wrote a magazine article (for this year) on Christmas. Upon receipt of payment, I blew it all on a black-dyed muskrat coat that thinks it's mink. It was the bargain of the year and I was thrilled. Every day I would go to the post office to see if The Coat had arrived from New York. Finally the box arrived. No anticipation was greater, no expectation more anticipated.

I tore open the package and there inside was *not* my minor muskrat, but instead a movie-star mink. A real mink coat with a price tag of five thousand dollars. Another tag revealed the coat also belonged to some woman on Long Island who was probably, right at that moment, crying her heart out over my muskrat.

The boxes had obviously been mixed and some poor Daddy Warbucks was probably getting the devil. I promptly put on the mink over my blue jeans and wore it from the kitchen to the bedroom—twice. Then I immediately put it back in the box and started proceedings.

I wanted my lowly muskrat instead of this lofty mink and it took approximately six letters, five telephone calls with frantic threats to salesmen and store buyers and finally a vice-president to retrieve my coat. I sensed early in the game I'd better get my muskrat before I returned their mink.

Now another fur coat has come into my life and this time it is the return of an old love. A long-haired raccoon that was obviously the cat's pajamas even before I was born. Even when I received it fifteen years ago, its days of glory were deep in the shadows of age.

Long before thrift shops were the fashionable haberdasheries of the young, my friend Jane had seen this coat in the Johns Hopkins Hospital Carry-On Shop. And she bought it for me. The price $2.50.

I wore it with honor, if not grace, and it managed beautifully not only to keep me warm, but to conceal the fact that the Hardies' fourth child was just around the corner.

It started splitting soon afterwards. After all, a great deal had been asked of it. I put it aside until a friend in Massachusetts mentioned how much her young daughter wanted a raccoon coat.

Now it has been given back to us. And what it really needs is a gift certificate to a series of steam baths and a furrier *extraordinaire,* but with needle in hand, I sewed again all those drafty pelts. I sewed and I sewed and I sewed.

Then I gave it as a birthday present to Beth, our fourteen-year-old daughter and fourth child. She *should* have it. After all, there was that time when she and I shared the wonderful mystery of wearing a raccoon coat together . . . just the two of us.

December 1971

Christmas is a child's pageant with small angels in tilted halos of tin foil and wire-hanger wings. Christmas is a round, wide, wicker basket in the narthex of the church rising high with cakes and cans of food and one perky poinsettia sitting on top because Miss Alice, who put it there, said, "You can't live by bread alone, y'know."

Christmas is the day George Washington stood up in the boat and Christmas is the little boy who found grass under the snow for the camels, as well as the reindeer.

Christmas in Madrid is Papa Noel and sausages wrapped in silver paper. Christmas in Maryland is special fish for a special time in the fish stalls of Baltimore's Lexington Market—cuttlefish and eels and smelts. Christmas is when you suddenly become the mother of Joseph as he walks on stage in yesterday's grain bag and your best silk scarf.

Christmas is whatever you put into it, however you feel, a birthday party for everyone. Sometimes as unexpected as the smile of Scrooge, often as deliberate as a maiden aunt's shopping list. Christmas is a light in the dark of winter. Christmas, for me, has always been a tree.

When I was younger, at home in Boston, the tree had always been our Christmas Eve and the height of the tree measured my father's temper—usually too tall. It was always a night to remember and the tree, when finished, although the crew was exhausted, was the most magnificent, the most glorious, the best.

Christmas now is choosing our tree, with everyone casting a vital vote. We pile into the car and in a minute, we're at the Butler Volunteer Fire Department. Tree after tree is examined from stack after stack. We twirl, we hold, we test the boughs. We look at these evergreens as Flo Ziegfeld may have looked at hopefuls for his chorus line. But we don't choose Follies girls, we carry home the plumpest Scotch pine we can find.

Then we wind it with golden beads, loop after loop, dot it with red balls and blue balls, tie it with tartan ribbon from the highlands of Scotland. At the very top is a green parrot. He hasn't a name, but to us, Christmas is a green parrot which never talks back.

Louise and Beth set up the crèche, which over the years has become a true mélange of memories—the ceramic angels from Portugal, the wooden camels from Jerusalem, the splendid Woolworthian Wise Men. There may be more beautifully carved crèches in Munich, more handsomely painted ones in Italy, but it's hard to beat a cardboard manger from the five-and-ten purchased by four children with an international cast of angels.

I look at our tree every night in the dark, the lights alive. And it's hard to let it go, even after the holidays are over. Often when the first Valentine hearts appear in the store, our tree is still shining.

Merry Christmas from the top of the tree to everyone.

December 1971

I want a neater New Year. And napkins have a lot to do with it. Napkins are like husbands who travel. You think you can get along without them, but you can't.

❧   You find this out about the second day. And there is no real substitute. For napkins, I mean. There is nothing, absolutely nothing like a good old-fashioned lap-covering napkin. And that goes for husbands, too.

Whenever the table is set here at Thornhill Farm, I find the rotating staff most often forgets the napkins. (And they do rotate to the farthest places the minute I ask someone to set the table.) But our children aren't the only ones who neglect napkins.

Over the holidays, we were out for lunch and the hostess served the most delicious homemade soupy soup filled with the vegetables of past memorable meals. But there were no napkins. What do you do? Lower your chin or keep a stiff upper lip? Or pass your sleeve ever so slightly left and right in the vicinity of your nose? In this case, in the middle of a sliding noodle, the napkins were remembered and passed.

It's a test, in a way, the Missing Napkin. Much like the Invisible Ashtray of the State Department. I once heard that young men hoping to enter the State Department are interviewed and offered a cigarette, only to find that there is no ashtray.

Those who use their initiative and put the ashes in their

trouser cuffs or suffer third-degree burns by crushing the cigarette in their palm are Out. Whereas one who merely and sensibly asks for an ashtray is In.

I am now offering my Missing Napkin trick to the State Department—Egg Drop Soup with or without napkins.

I do hope the napkin doesn't disappear into the folds of the past. In Denmark, especially, I've noticed they know how to put a napkin in its place. Beautifully so. In Denmark, a napkin usually stands proudly on a plate, the white linen sculptured into a shape, or curves seductively from a wineglass.

I've even inveigled apprentice bus boys to make me napkin patterns out of paper, but I've never used them. How could I make those sitting swans, or stiff white collars, or taut sails or petals of a rose that are really napkins in disguise?

I realize our children think there are many more important issues in today's world than blanket coverage of laps while eating. But I feel if they are going to try to tidy up this world, they might just as well start with clean hands.

January 1972

Duntml:inline_markdownring the other war, I made my father sign the paper allowing me to be a blood donor. I went to the Red Cross, lay nervously on the table, pumped the rubber ball they put in my hand, drank the orange juice, then walked wobbly out. I thought it was the least I could do for my country. And it was the nearest I could get to the front.

Over the years, I've given lots of blood. It's an ego builder, naturally. It makes *me* feel better. And it's so easy. Besides, Tom can't be a donor, as he had jaundice in that same war. And after giving blood, I've been guilty of trickling out such upmanships as "You can sure tell good blood when you see it."

Besides blood, I give tears easily, too. Freely and flowingly. Ask any member of my family. I'm Tear Duct Dee to those who know me best. But I'm tired of being called emotional. Why don't they trim it with lace and call me sentimental? But no, I'm mainly an emotional mother.

Since blood banks are well established, I'm going to start an Emotion Bank. I have gallons to give away.

Dorothy Parker's much quoted and copied line about a performance of Katharine Hepburn that "she ran the gamut of emotions from *A* to *B*" is indeed a slight alphabet. My emotions stretch thinly to *Z.* ... Z is for *Zut alors,* which is French and loaded with emotion.

Of course, to qualify for my Emotion Bank, there are a few

stipulations. I take only the ones who need me. The unruffled, the calm, cool, collected, the organized. I am particularly looking for those who are in charge of every situation. I feel they must be desperate. Wouldn't they like to be completely confused, lost just once?

I'm looking especially for women who haven't yelled at their children in months, who leap out of bed every morning with vigor, who always remember to put back their husband's razor, who have can-to-can cupboards, a clean calendar, a twenty-four-inch waist, not a wrinkle on their face and never a fallen soufflé. I want to give them most of my tears, some of my laughter and a few of my cares.

The Beautiful People or the Cat Pack, as *Women's Wear Daily* now calls them, seem to be a worthy group for my Emotion Bank. They look as if their expressions couldn't change even if a hippopotamus walked into their Louis XV living rooms.

I'm going to keep some of my emotions for a rainy day. I'm not going to give away all sadness, because then how would I know joy? Nor will I part with all anger, for I might miss the delight of surprise.

Thinking it over, perhaps I'll keep my emotions to myself. Or whom am I kidding?

January 1972

L ast weekend Tom took over the kitchen. In fact, he com-
mandeered it.

And if this is a preview of things to come in the
New Year, I see a larder filled with luxuries. *I* would never
buy and store scents to delight any wife. A green thumb in the
garden is one thing, but a green thumb in the kitchen—especially
when it's not my own—is a thing of beauty, a joy forever.

Praises aside, he didn't do this for my palate or his children's
culinary education. He did it solely for himself. He likes to eat. He
thinks food, like women, should be slightly mysterious and should
provoke as well as provide. In other words, he is sick of pork chops
plain and after twenty-one years, he admits he detests salads.

He now demands kitchen privileges every once in a while,
but this time he wouldn't even let me in. So instead of biting my
nails, I settled down with *The Wreck of the Whaleship Essex,* an
account of the survivors of a whaling ship broken in two in 1821
by a spermaceti whale. It tells, among other things, how they ate.

There I was learning that turtles "are a most delicious food,
can live a year without water or food, but soon die in a cool
climate," while Tom was in a hot kitchen with Elizabeth David
. . . in paperback.

Elizabeth David, a prominent English writer and cook, as
the book blurb said, treats "food with reverence, understanding and,

above all, care." I think she cares a lot about has-been morsels, for the first night we had mutton, the second, an old duck.

It took Tom about four hours of dramatic labor to make Navarin Printanier, which finally boiled down to stew. In the dead of winter, we had this lamb ragout to which "spring vegetables give special character." We all ate in silence, as we were weakened by hunger.

Lunch the next day was simpler—Shrimp à la Crème. While Tom was in shrimp, my whaleboat survivors were eating delicious small clams from the underside of their boats. They went on to find an island and tropical birds, while Tom started on the duck.

Canard en Daube floats in white wine, brandy and water. The poor duck is then punctured all over and bacon, wrapped around parsley, shallots, chives, garlic, a bayleaf, thyme, basil, salt, pepper and grated nutmeg, are shoved into all the incisions. The perfect dish for peanut-buttered American children.

Somehow a duck looks more defenseless, far more naked than, say, a turkey. But he was properly covered and cooked slowly for three hours. Then came the moment of truth, the dinner hour.

The duck simply fell apart. On the platter we had something resembling a prop from Death Valley Days. A cadaver. By persistence and searching care, we were fed. By this time, I had finished my whaleboat and I won't tell you what they ate just before being rescued, but maybe that's why the duck didn't seem too appealing.

By Sunday Tom was exhausted and couldn't eat. He also had an upset stomach. As for the rest of us, we feasted on BLT's on toast.

January 1972

T he other morning, Beth told me the back of my head looked like Pericles. How wonderful, I thought, Beth thinks of me as a Greek myth.

What a marvelous way to think of one's mother. It's worth all those years of struggle. My fuzzy-wuzzy washable bathrobe suddenly turned into a toga of fragile, floating chiffon. I was cooking grits, but I really was on Mount Olympus.

Pericles, hmmmmm, I don't remember *that* goddess. After breakfast and some surreptitious research, I discovered that . . . Pericles was a Greek general who always wore a helmet because he had a long head.

At least she didn't mention Caesar. He wore a wreath because he was bald. Pericles's face was handsome and he is, after all, responsible for the Acropolis, so why would I complain about looking like a helmet?

It's strange how other people see you. No need to elaborate on how your own children see you (wicked witch of the west), but other people. A few months ago, four friends called to tell me we *had* to see the movie *Touch*. There was someone in it who was so like me . . . Elliott Gould?

No, it was a Swedish actress. Well, you don't think I made everyone eat hours earlier, and fast, so Tom and I could drive miles to a movie in the middle of the week to see Bibi Andersson? Fast . . . I had the whip out.

After all, how many times in your life are you told that you look like a Swedish movie star? When we arrived at the local theater, I pulled my coat collar a little higher and put on my sunglasses. After all, I didn't want to be mobbed. . . .

The movie hadn't been on five minutes when I realized the only point of similarity is that Bibi and I both have Swedish mothers.

But we tried.

"Tom, do you think we look alike?" I whispered hopefully.

"Well, maybe when you were younger," he said encouragingly.

We kept trying and the more we tried, the more she kept taking off her clothes. And the more she kept taking off her clothes, the lower I would sink into the depths of the theater seat.

Our jawbones do angle a bit the same, a Scandinavian square, but the physiognomy ends there. Bibi is quite a *flicka* (girl) as they say in *Svenska*.

As I slouched, enveloped in Tom's overcoat, my scarf and half an eye peering onto the screen (after all, I didn't want to miss anything), I remembered what Nancy had told me on the phone. . . .

"I hope you won't be angry with me, Dee, but honestly, she acts just like *you!*"

In the movie, Bibi probably had her baby and finished her Italian lessons or perhaps finished her Italian lessons and had her baby, I don't know. But the next movie I went to was *Peter Rabbit and the Tales of Beatrix Potter.*

I once had a friend who looked like a rabbit, but I never told her.

February 1972

I always go to the hairdresser's loaded with good intentions, worthy ideas. I take enough equipment to last a month in the curlers—bills to be paid, letters to be written, the book I should read, some two-year-old needlepoint. But I am almost always seduced almost immediately by the slick-slick magazines.

Five years ago, if you wanted some racy reading, you turned to the pages of the flimsy movie magazines. Today, the field is wide open. All those womanly magazines worrying about marshmallow molds and how-to-make-an-oilcloth-apron over morning coffee seem to have left town. The homemaker is taking a backseat—alone.

According to recent research I did under the dryer, I found that women *were* emphasized, indeed. But where are those women? The articles made Hollywood look like Hometown U.S.A.

Probably because it had a pink cover I picked up *Cosmopolitan*. (The cover should have been red.) "Oh ho," said a woman in the next chair having her hair teased, "That's the female *Playboy*!" She obviously knew something I didn't. But by the time I read the cover captions, I felt *my* hair was standing on end. . . .

For example . . . "Girls in Prison—Savage, Wild and Horrifying," "A Survey of Co-eds Who Seduce Their Professors," "How 'Respectable' Wives Coolly Cheat—Wicked Strategy to Make Any Husband Wonder and Worry," "How Good a Lover Are You? (Quiz)" and "38 Ways to Meet Your Man."

Horrors, I thought, what is the world coming to? . . . Purely as a sociologist, I felt I should read the magazine. As a matter of fact, wild bulls couldn't have taken it away. Then came the quiz.

Once upon a time, quizzes helped you decide whether to live in a blue room or a green kitchen, what eyeshadows were best for Libras or the toys to give a three-year-old. This quiz was quite different.

But as a wife and a mother, I felt I should answer it. I soon discovered I was in the wrong pew. This quiz was definitely for the single woman, the woman of today. I held the magazine close and read the answers upside down in case anyone was looking. . . .

I didn't do so well. I was politely told I had "potential," but I should read *The Sensuous Woman*. That was the end. I read that *Woman* two summers ago and thought it was hilarious.

It wasn't until I was halfway home that I remembered I had left my answers written on an old airmail envelope addressed to me in the middle of the magazine, right at the quiz. My reputation as a sociologist, mother and wife quickly passed through my mind. I was sinking fast.

Coolly and wickedly I whipped the car around and drove like fury to the hairdresser's. I then calmly entered the beauty establishment and nonchalantly said I had forgotten a letter. Beads of perspiration were on my forehead as I discovered the magazine was as I had left it. I immediately left with my envelope and my secrets still my very own.

April 1972

About the closest I've ever come to envying the nautical life was when Dick Powell, in a sailor suit, sang to Ginger Rogers, also in a sailor suit.

I remember spending the next week, circa 1939, tap-dancing up and down stairs saluting. Ahoy! . . .

Many years later I discovered the S.S. *France* was my kind of ship. And that's that, as far as going out to sea.

Until a man was suddenly fifty. (I think one is always "suddenly fifty.") And when that time comes a man takes those years in his hands and decides to do what he has always wanted to do . . . buy a boat. Why didn't he just let his hair grow?

And so I have been shanghaied aboard the *Victory*, a small sailing ship. And although she is still on wooden blocks we have spent the winter sailing her from port to port. We've made the most astonishing cruises. Sir Francis Chichester beware. . . . She has become, even before we've set sail, my husband's winged victory.

Granted, *Victory* is quite an imperial name for such a small boat. But I like its ring. And why not? If it was all right for Horatio, Lord Nelson, it's all right with us. We've got the Battle of Trafalgar behind us. And they didn't laugh too much when we registered her. Beth did suggest *Clam* and maybe she's got something there. We'll see how she sits.

Last weekend was the beginning. We painted her bottom, I mean hull. The admiral/owner has a bad back so Tommy and I sprawled awkwardly under the broad bottom, and I mean bottom, and painted wide strokes of red. The admiral kept telling us we were just like Michelangelo, but I didn't feel a bit like Michelangelo. But you really didn't mind because everyone around you was sprawled, too. Next to us *True Love* was getting a second coat, and on the other side *Poop Poop A Deck.*

While we were painting, the admiral spent his time ashore investing in a depth finder, a compass, an anchor, line and who knows what else. I suddenly started thinking about the birthday party Richard Burton recently gave Liz. He donated the same amount of money he spent on the party to a charity. Why not, I asked Tom, give the equal amount spent on the boat to a local charity, me, the Old Sailors' Fun Pension? He didn't see it at all. . . .

After a long day under the bow Tommy rolled over and said, "You know, Mom, this boat is Dad's fifth child."

"Oh no," I answered, "it's his second wife."

Maybe it's better this way.

May 1972

Here, my magazine columns begin, June 1980, House & Garden. *In the hiatus of eight years our family had diminished, and in other ways, grown. I, by the loss and gain, had changed as well. I think these next columns reflect that change. They are not so light-hearted as the newspaper ones that ended in 1972, but I do hope they too have heart.*

Every summer I have an intense affair with my raspberries. And the pleasures and passions received from them are far more emotional than any pea picked, any carrot pulled from the vegetable garden. The first tomato, round and red, I must admit gives a certain sense of pride. It's the first merit badge. But soon they become overbearing, and I give them away easily without regret. My raspberries are the aristocrats. Elegant, evasive, more difficult, more treasured.

They hide like children who don't want their hands washed. But knowing what's good for them, I invade their privacy. With overwhelming self-confidence, obvious greed, I must be quicker than the birds, and more clever, hoping they feast on the nearby mulberry tree.

Four weeks of my life, the last of June and the beginning of July, are ruled by this precious crop. Other summer fun fades. And quite frankly, my berry fingers are better than my backhand. I think only raspberry. In the morning, before it gets too hot, I start picking.

I fashioned a comfortable working basket by tying a long rolled cotton scarf to each side, the loop going around my neck. The basket hangs at my waist, leaving both hands free. And while I pick, I hoard, reluctantly offering to anyone passing by perhaps one or two berries, no more. Only after the berries are made into jam do

I become more generous. Somehow then the deed is done, I have captured as many as possible and can begin to share.

Probably part of my devotion is a determination to keep the family line continuous. I inherited my raspberries from a son who inherited them from a grandfather. Other family possessions are passed down, fine silver, old tuxedos, but the berries come alive each year, every year. My son would care as I do.

It takes a good hour each day to pick the raspberries. Strawberries, which I no longer have, look up at you, but for the raspberries I get down on my knees. And the taller branches I bend back into wide curves, like Fred Astaire leading Ginger, to find the hidden red domes of the berries below. There must be a raspberry Mafia out to get me, because my arms become scratched, my feet tangle with lower branches. But a full-berried basket is worth the risk. My eye measures five cups of berries, four jars of jam.

Peace only comes when the berries are bubbling on the kitchen stove. I'm stirring the pot as country women have been doing for centuries, repeating a pattern of love, making sweets for family and friends. I boil the jars saved over the year, containers for artichoke hearts, bouillon cubes. Sugar is measured but as little as possible, paraffin is heated with great care. Jar lids become camouflaged with flowered fabrics, labels written with careful calligraphy, each day the cupboard shelf grows closer with jars of jam.

At last the day comes when my summer collection is complete. And there they stand and wait. The joy and pride is the giving, one by one, slowly over the year. A surprise jar for a honeymoon breakfast, others for winter teas. The day I pick the last berry, the first peach always seems to be ready. But it isn't quite the same. Maybe peaches are just too easy. They practically beg to be taken, while raspberries tease.

In late September, early October, we have a second crop, but not as bountiful. And as my closet is already filled with over fifty jars of jam, I make an 1835 dessert with fresh raspberries, which I found in *Maryland's Way,* a cookbook published by the Hammond-Harwood House in Annapolis, Maryland.

2 cups raspberries
½ cup sugar
½ pint whipping cream

Clean raspberries; add sugar to fruit and let stand to extract juice. Mash berries slightly, and bring slowly to the boil. Cook until soft, and pass through a sieve. After it is cold, whip the cream and add the fruit. Put on ice for 2 hours. Serve with wafers or sweet biscuits.

June 1980

The apron I remember was not my mother's, but my father's. It was long and white and he bought it from the butcher. He wore this white badge of courage only when he gave his first-class clambakes. It was his big event, his singular culinary achievement, and he loved getting all of summer's delicacies into one huge pot. And as the clam inspector was his friend, we had the best of all clams.

When I married, my father gave me some of those long, white aprons, and I have been tied to their strings, their honest lines, ever since. My original aprons, of course, have worn out, but any others—with ruffles, tassels or crafty trim—make me uncomfortable. So I've copied my father's design. Not that I'm always in the kitchen, but I seem to be often in an apron.

And in provocative company. Marie Antoinette wore one, we all know, when she was playing milkmaid at the Petit Trianon. Even earlier, a notorious couple "sewed fig leaves together and made themselves aprons" (Genesis 3:7). The inventory of any proper Dutch wife settling in the New World included "a purple apron and four new ones," and in the 1880s fashion dictated a tea apron as well as one for tennis. Mine, however, go to work.

Aprons are my armor of daily life. I wear them waxing floors, gardening, arranging flowers, making scrapbooks, decorating before a dinner party, laying the fires, wrapping presents, typing and, of course, cooking. "Everywhere," a friend once remarked, "except to bed." That's not quite true, but to me a fresh apron in the morning gets one going—it's a clean slate.

They're always the same design, but of various lengths. I've made a family of them in a day, the butcher apron blooming in different colors and patterns. An easy accessory, you can make an ample straight-bib apron from one yard of forty-five-inch mate-rial—much more satisfactory to me than those in stores stitched in plastic, mini-sized or covered with clever sayings and frogs.

But my aprons must have certain priorities. They must have bibs with the neck cord sewn loosely enough so the apron slips easily over the head, and the side strings must be long enough to wrap around the waist to tie in front. I first saw this in Austria where young women tied their aprons in perky bows in front. I consider it more convenient, but the *Fräuleins* told me that the front bow knot was to announce that they were unengaged, unattached!

If I'm going to do a lot of cutting, like wrapping Christmas presents, I tie scissors on a ribbon to my apron strings—childlike, but never lost. And no pockets. None. Cries of treason may now be heard. Pockets are the kangaroo pouches of most people. How-ever, my pockets only gather cookie crumbs and soggy matches. Less is really more when it comes to functional aprons. If you must have pockets, there is enough material in that yard to cut pockets from the two unused corners. My latest apron is reversible, made from leftover material from summer party tablecloths. One side is of navy blue and peach flowered chintz, the other side, tiny peach and white polkadots. Without pockets to get in the way, you can wear it on either side.

In a fabric store I can't resist buying yards of different materials for aprons, like going into a garden to pick flowers. Although the pattern design is always the same, I can be as wild as I like in the bouquets. And they make wonderful Christmas gifts, tied up with wooden spoons. I often give the identical apron, in bold stripes, to both husband and wife, and gardening friends get aprons hemmed well above the knee. And to make them for children is quick joy.

November 1980

T odd, our beekeeper son, has given me a most prestigious honorary degree, the "M.I.L." The title came about because of a wonderful new daughter-in-law who didn't know what to call me. Ever since Diana was sixteen and first came home from school with our daughter Beth, I've been "Mrs. Hardie." Now she's twenty-three and I'm her husband's mother.

When the honey started flowing, I made my maiden *belle-mère* visit to see Diana and Todd in northern Vermont. (The French, when it comes to families and affection, often say it better—"mother-in-law" becomes the far more gentle *belle-mère*.) With 143 colonies of bees, they needed all the help they could get. Their farm sits by a stand of sugar maples within view of Canada, and they can cross over the border to *fraise* farms to pick strawberries. They are surrounded by towering cobalt-blue silos painted bright with American flags, hay bales rolled like giant shredded-wheat biscuits. And in the summertime there are band concerts and ice-cream socials.

Their small Edward Hopper farmhouse was lived in for almost sixty years by two brothers. When I arrived, it would mean two women under the same roof for the very first time. Actually it was a ménage à trois. Perhaps I was taking the art of mother-in-lawing too seriously. My friend Carol thought I was. A mother of four sons, she assured me that all I had to do was "keep my mouth shut and my pocketbook open." Not exactly delicate advice, yet sensible.

But I had a hard act to follow. My own mother-in-law, now ninety-two, was a whirlwind in our prime. Even as our family grew bigger, she would race out to our farm carrying crab gumbo for Sunday suppers, keep the girls in Liberty lawn smocked dresses and the boys in good manners, and when I was particularly tired, she would take them all away for a toot at the zoo.

For my trip north to the apiary I couldn't bring any old family recipes—crab doesn't travel well from Maryland to Vermont. Instead I brought other cottage industries—our Maryland raspberry jam, and framed photographs of Todd as a little boy. The first evening Diana made a delicious herbal eggplant casserole, and later, as a lovely surprise, she turned down my bed and put wildflowers by my pillow.

For a week we worked and played. We spent days in the nearby honey house, which is about the size of a telephone booth, making bee frames, extracting honey, sometimes letting it drip over a slice of homemade bread, then eating it with our sticky hands. Pure childhood nectar.

I tried to be quiet and tidy, and whenever I saw even a spoon in the sink, I quickly washed it up. And it was a wonderful week of reciprocal love and trade. Diana and I found time to buy a clawfoot bathtub of regal proportions, which she painted lilac—a color which prompted, I think, their first domestic disagreement.

And I helped her decide where to put the swing on the porch, the trellis of roses and what hedge to plant that would be a windshield for the vegetable garden but not "block out the sunsets."

Diana taught *me* how to make a basket from the vines of Virginia creeper, how to make a salad from the young buds of day lilies, how the rings of a fallen stump tell the rainy years from the dry—wide rings of growth from rain, narrow ones from drought—and how to recognize Wild Richard, a charming flower I had never seen in Maryland.

And now, with only the *slightest* hesitation, she calls me "Dee." As for being a *belle-mère,* I decided right then and there, in a honey house in Vermont, it was like being in clover.

For those Vermont socials, Diana makes this home product:

> 1 quart heavy cream
> 1 cup milk
> ⅔ cup honey
> 1 teaspoon vanilla
> 1 egg

Put half the cream and all the milk, honey, vanilla and the egg in a blender. Pour mixture into a bowl and add the remaining cream. Mix. Freeze 1 hour. Remove and beat. Freeze again. Serves six to eight.

June 1981

My heart leaps up when I behold a rainbow in the sky, but it does a *lot* more when I see a simple white frame house along a country road, with the American flag flying from the porch. And here at Thornhill Farm, flags have always been part of our regalia. Right away you know how the wind blows—and the house stands taller.

Perhaps it all started in Paris where we lived the first year of our marriage. The French fly flags at the hint of a holiday, an accessory of pride. Even on their autobuses. Looking like moving Raoul Dufy paintings, small tiaras of flags flutter high from the front of the buses. And it *was* fun being part of a parade riding along the Seine.

Here in Maryland, we had Mary Pickersgill, who made a flag in 1814 that was so big, thirty by forty-two feet, that she had to finish sewing it in a brewery. This was the flag that was "still there" over Baltimore's harbor after twenty-five hours of British bombardment—the banner that inspired Francis Scott Key to write what is now our national anthem.

At Thornhill, our flags have never been quite so heroic, but we've certainly enjoyed them. One spring, we asked some foreign exchange students to a "B.Y.O. Flag Party," suggesting paper or fabric at least a yard long and wide. Makeshift, perhaps, but marvelous pennants arrived.

Argentina came, as well as England, France, Spain and on

around the world. We stapled the flags to garden bean poles, climbed a very tall ladder and stuck the standards into the inside beams of the barn. Suddenly our country hay barn became a medieval banquet hall filled with international flavor. The party flowed and the flags flew. Even today our barn pigeons perch imperially on flags of many nations.

When our own children were young, we used the patterns of flags to teach them how to do needlepoint. Colorful and easy to design on a large canvas, the lines of foreign flags are straightforward enough for a child to follow. My friend Mary Jane started it all by coming from New York for the weekend with canvas and thread for a small flag rug. Anything to keep the children quiet, she reasoned, and if our son Tommy really wanted to be a doctor, he should learn how to stitch early.

On needlepoint canvas, she drew the flags of countries our family had visited. Tommy enjoyed it the most, and there he would be doing his needlepoint while listening to an Orioles baseball game on the radio. Eventually other projects came into his life—making glasses out of old wine bottles, collecting paper to recycle and, I think, girls. Although the rug was never finished, we did salvage some of our young needlework by making the completed sections into pillows. Right now as I type, I'm sitting on Italy.

In July, especially, our American flags fly forth. Ten of them came from a dusty antiques shop in Concord, New Hampshire. Each is about a yard long, with forty-eight stars in the top left corner and "Wonolancet Club" in small letters on the lower border. Since we had forty-eight stars as far back as 1912, I like to think these flags have celebrated many a glorious Fourth, complete with fireworks and dancing under the stars. And as they only cost one dollar, I felt the least I could do was to have them cleaned.

It's not often one says, "I'm taking my flags to the cleaners." And I didn't. Instead, when Monday came, I asked Homer, who has been collecting here for years, if his laundry did flags.

"Of course," he said with his usual country brevity. Since I had ten, I asked how much they would cost.

"Flags are free," he answered.

Could this really be, I wondered, or was it just small-town patriotism, a vestige of old-time America? Long ago, George M. Cohan's nephew taught me how to dance, but he never told me about flags. And so I called several dry cleaners in Baltimore and discovered that yes indeed, the cleaning of an American flag is always on the house. Suddenly, somehow, the whole world looked a lot better. Flags are still free, it seems, at least at the cleaners.

July 1981

A woman who *thinks* she's organized, but can momentarily lose almost anything, is a hazard to her family's health. When I misplace, I mistrust—wild accusations fly forth. Then two months later when the silver christening cup shows up happily ensconced in a shoe box—*my* shoe box—I feel like a fool. My filing system, granted, is not perfect. My husband even changed his personal postal address to his office, tired, he said, of searching for his mail under my car seat. Maybe I did it on purpose. There are some things better to be lost. And last year I *tried* to lose Thanksgiving.

For some, traditions are like pigtails. When you grow up, you cut them off. But not for me. Our country Thanksgivings have long been pleasant feast days. For Aunt Alice, it was a pilgrim's progress, with her driving up every year from the mountains of North Carolina, a scraggly tree perched on the car roof. The tree then waited for Christmas on our side porch. While the turkey roasted, we'd go to Saint Johns, our country church, to watch the blessing of the hunt and hounds—a colorful tableau of pink coats and top hats and fine horses.

Home again, we enjoyed our own special act, the carving of the turkey by my father-in-law. Harry, as even his four grandchildren called him, was a quiet, courtly man, the family surgeon when it came to turkeys. When he carved, it was a ritual with the pace and precision of any Oriental tea ceremony. First, the knife to be tested, then off with the legs, delicate slivers of white meat, a bouquet of dark meat, and the dressing, all beautifully mounted on individual plates.

Then, as life and death and marriage and mileage have a way of doing, Tom and I were faced last year with our first Thanksgiving without any family at home. Once your children marry, you become an Alternating Holiday. As it should be, but I wasn't looking forward to it. Louise was going to be with Scott's parents, Todd with Diana's, and Beth was in the Colorado mountains teaching city children about nature.

I should have taken it in my stride. After all, for years I tried to avoid cranberry sauce though I was raised in New England, and I find it alien to have sauerkraut with turkey—the custom here in Maryland. But last Thanksgiving I just wanted it all to go away.

Instead, *we* went away. There was a business trip to Puerto Rico, and Tom said yes, it could be prolonged until the day after Thanksgiving. We could, quite simply, "lose Thanksgiving." How clever we were, I thought. Instead of browning the turkey, *we'll* sit in the sun. Freedom at last from responsibilities. Cha Cha Cha and *fresh* pineapple juice, all the plantain we could eat. We flew to San Juan with great expectations and tropical dreams.

When the morning of the last Thursday in November arrived, *I* knew what day it was, but pretended to forget. I'm not sure anyone else knew. Especially not the children in the swimming pool crying out in Spanish, or the trade winds fanning the palm trees. When the hotel announced that the U.S.S. *Forrestal* was in port and anyone who wanted a homesick sailor for dinner could call a certain number, I really knew what day it was, and suddenly I missed the old bird.

More than that, I knew that it wasn't so exotic running away. A country girl from Maryland in Puerto Rico on Thanksgiving was a misplaced person. The lovely part about traditions, I realized, is that you get used to them. They become part of the texture of your life, the blue blanket grown up. I could easily have cried in my drink.

Instead, we had a Thanksgiving dinner of *langosta frita en mantequilla* and *pulpo en ensalada.* It was a lonely meal. Right then I decided I was going to save lobsters for summer eating, and that I really didn't like octopus in salads.

From now on I will somehow find a family and friends to sit around that Thanksgiving table on the farm. On the table there is going to be a big bowl of light-green limes to help me remember fragrant Puerto Rico, but sprinkled with lots of deep-red cranberries to remind me where I *really* belong.

November 1981

About every seven years, my husband, Tom, starts to itch—for a new adventure. Maybe that's what keeps him young. When we *were* younger, he raised sheep with his sons and they were shepherds of the fields. And every wool blanket on our beds came from our barnyard. Then he read all of Georges Simenon and even Ian Fleming in French. Next he decided he wanted to be a sailor, bought a small boat and suddenly "left" and "right" disappeared from his vocabulary. Everything was "port" or "starboard" and he wanted all of us to call him "Cap'n." *Now* he's gone into weaving.

Without even knowing his warp from his weft, he came home with a loom as casually as most men bring home the evening paper. And at Thornhill Farm, what was always his office he now calls the Loom Room. That he is not a domestic animal, or even what you'd call "handy," makes his weaving even more of a strange interlude. He is, however, a curious man, open to all new ideas—until they explode. On his first attempt at cooking, he put the casserole *on* the stove rather than *in* the oven. He learned about culinary combustion, and I learned never to leave him alone in the kitchen on a Sunday afternoon.

Weaving, I hope, is a safer venture. His leader is our daughter Louise. A weaver for some time, she makes glorious cotton rag rugs. I like to think she inherited this talent from my Swedish grandfather, who designed textiles in the Fall River mills long ago. Tom is far more concerned with showing his daughter that there is still some life left in the old boy yet. Age, it seems, bothers men more than women. It certainly makes them do unusual things.

This businessman, normally connected to a telephone the way a baby is attached to the umbilical cord, spent a precious week in a remote Pennsylvania farmhouse learning how to weave. I still find it hard to believe—but very appealing. Surprise, after thirty-one years of marriage, is a marvelous ingredient.

Before we left for the school in East Berlin, Pennsylvania, Tom practiced weaving at home with Louise. He would flip the shuttle back and forth across the loom, then look up with a boyish smile, more a grin of discovery.

I think he thought he was back on the playing field, cradling the ball in his lacrosse stick. His first production was meant to be woolen scarves for our children, but somehow they stretched into small rugs. He was thrilled.

School was a different game. We spent most of the time

working with silk thread, weaving intricate samplers that would look at home in a Bavarian chalet. "Discipline," we were told, was what we needed, and cotton rag rugs, which we really wanted to do, were considered déclassé. Learning how to weave in middle years was like entering a foreign country. We had to get past the customs, learn a new language—heddles, harness, threading, sleying.* It was exhausting.

At 8:30 in the morning we were over the looms, and by 8:30 at night we were in bed. One evening we went into Hanover, a small town with shoe factories, whose last historic moment, *before* Tom took up weaving, was when the Union troops came through because they needed new boots. We drank a little, relaxed a little and managed to survive the week.

Now we've just finished "dressing," or warping, our first loom. They say it gets easier, but it took us all weekend, and by Sunday night I was bleary-eyed. When Tom was in sheep, I managed to burlap-bag the wool to send to Texas where the blankets were made. When he was in his French period, I cooked Madame Maigret recipes, and when he took up sailing I managed to get by dropping such sentences as "With reefed mainsail we found she would lay north by east fairly comfortably." But warping a loom leaves me speechless.

The rainbow, however, is still to come, and our first cotton rag rug is going to be lavender, maroon and melon for the guest room. And I have more designs on my mind. The most important is that from now on Tom can "dress" the loom and *I'll* dress the house, with our own rag rugs—everywhere!

April 1982

*The book we found most helpful was *The Weaver's Book* by Harriet Tidball (Collier Books, 1976).

Our first pony was named Kelly, and he cost, at the fairgrounds auction, $150 with payment heavy in pennies. Welsh and wide, he was fat enough to carry two children at a time, and docile enough not to know the difference. Our special adventures on Sunday afternoons were pony picnics. Some would ride, others walk to a far field where our destination was a small stone ruin we called the Indian Fort. It was probably an abandoned still, but that never crossed our minds. To us it held corners of secrets, and it was spring. Now it's spring again, and I need another pony. I am about to become a grandmother!

A pony should be part of this new parade into childhood. It's almost de rigueur. We live on a farm. I also need all the help I can get. As I never had a grandmother to play with, I'm not at all sure of my first steps.

Tom claims I have been practicing for years. When he says this I wonder if I'm looking for my own childhood, or perhaps that of our four children. They were happy years. Maybe my husband knows me better than I realize. I *do* have a salt-box dollhouse, a brigade of tiny tin soldiers, a trunk full of puzzles and books, a shelf of teddy bears and Fiona Barley, an old English doll, all waiting in the wings—obviously for a small leading lady, or man, to come our way.

My friend Alice, who has three grandchildren down the road on the family dairy farm, says being a grandmother is the "icing on the cake" and she enjoys every crumb. Katey says it's "joy mixed with terror," especially when you hold that glorious baby for the very first time. She also told me about the grandchild, sitting in the dressing room while her grandmother tried on a new dress, who asked: "Grandma, who let the air out of your arms?" No room for vanity with a grandchild around, claims Katey. Since I consider these two women grandmothers cum laude, I listen when they speak.

When Louise spoke and told us she was pregnant, I cried happy tears. I suddenly found myself taking long afternoon naps, gave up practically all my vices, developed a craving for the chocolate of a Mr. Goodbar at three in the morning. That was the fourth month. In the fifth month I stopped looking at babies, didn't dare ask about gingham overalls, size 6 months, stopped peeking at pinafores. It was just too overwhelming, too wonderful to think that soon we were going to have one of our own—Louise and Scott's baby.

In the seventh month, we had a serious conversation about names. Not names of the baby, but what the baby was to call us. I told Louise about a friend who, when asked this same question by her son, told him she wanted her grandchildren to call her "Perfect." And now there are two little children who do just that. But I opted for "Grandmother," pure and simple.

Tom, the future grandfather, said that he didn't see himself married to a "Grandmother," and he thought "Cap'n" would do for him. It looked as if it could be easier naming a pony. I shopped around, asked my friends what they had called their grandmothers. "Baboo," "Oma" and "Umpa" came forth. I'm still pushing "Grandmother," but "Duchess" *does* have a nice ring.

Even more searching was the afternoon Louise and I spent in our barn, trying to recycle the past. We found the children's old maple spool crib stored there, but it only had three sides. The playpen was, Louise considered, unsafe. Then I remembered, once out of diapers, it had graduated to housing early Easter bunnies and occasional rambunctious puppies.

In the tack room, however, we found a real treasure—the pony bridle, ready to go. Now my friends are looking around for a pony who needs a grandmother!

May 1982

L ast June, in a wild emotional frenzy of weeding, I thought about divorcing my vegetable garden and giving complete custody of it to my husband. I didn't even want the right to visit every other weekend. It was simply that the vegetables and I seemed totally incompatible. The moment that I left them for one short week, they started running around with weeds, tarnishing my country reputation.

If you live in the country, and *don't* have a vegetable garden, country friends think you are some kind of turnip—a very ordinary crop—and city friends just can't believe it. "What!" they say with urban airs, "No vegetable garden this year? You should see what *we* get from one window box!" And so it is a rural obligation, an American duty, to sow seeds if you have even a half acre of land. But there are times when I get tired of trying to be Mother Earth, and late last June was one of those moments.

I took a week off to visit my parents in Boston, and Tom took the time to work late at the office. The vegetable garden was left foolishly alone. I really should have known better after all these years. You *never* turn your back on your vegetable garden, especially during the monsoon season in Maryland. But when I left it was all so tidy and trim.

This was a calculated garden, planned parenthood. In earlier years we had much larger agricultural spreads, from rutabaga to melons. But we also had a crew of four young farmers who rejoiced with the birth of each radish, and thought snapping string beans almost as much summer fun as catching fireflies.

And now that we're on our own, we've cut down on the crops. We tried to size up the garden, rather than have the garden outsize us. With great expectations we plotted with seed catalogues in February, and with confidence we planted in the spring. This was to be our adult garden—rows of fernlike asparagus, showy snow peas, both particularly choice for dinner parties, no carrots, but beets, broccoli, tomatoes, and cucumbers, of course, and the best of Bibb lettuce. I edged the entire garden with nasturtiums, which grew fat and fast, making me look a much better gardener than I really am.

I was proud of our efforts, probably too pleased. Then after a week's absence and constant country rain, I came back to a jungle, promiscuous weeds, a full-scale invasion of the unwanted. There was some comfort in the sprightly nasturtiums, but that's only because they were the only plant that I could recognize. Ralph Waldo Emerson, a philosopher favorite of our quotation-collecting son, once wrote: "What is a weed? A plant whose virtues have not yet been discovered." Well, he's all wrong. Weeds have *no* heart!

Now when Scarlett O'Hara found her vegetable garden in shambles, albeit after a longer time, she merely tore down the deep-green velvet curtains, made a fine dress and cajoled Rhett Butler into helping her. I can't sew that well, so instead I sprang into the garden with savage determination. It was discouraging. For two days I weeded the way a Moslem prays—on my knees, back doubled over, head down. Slowly I rescued my purloined vegetables from the strangling weeds. I forgave them for their foolish ways, felt rewarded seeing them spring back to life. We had a reconciliation.

The rest of the summer was bountiful, and we all lived in harmony. Even the scent of the tomato plants seemed stronger now that we were together again.

Thornhill Tomato Preserves: Collect 7 pounds of ripe tomatoes. Cook them down and drain. Do *not* add any water. Add 2 pounds brown sugar, 1 pint vinegar, 1 teaspoon each ginger and allspice, 3 teaspoons cinnamon, the juice and grated rind of 1 lemon, 1 teaspoon salt. Cook down until thick and put in jars that have been sterilized. Seal with paraffin.

June 1982

W hen our two Saint Bernards started chasing sheep, the *neighbor's* sheep, we had to give the playful pups away. They had become a menace, although they didn't know it, and the rules of the country are often cruel. Tuffy now lives with a marine biologist in Florida, and Rosie is with an oyster inspector on the Eastern Shore—both, I am sure, happy as clams. But I was crushed. To compensate, my husband gave me another pet. He gave me a small white wooden boat.

Crazy, I thought, what am I going to do with a boat in the country? But there was a method to his madness. With a boat waiting for me in the Nantucket harbor, we had to go down to the sea again, especially in August when it was to be delivered.

And when you are married to a man who loves the sea as Tom does—although he decided long ago to settle his family in the deep country—you've got to get your feet wet. This new little white boat, a Beetle Cat made in South Dartmouth, outside New Bedford, Massachusetts, was a matey way to take a first plunge.

A Beetle Cat, twelve feet, four inches long, is usually child's play. Its beam is broad, almost impossible to tip over, and it's the boat the young learn to sail. It becomes a family mascot, a picnic boat, a childhood memory. And the mention of it can bring smiles to old men. With one sail and gaff-rig, it has a nineteenth-century flavor. It's an owl-and-the-pussycat kind of boat.

Sailing a boat, I kept telling myself, *is* like taking a long walk in the country. No telephones, no troubles, peace for at least an hour while you're running with the wind.

The gift wasn't completely unannounced. Tom didn't cover my eyes, lead me to water, whip off a blindfold and say, "There you are, a boat all your own!" If I was going to be given a boat, I wanted a boat with style, tradition, a classic. No fiberglass bathtub for me. I wanted a proud wooden boat.

I had read an article about Beetle Cats, made by Concordia, how they are still entirely of wood, cedar and oak, still constructed with the same techniques used in boatbuilding for over two hundred years, still built by the same man who has done it for the last fifty-two years. Leo Telesmanick at sixty-five couldn't find anyone to take his place. It could be the end of an era. I was touched and saddened. And if Tom really wanted to give me a boat, I wanted to be part of this fleet, one that soon might be part of the past.

We made a pilgrimage, and went to see him. We walked around his sheds, touched a boat being built upside down on a mold that someone described as the "reconstructed skeleton of a hippopotamus." It was all *very* businesslike. Once we made the decision, I relaxed. I looked at Mr. Telesmanick and admitted, "When I read that article in *The New York Times* over breakfast about you and perhaps the end of your wooden Beetle Cats, I cried." He looked at me, this tall, stern Yankee, and said simply, "So did I." And then we both proceeded to shed tears. It was the strangest moment in the most wonderful way. We had a bond. He loved building boats, and I was going to love his boat. He was also surprised but looked pleased when I chose a purple sail.

Years back there was a large fleet of Beetle Cats on the island of Nantucket, off the coast of Cape Cod, each with a different-colored sail, and they were called Rainbows, as they are to this day. I chose the color purple as I like it, and frankly wanted to be noticed. I didn't realize what company I was in. A few months later I read, "Purple the sails, and so perfumed that the winds were lovesick with them." So wrote Shakespeare of Cleopatra's barge.

I named my boat after myself—*Deeds*. No *At Lass* or *Sea Witch* for me. And *Deeds* and I had a good time last summer, getting to know each other, coming about. But I never gained enough courage or skill to sail her alone. This is the August of independence, or maybe just messing about. As Water Rat says in *Wind in the Willows,* the lovely English classic, "There is nothing—absolutely nothing—half so much worth doing as simply messing about in boats . . . simply messing . . . nothing seems really to matter, that's the charm of it."

August 1982

We've always been rather blasé about our apple trees. For years we've taken them for granted—and for apple pies. And they're scattered about the farm as if Johnny Appleseed passed by on his way to the Ohio Valley. There are two trees by the raspberries, and these we shake with a rake for an avalanche when we feel like baking up a batch of pies, or a simple Apple Crisp for a supper sweet.

Another tree is far down in the meadow, remembered chiefly because after a long country walk, it was under this tree Uncle Henry showed us how to wiggle our ears. The fourth tree is in the corner of a pasture, its branches low enough for the neighbor's cows to stretch their necks for a lazy morning snack.

Growing up, our children seemed to prefer the chestnut tree, perhaps because its limbs are easier for climbing, the chestnut itself more of a mystery to the young. The pear tree, with its bending boughs, was also a favorite. You merely reach out and the tree still hands you a luscious September pear.

And the maples have wonderful leaves for pressing, especially on a rainy day. We once pressed sixty leaves from sixty different trees on Thornhill Farm for a school project. I wanted to title the scrapbook "Leaves from Family Trees," but although Todd was only eleven, or maybe because he *was* eleven, he refused my pun. I was crushed. Literary rejection from your own child!

With all those trees, I couldn't see the forest, I guess, of ideas that come from apples. But this year I was tempted, really tempted by an apple. And it took Marny, a young woman who works with food in Boston, to teach an old goose like myself how to make a graceful swan from a round, red apple.

At a late summer party on Nantucket, I was overcome with desire. Sitting elegantly in the center of a party plate surrounded by pâté was a swan carved from an apple. Suddenly a "whiteness of swans," as a gathering is called, flew through my head. With all those apple trees at home, I thought, why couldn't I have a dinner party with an apple swan at each place?

Marny Lanagan, I discovered, was the hostess's niece, the sculptor and, the next evening, *my* teacher. We carved together and she delivered, time after time, a graceful swan, while I carved what might be considered a series of lame ducks. She encouraged me to think that in time the way of swans and apples would be as simple as you-know-what kind of pie.

The time came much sooner than I expected. My friend Alice, who can do just about anything, has yet to learn how to say "No." Announce a church auction, and she collects the treasures. Give a house and garden pilgrimage, she makes the box lunches. Have a benefit cooking class, she's—well, that was her Waterloo.

"Dee!" she asked desperately in an 8:00 A.M. telephone call, the time when telephone calls in the country *really* mean business. "Can you make a radish into a rose?" Without hardly missing a beat, I said, "No, Alice, I can't, but I *can* make an apple into a swan." Her relief was so obvious I felt as if I had the powers of a Papal blessing.

What a fraud I was, but what a friend is Alice. She brought the lunch, I supplied the apples. With the stem end of the apple facing toward me, I cut off a half-inch slice from the lower bottom.

This I saved to carve the head and neck. I sat the apple on its flat side, and in the center top, now the swan's back, I cut shallow graduated V-wedges, small to larger, about five. I did the same on both sides of the apple. I put these wedges in lemon juice (one lemon to two cups of water), as it is an adhesive and also keeps them from turning brown. I then took the wedges and fanned them out in the center V of the apple's back, and then did the same on each side. *Voilà,* you have the swan's feathers. I carved a head and neck from a curve of that first bottom slice of the apple, stuck it in with a toothpick, added a clove as an eye.

After five apples, I was a pro. I've admired royal swans in England, rural swans in Vermont, but Alice's are the swans I'll remember.

September 1982

O ctober is a special month for me, as I was born right in the middle of it. So was Oscar Wilde, although probably a century too soon, and Eleanor Roosevelt, Sarah Bernhardt, Pablo Picasso. It's a vintage month filled with provocative people from the past. It's also the month when the country sparrows swoop onto the meadows searching for seeds, the maples are extravagant with their gold and I have reason to make a little whoopee as another year has passed.

I *always* celebrate, one way or another. When I was fifty, I painted my toenails red. This may seem tame, but it was a startling moment. The next year I asked Tom to take me to a marathon of movies. During the fifth movie he bailed out. Which is exactly what he should have done, as it was a bomb. This year I think I'll have a fireworks display. Sparklers make wonderful candles on a birthday cake. Although fireworks are prohibited by county law in July, I wonder about October?

One does get bolder as one gets older. And I find I don't care half as much about what people think of me. This may sound brazen, but age does give you certain rights to declare your independence. And my priorities, easily counted on one hand, are in order at last. Just one smile from our seven-month-old grandson Albert makes my world wonderful.

When I was younger there was this hybrid vigor—half Swedish, a quarter each of French and English. I had to prove myself. Not for them, those brave pioneering, probably terrified, immigrants but for myself. Now I'm years older, and I'm going to take it easy. I am a woman *entre deux âges*, which is the French way of politely telling me I'm neither too young nor too old. A very happy place in the sun.

My friend Genevieve, who lives in South Carolina, sixty-eight years this December, celebrates with "investments in elegance." Last year she went to New York City for four days. This was the itinerary she wrote me: "Ostensibly to see *Nicholas Nickleby,* but it also included Tiffany's, Bloomingdale's, a long stroll on 57th Street, a visit to the Metropolitan Museum, St. Francis of Assisi Church, famous for its breadline, one bus ride on Lexington, one subway venture with disaster. . . ."

I, on the other hand, would like some country favors, some wishes one can fling out on a birthday if at no other time.

I wish I had more country style. Although I have lived at Thornhill Farm for twenty-seven years, I still have a city conscience about slipcovers. I'm uptight, you might say, about slipcovers. I like them trim and tidy. Whereas *real* country is to accept them, with a nonchalance of ease, rumpled and weary, ready for the pounce of five or six dogs, and in the distance a field of daffodils.

Country style, I've discovered, is much more than a pine

cupboard filled with spongeware bowls and the horse weather vane on the blanket chest. *That* can be photographed, that can be defined. Real country style is more illusive. It's something you're born with. Like our house. Settled, small, honest, born in 1843, our house knows its place and can handle the trivial fancies, or pretensions, of its owners of almost the last three decades.

But its owners can also dream. I'd like to have ridden, if wishes were known, sidesaddle with the arch of my long black skirt elegantly swagged on a high horse. And it would be lovely to have someone weed, without notice, the raspberry patch.

Then there are improbable presents I'd like to give myself. A long pearl necklace, 8 1/2 millimeters each pearl, please. And evenings of waltzing every once in a while. It's so easy—one-two-three, one-two-three. Johann Strauss, Jr. was born October 25, but I loved waltzing long before I realized he was a member of our club.

Another member is James Lawrence, born on the first of October, a hero of the War of 1812, who said in his moment of glory: "Don't give up the ship." And *that* says it very well indeed for all of us.

October 1982

In the country we call them stolen days—days when heavy snow pushes life back to a more leisurely pace. This happened to us in February, and we had no way to get down our hill. As we had an unexpected holiday, we seemed to do unexpected things—Tom offered sherry before lunch, I read an entire P. D. James mystery before dark and together we erased with ease the timetables of a day.

The next snowfall wasn't so casual. We had played *enough* double solitaire and felt liberated when we heard the deep rumble of John Pearce's tractor plowing us out. But just in case, we piled the laundry into the washer before the 'lectric, as it is called here in the country, faded away. We lined up the candles, set the boots by the door and threw bales of hay from the barn for the six deer we had seen the evening before, wandering with great dignity but obvious dismay around the snow-crusted cornfield, foraging without hope.

As the month grew older and colder it snowed again, and with the snow came an elegant armor of ice. Even small oak leaves were encased in icy shields. Carefully, I would take the molds from the leaves and use them as ice cubes in apple cider. This particularly delighted the young visitors who had walked over the fields. Everything sparkled, and the bowed branches of the chestnut tree were like country chandeliers.

But when I turned to look at our boxwood bushes, all the

winter magic seemed to disappear. I had forgotten to clothe them for winter. They were like fallen women in a nineteenth-century Russian novel, their limbs in a state of dishabille, the ice bending them to their knees. I had neglected my old friends, forgotten our annual winter drill.

The boxwood had been at Thornhill Farm almost as long as I had. When we first moved to Maryland my mother-in-law, who always called me her Yankee daughter, gave me a white birch tree so I wouldn't be homesick for my native New England. She also insisted that every farmhouse needed boxwood bushes, and before you could whistle "Dixie" she had planted a row of box shrubs in front of our house.

Energetic, not quite five feet tall, this Southern lady born in Mississippi, had strong roots. Although she lived most of her adult life in Maryland, one of her greatest treasures was her Georgia grandfather's calling card which not only gave his address, but a complete list of his Civil War battles. For her the South rose again when she planted those boxwood bushes at Thornhill Farm.

Every spring more were added by our children. After Rogation Sunday, when the crops were blessed at Saint John's Church, the entire Sunday school received tiny boxwood bushes to plant at home. When winter came one of the season's first rituals was to cover the boxwood with burlap grain bags to keep them warm. As they outgrew the bags, growing wider and taller, we tied them tight with corsets of twine. When the snows came we banged the bushes with a broom to keep them in line, scattering the white caps from the tops of the shrubs.

We did so well that the first row of boxwood has grown full and close, practically holding hands with each other. And each spring the primroses peek out from under a very green roof of boxwood. At Christmas we prune them by breaking off the inner branches to make endless wreaths and garlands.

Looking at the boxwood caked with heavy ice, now minus bags and twine, I slowly realized the inevitable. You can't worry about your boxwood once it grows up. And the boxwood, like our children, *had* grown up. We had loved and nurtured them, clothed them, given them, I hope, some style. Now they were probably better off on their own, I reasoned, but not without some pangs, some slight resentment.

However, being a mother, that still didn't stop me from heating a teakettle and pouring warm water to melt some of the ice on my fallen friends. And the next day, helped by warmer temperatures, the bushes had almost sprung back to size. Maybe that spanking by winter will make them stronger. At least it made *me* a little wiser—a bit of cold comfort at the end of winter.

January 1983

For years I've been leading a double life. Thornhill, of course, is my heart, but every August I become involved deeply, even emotionally, with a house at 39 India Street on Nantucket Island. I wonder if this is how a woman feels when she has loved more than once?

I always feel a bit unfaithful when I am about to leave the farm. How will the flowers do without me? Will the vegetables behave? But very quickly I become embraced by easy town living on this island Herman Melville once called "an elbow of sand."

I can walk to the sea, build sand castles with my grandson Albert and, whenever I please, ride my bicycle around endless ribbons of nineteenth-century streets edged with the fine houses built by captains and crews of whaling ships. It's a whole different world.

There is an anxious moment when I first open the door of

39 India. The house has been rented for a month. Sometimes I find a bouquet and the beds are neat. I'm ecstatic. If not, I tear around until I make the house mine again. Then we settle down for summertime.

This townhouse takes care of itself, as I never seem to allow Thornhill to do. While our farmhouse rambles, 39 India is straight and tall. Built by Gorham Macy in 1835 as a wedding present to his son, it's the kind of house you could copy in cardboard for a child's school project—square house, peaked roof. It reminds you of an old-fashioned wooden-block puzzle that you can take apart and put together in no time at all, room by room. In this house you know where you stand.

It's a bit stern perhaps, but the weathered shingles are warm and I always put bright red geraniums in the window boxes. And over the years I've learned to live with another house, once never dreaming I'd be the mistress of two.

When I first saw the house, fifteen years ago, the real estate agent said, "Everything goes with it except the organ." That was a blessing. Owned by the widow of a Baptist minister, there were Bibles and hymnals in the attic, and the basement ceiling is still supported by old posters that say "Jesus Saves."

Eventually we made it ours, putting a Hans Hofmann print over the fireplace, making curtains from sheets, painting old wicker white. And now every summer we are all together again as we once were. We sit in the backyard, the size of a handkerchief, and treat ourselves to lobster one night, bluefish the next. We sail in a picnic boat to points of Coatue; we lean over the back fence for chats with neighbors we can touch. Sometimes we exchange a bottle of wine with India House, an inn nearby. Tom calls 39 India my dollhouse, but I think of it as my New England conscience.

It makes me remember the past, who I am. And if you were born in New England, as I was, it's good to go home again, hear voices say "patten" for pattern, "summa" for summer, and know when they say "steamers," they really mean clams. But by the time early September arrives it's time to leave. The summer affair is over, and I'm all ready for the fall harvest at Thornhill.

August 1983

I arrange my spices alphabetically in our kitchen cupboard, and I do the same with my friends in my address book. These days, however, Rosemary and Thyme seem easier to find in a pinch than those friends who are always on the move. And after years of putting these friends in their place, the time has come to edit my address book.

For better or for worse, for divorce and marriage, often for work, sometimes for play, my friends have changed their geography. They are either going up in the world or coming down to smaller quarters, and their changing addresses seem to be their one constant way of life.

This came through clearly when we were sending out Christmas cards, our one big mailing of the year. My address book, stuffed as well with torn flaps of envelopes and new addresses, looked like an old ledger with lines drawn through entries on every page.

There are lots of friends, of course, whose addresses I know by heart. I began to think *that* group should be our Christmas list. But they too have ZIP codes, those villains who usually must be researched. An address book, after all, is an appendage to the art of keeping in touch, knowing that old friends may be far away but always in reach *if* you can only read your own writing.

Or there is the telephone that punctuates most people's lives. But for me it is only an emergency valve. If I want a *real* visit, I write a letter. Love, I think, is more emphatic if you take time to write. And I treasure letters from our children, putting them in a basket, deep in a bookcase, which they might someday find and read.

These children, however, have not made my address book any younger, giving line upon lines. Although grown, they still seem to be in transit. Look at Beth's itinerary. In the last three years our younger daughter has lived in Colorado, the Virgin Islands and now Lake Placid, New York. All winter gardens for some, but where Beth has taught school nobly and with heart. I've learned to *pencil* her in.

My Aunt Eunice, a grand matriarch, is in ink. She is the only person I know who lives at the same address where she was born, eighty years ago. Her address reads, as it does in my memory, 34 Adams Street, Fall River, Mass., ZIP code immaterial. She knows, as does the postman, where she lives.

But she is an extraordinary island in this day and age. And when I started to revise my address book, I thought perhaps I should begin with a clean slate. I looked at leather-covered books in stationery stores, admired their crisp pages, clean with empty spaces with hope for years to come. Then I realized I didn't really want to start over again, to erase away the past.

There are too many good friends, some I'll never see again, too many good times tucked away in those pages. The actress Helen Hayes once said she wouldn't dream of taking the lines from her face—they show the routes of her life. Well if Helen Hayes can face it, so can my address book. And so here's to a new year, perhaps new friends, but always the old memories, thanks to my address book, battered and bowed and brave.

January 1984

Thornhill hibernates in winter, as does all our Maryland countryside. We become insular. We tuck in and thaw out by the fire. But we always know there is April. And April is our jubilee.

On every Saturday afternoon in April there is a steeplechase, a race of country horses over farms and fences, ridden by gentlemen jockeys in their racing silks as bright as the first gardens of spring. It's not only a sport—it's a social gathering.

The races are free, the grandstands are grassy slopes sprinkled with tiny grape hyacinths and everybody comes. City meets country; country neighbors visit with friends they haven't seen in months.

In England races such as these were called steeplechases because the course was around one country church spire to the next. The name continues in America, especially in Maryland where it's been a tradition since the turn of the century. And it's a lovely way to spend an old-fashioned day in the country—time standing still, if only for a bit.

Most of our neighbors, at one time or another, have had entries in these races, making it more exciting for us. But for our own family, our horse life limited, these races have always been a spectator sport. Not that we haven't tried.

First there was Hammersmith, named after a bus stop in outer London. A bay, seventeen hands high. . . . Tom rode him, the children enjoyed him and we have vintage black-and-white photographs of four children joyously astride one horse. But when Hammersmith started eating his bridle as if it were spaghetti, we thought it best to return him to his original donor, our neighbor Gillian.

Then there was Colonel, a gift horse we should have looked in the mouth. He died mysteriously by falling against a barn post. Right then and there our equestrian life abruptly ended. We never replaced the post or the horse. But that doesn't stop us from going to the races every single spring.

In April these horse races become everybody's world. Car after car pulls into parking lots that only the day before were pastures. And since our nearest race, the Grand National, is within walking distance of Thornhill, this is the time of the year we entertain. We use hay bales for benches, have lunch on the lawn. After a week of tidying up the garden, sprucing up the house, we hope we are looking our best. We are unabashedly showing off.

In Australia steeplechases like ours are called picnic races, and often we too take our guests on a big, grand picnic. We always start with "devilish" eggs, making them more Maryland by adding crab.

There's nothing quite like it, sitting on a hillside watching the elegance, the style and stretch of horses in the distance. It looks like a Degas painting, or perhaps an English print. But once I taste the crab, I know *just* where I am.

April 1984

I am an accomplice, not so innocently, to what might turn out to be a heated domestic discussion. The accessory is a tall pine cupboard, circa 1840, that my friend Cynthia bought, but hasn't quite had the nerve to bring into her own kitchen. And so it stands in our red bank barn, hidden between bales of hay. And until now, only the barn pigeons knew our secret.

I don't feel a bit guilty; I even encouraged Cynthia to buy it. It was just what she wanted, at what I thought was a most agreeable price. (I find I'm very good at spending the money of others). The dealer in New Market, a town about an hour from Thornhill filled with more than forty antiques shops, was so delighted to make a sale that she gave us each a box of balsam incense. It was a very nice day in the country.

Part of the pleasure, I realized, was the pursuit—finding that piece of furniture. I discovered the fun of the search, the sport of bargaining. It was a new game for me, and I decided to join in by announcing that Thornhill needed a blanket chest. There were none in sight so it was a safe statement.

I had never seriously done any antiquing before since Thornhill has been comfortably furnished by Hardie generations before us. We are, indeed, a full house. But I was bitten, now convinced that we needed a chest for blankets so they wouldn't tumble down from closet shelves every time I opened a door.

I also reminded myself that our children were slowly

removing house furniture, dressing their own with our family re-
tainers. Maybe it *was* time to start replenishing. Shades of rational-
ity! Todd *does* have his grandfather's rolltop desk, Louise the brass
bed of her grandparents. And on the back of a painting of wild
poppies is a legend—"This painting was given to Beth when she was
ten. Dee Hardie, New Year's Eve, 1981." When I wrote that I was
either trying to start the new year right with Beth, or perhaps it was
the champagne. Whatever, we *all* know where it is eventually going
to live.

It wasn't always like this. Some years back our children
spurned possessions. They were filled with ideals, couldn't have cared
less about furnishing a house. But if you wait long enough, things
do change. Now it's Todd who wears a coat and tie, and I'm the
one in overalls. The better, I tell myself, to prowl around antiques
shops.

And that's what I've done all over Maryland, but it was in
our own village at the Butler Peddler that I found our blanket chest.

It now sits at the end of our bed, a blue hope chest initialed
in red and painted with the year "1860." Known also as an immigrants' chest, it comes from Sweden as did my own grandparents.

To me that's magic. I found a chest that my own Anna and
Adolph could have used journeying to the new world. And whenever I look at this chest, I feel a strong family connection. That's
what antiques are meant to do—make you remember, help you
belong.

July 1984

Every fall I tuck in tulips around Thornhill Farm. Over the years I've learned a few tulips in the right place are worth twenty in the wrong. It's the site that counts—the white lily-petaled ones against the green boxwood, a clump of pink by the beige fieldstone wall. And in the iron urns that sit on either side of our front door I plant bulbs that promise spring tulips the color of deep red wine.

When spring comes these tulips are my first hurrah, my first garden party. They're the awakening, the hope. Together we have survived winter. But last spring not all my guests arrived. The urn tulips didn't show their faces, not even a tiny spear of green appeared. It could have been the winter, a fierce one, and I finally gave up waiting. I planted, instead, annuals in the urns.

I put in lavender-blue pansies and petunias, their deep-pink centers reaching over paler petals. It was a new variety called Summer Madness, and I *was* delirious as their blooms immediately covered the tops of the urns.

Then one morning I looked out and their heads had been cut off. The next day I saw the culprit, a cunning chipmunk carrying away the petals. I was furious. I was also determined not to lose out to the chipmunk, a tiny rodent who looks like he wears a smooth raccoon coat. And just as I was about to plan my attack, the raids stopped.

Chris, a young friend studying for his Ph.D. in zoology,

suggested that my adversaries were in their burrows, long tunnels in the ground with adjacent rooms, a bit like Hitler's bunker, eating away at nuts.

I knew better. My chipmunks were underground gourmets, and I knew what they were eating—*my* pink petunias and pansy petals. And soon they were coming up again for a second course as my annuals were again losing their heads.

A nurseryman told me to put mothballs around the plants, or get clippings of human hair from a barber. The last resort—a shotgun.

I tried home ground. My friend Kitty suggested two tablespoons of Tabasco sauce to a gallon of water, while Catherine was convinced dried blood, a fertilizer and a repellent to rodents, was the only answer.

The plot was thickening. Little did the chipmunk realize I was waging war. I decided to attack on all sides, use every weapon. I had lost my urn tulips, possibly to winter freeze, but I didn't want to give up on my annuals, which have often cheered me into December.

I sprinkled the top of the urns with Tabasco, gave Tom a haircut he didn't need and used his locks as the next layer. Then came dried blood, and as a frosting I put mothballs around the plants.

I used *every* idea that was given to me, and I won! The chipmunks never nibbled again.

Sometimes you learn, simply by a pansy, or perhaps a petunia, that it *is* the survival of the fittest. And if it takes a trick or two, with a touch of Tabasco, why not!

September 1984

We live in an old house with old ideas. We *still* have a dining room. And I certainly don't agree with my more modern friend who keeps telling me a dining room is like an appendix—something you don't need at all. When our children were younger it was the *one* room where we all acted grownup together.

Christmas week our dining room is the centerpiece of our celebrations. There's always a small spruce in the corner, and I dress the table as lavishly as I decorate the tree. On the twenty-third, our wedding anniversary, the table shines with white and silver. For Christmas Eve, I bring out the red and gold.

That's fun. I love embroidering the glow of Christmas around holiday meals. But off season, that dining room table is my nemesis!

Not that I haven't tried to conquer its sedentary ways by camouflage—sewing endless cloths of chintz and lace to lighten its look, for day as well as by night. (Its legs are like elephants'!) But suddenly I'm tired of trying to make a movie star out of a bit player.

This mahogany table, round and stout, was made in 1898 for the young house of my husband's grandparents. And it sat heavily in New Orleans's Garden District until it came to us when we married. Although it has none of the amusing flourishes of the Victorian era, it has certainly served its purpose—much in the manner, I suspect, of a good Victorian wife.

Even when we first received it there were rings of age and wine, the legs nibbled by puppies of the past. And when we open it to put in leaves for a dinner party it is like a tug of war—Tom on one end, I on the other, the heavy table parting slowly, reluctantly. But legacies are legacies. That table is a link with Tom's past. You *don't* turn your back on family portraits. Traditions.

Ha! That's what I thought for the last thirty-four years. But now I've come of an age and figure I'm old enough to introduce new heirlooms, my *own* heirlooms. Legacies, I realize, can sometimes be more of a puzzle than a continued pattern, better kept in the past behind the potted palms.

And what *I'd* like for Christmas is a dining room table, my very own. I'd like it to be oval, the right size to embrace four, or with wings, stretching to seat twelve. And please, the well-shaped legs of Queen Anne.

Fruitwood would be nice, but even more I'd like to see the shine on its face, the patina, the polish of wood. I'd like to see a naked table by day, one I could costume by night—if I wish.

Tom's parents enjoyed every meal in their dining room, and he remembers it well, and with some envy. What he forgets in his dotage is that under the Oriental rug was a button that, when pressed by his mother's toe, summoned someone *else* to serve the omelet.

With a table of *my* own choice, I guarantee reliable service. It's time to start the next course. Something different. The new year is near.

December 1984

I never had a grandmother. There were the tributaries, certainly, some aunts, some uncles, but never that river with its current of love—that flow of affection when you haven't seen each other for at least two weeks. Never a grandmother to tell me to stand up straight, never a grandmother to ask me to tea.

To be quite honest I don't think I realized I was an orphan grandchild. There were plenty of older cousins who were my idols, as well as Tom Mix and his horse every Saturday afternoon at the movies for ten cents a show. But now that *I* am a grandmother I realize it's the role I've been waiting for all my life. And I'm probably overacting. Tom says I'm going through my second childhood, but why not! And tell me, if you can, a better way to retwig the empty nest.

In a small bedroom at Thornhill the wallpaper is newly striped lavender and white, and around the top is a border of mice doing the minuet with flowers. There's a Victorian sleigh bed that had to be hoisted through the second-floor window because it couldn't curve around the 143-year-old stairway. And beside it is a miniature bed with a china doll named Fiona Barley. This room is Edith's room, although she is only a year old, a room poised for a granddaughter.

Albert—her brother and our three-year-old grandson—established his territorial rights much earlier. When he comes to visit he goes right to his trunk of pop-up books, pats his wooden horse stabled in the library and is almost greedy about *his* chair, the small caned chair of his great-great-grandfather.

Even our closets, I find, are controlled by the next generation. Every year when I try to tidy them up, I'm often stopped by thoughts for future fun. Would Edith like this seedy sequin dress as a costume? Would Albert enjoy wearing his grandfather's flying jacket from World War II? And so I save those memories from the past and forget that Salvation Army van stationed at the shopping center.

Now that Albert has suddenly learned the magic, the wonder, the wand of a completed sentence, I must be careful. He understands. He mimics me, he parrots, he learns quickly. And I want him to learn the right stuff. When he leans against me and says, *"My* Momma Dee," he rules my world, but I must help guide his.

I want Albert to be kind and wise. I want him to know what Henry Beetle Hough, the venerable editor of *The Vineyard Gazette,* once wrote: "The good life means love, manners, taste, tolerance and hard work."

Great expectations, perhaps, for Albert and Edith, children so young. But whatever, they will always be my valentines, for them there will always be a Thornhill. And *that* is really the heart of the matter!

February 1985

When I was thirteen I became the owner of my very first teapot. I bought it for three dollars, a goodly sum when making only twenty-five cents an hour trying to teach my younger sister, Robin, how to spell. But I couldn't resist that teapot. And I still have it. It is a small black pot splashed with bright pink rosebuds. On the lid, printed in gold, is a noble legend—FOR ENGLAND AND FOR DEMOCRACY. And if you turn it over, you see on the bottom, "World War II, Made in England, Escorted to the U.S.A. by Royal Navy."

My mother, an inveterate coffee drinker, couldn't understand my youthful extravagance. But I knew. I knew my teapot had outwitted the turtlenecked sailors on those German U-boats, especially that captain peering through his periscope, trying to sink British teapots. I was thrilled. I thought I was helping win the war!

Over the years that small teapot has been joined by a coterie of other teapots, all held together by the common bond of one social grace—the drinking of tea. I have eight of them, inherited, inveigled, all beloved. They sit on top of a pine cupboard in the kitchen, waiting to serve.

For my *very* young friends our tea parties are in the spring under the pear tree. Their tea I lace with milk and honey. And for my older friends, as we sit around the fire for a spicy gossip in the cold of winter, I've been known to add a touch of something to the pot. Sneaky perhaps, but it loosens the tongue, and is *so* delicious.

Tea may be my own particular placebo, but it does seem to give comfort in any situation, in any season. The company of tea is ageless.

But making a pot of tea at Thornhill isn't always in the bag. I often use loose tea—Darjeeling because it's delicious, or Prince of Wales simply because I love the name. And I always use bone china cups and slim silver spoons. A little grandeur, a little style, doesn't hurt any girl, no matter what age. Sometimes the best tea of all is when Tom comes home early and it's tea for two.

I fill the kettle with cold water and bring it to a boil. While waiting, I fill my pot with hot water from the faucet. I slosh it around, then empty it. Next I put in a teaspoon of loose tea for each person, and "one for the pot." Then I fill it with the boiling water and let it steep for five minutes.

With the tea, depending on the age of my guests, I have lacy oatmeal cookies or rounds of bread topped with watercress from our stream, or with tiny shrimp mixed with butter and herbs from the garden—minced lemon sage or pineapple verbena.

Now that it's March I make a country tea from sassafras roots I've dug from our woods. I scrape off the bark, cover the roots with water and boil for ten minutes, then sweeten them with Todd and Diana's honey. Diana says sassafras tea is a spring tonic. And so it is. When that sassafras scent fills the kitchen, I rejoice. I know another spring is *almost* here.

March 1985

Often the most remote, silent prize is the most taken for granted. It doesn't seem fair, but that's the way it is. Take our woodlands, for example. On the far back border of our land are ten acres of green velvet mosses, wild flowers in May, a hillside of laurel, a vast treasury of trees. And we hardly have time to even walk in their shade.

It hasn't always been like this. When our children were younger we would go to the woods for pony picnics—one pony, four children. That was where they hid from parents and bedtime. It was their private club.

Even the Quakers who built our farmhouse used the woods, hiding their two workhorses there when the Yankees marched through on their way to Gettysburg. And to this day, the horses trot on the woodland paths used by our equestrian neighbors in every season.

I go to the woods, always, in May. It's our reunion. The wild flowers have come, a floral clock. And if I don't make it by half-past May, I've missed the first awakening. I walk through the woods with my neighbor Genie, a true naturalist. Over the years she has taught me all about my wild garden, a garden that needs no care, asks no favors or fertilizer, gives nature's small wonders as simple gifts.

We walk carefully, eyes down. First we see the slender fiddleheads of ferns unfolding, then a generous spread of Mayapples, the flower like an open white peony, and over each their own leafy umbrella. On small banks we find the pink of sweet rocket, the yellow celandine like tall buttercups, the white star flowers of bloodroot. And if we're lucky, sometimes the lavender of a wild geranium stands out. My favorite though is the pale green of the Jack-in-the-pulpit, the top of the blossom shaped like the elegant head of a bird.

Genie tells me about the trees as well. By the weave of the wood, the braid of the bark, she shows me oak, hickory, poplar, a beech. And even if the tree is dead, there is life. The higher holes house owls; the lower ones in stumps are the domains of raccoons. *Our* woodlands are *their* kingdom.

This May, Catherine, another good friend, is joining the pilgrimage. Catherine has created her own wild flower garden in a small dell near her house. Some of her flowers volunteered—black-eyed Susans, Queen Anne's lace, but she planted others, such as spring beauty and hepatica, which bloom early before the trees leaf out, a necessity as even wild flowers need the warmth of sun. Now she hopes to transplant some of the wild of Thornhill to her garden. And she's giving me, in return, more cultivated relations—lilies of the valley, which Catherine claims run wild with the wild, their small white bells always blooming right on time for Mother's Day!

Next year I'm taking our grandchildren, Albert and his sister Edith, on this trek. They'll be old enough to walk through the woods by then, but perhaps not *quite* old enough to know that even the wild, sometimes, at Thornhill, are still born free.

May 1985

On the Fourth of July my father always put out the flags and made a pot of clam chowder. It was, as he called it, "the beginning of the chow-da season." For me it was the beginning of summertime in New England.

This July festivity was my father's act, his specialty. He even had his clams auditioned, as he had an agent. A friend just happened to be a clam inspector and so my father and his pot only received the most plump, the most succulent clams around.

Every weekend, from July 4 on, my father dove into that pot and made the best clam chowder in all of Massachusetts. At least that's how he billed it. He even had a costume. It was a long white apron he bought from the local butcher when butchers still wore straw boaters and paper cuffs.

Yet aside from my father's Saturday sortie into chowder, he didn't much invade the kitchen. Still there was a fixed menu every weekend. My mother, good 1930s wife that she was, cooked it, but I feel my father ordained it. There was fish every Friday, baked beans, soaked the night over, for Saturday supper. And before church on Sunday my father lavished cold beans on bread for breakfast. Sunday dinner was roast chicken or a lovely leg of lamb.

It doesn't sound like a very original menu, and I never took to my father's bean sandwiches, but it was comforting, as childhood food often is. We knew what to expect. We also knew never to speak at the dinner table if the baseball scores were on the radio at the same time. The Red Sox were as important to my father as the ingredients of his chowder.

His chowder is never touched by tomatoes, as in Manhattan. Heaven forbid, that's sacrilege. Clam chowder means heavy cream and fine onions, diced potatoes and the more clams the merrier. I never even give it the company of a cracker. We like our chowder rich and pure.

In a way I'm a renegade from my New England heritage, moving to Maryland, but *not* when it comes to chowder. In the summer I make my father's Massachusetts chowder, and what's more, when I make Maryland oyster stew in the winter, I always add, on the sly, bottled *clam* juice. It's my small wave to my father, and it makes *all* the difference. At least I like to think so.

And now I'd like to present my father's chowder:

    1 cup finely diced onions
  ¼ pound lean diced salt pork
    3 tablespoons butter
    3 cups chicken stock
1-½ pounds potatoes, peeled and diced, about 3 cups
    1 bay leaf
    3 dozen clams, shucked and their juice
    1 cup bottled clam juice
    3 cups milk
    1 cup heavy cream
      Salt and pepper to taste

Sauté onions and salt pork in butter until onions are soft. Add stock, potatoes, bay leaf and pepper. Cover, bring to a boil and simmer 10 minutes. Potatoes should remain crisp. Remove bay leaf. Mince clams, add to chowder with juices and cream and milk, reheat without boiling. Season with salt, and before serving add a knob of butter to each bowl. Serves six.

July 1985

Whenever we have a September dinner party I always go to the trees to decorate the table. I use yellow maple leaves as place cards, writing the names of the guests with a black felt pen, and in the center of the table I group our red apples and green pears. I also carve out a cylinder in some of the apples and stick in thick white candles for evening sparkle.

It's not always easy to find a perfect pear as the bees love to sample their sweetness, and now, alas, something is testing my apples, a bite here, a bite there.

Although *we* paid the mortgage, I always knew Thornhill was not really ours, knew that we were living on borrowed land. The true gentry of Thornhill, one soon realizes, is the animal kingdom, a kingdom that was established long before we arrived.

We see deer in the fields, chipmunks and squirrels on the lawn, and in the multiflora hedge that borders our road up to the house there is a vast population of rabbits, groundhogs and mice. Overhead, goldfinches and cardinals dip in and out of the branches with vivid color and quiet grace. *Our* hedgerow has become *their* condominium. And it is a pretty one indeed. In the spring it is sprinkled with white flowers, and now it is garnished with small red berries.

I first suspected these rabbits of eating my apples, but no, it is the lettuce in the vegetable garden that they look at with longing. Then I thought perhaps it could be the chipmunks. Instead I see them nibbling my rose petals. I finally saw the culprit in the act. And now we have, I'd like to report, a red fox in residence who obviously enjoys a free apple diet.

I moved toward the fox, and he, or maybe she, ran for cover, right into a deep hole in my compost pile, a huge gathering of many years of autumn leaves. My compost pile is now a den.

Not so surprising, as we live in the middle of fox-hunting country. And although we have never "ridden to hounds," there has been many an exciting Saturday afternoon when we've watched the hunt riding across our land. It is an elegant sight—pink coats and top hats, very much like an old English print.

This fox in my compost might outfox the hunt. He, or maybe she, has certainly outfoxed me, continuing to feast on my apples. And like a gourmet, just a little at a time.

Reynard, the only name we know for such an animal, must be in fox heaven as there is a spread of food around the den—the hedgerow berries, a variety of rose hips filled with vitamin C, the apple tree as well as my raspberry patch. And, according to my friend Kitty, Joint-Master of Foxhounds, foxes *love* fruit.

I enjoy watching a new animal, but Reynard better watch it when it comes to my apples. I need them for our *own* table. Unless of course it's really Reynarda and she has hungry cubs deep in those autumn leaves. Then the apples, with our best wishes, become part of another family tree at Thornhill.

September 1985

One of the splendors of winter, at least to my way of thinking, is the refreshing yet slightly seductive scent of paper-white narcissus. Standing tall in bowls or pots, gloriously white, they are my winter gardens. And by the middle of November I start my indoor gardening, setting bulbs in almost every room of Thornhill. When they bloom, about four or five weeks later, their fragrance is my very first Christmas present.

And I always order enough in the summer to give away as gifts. As my friend Kitty, who is in the business of bulbs, says, "Any idiot can grow them!" Which might explain my great affection for them. But no, it's more than that. It's their white in winter making it seem like springtime indoors; it's that wonderful fragrant whiff you catch as you run around the house trying to tie up Christmas; and it's their simple but stately grandeur that somehow makes the rooms of this small farmhouse seem more abundant, filled with life in the dead of winter.

When the paper-white bulbs arrive in September I don't put them to work right away. Instead I hang them in an old onion bag on the wall leading down to the basement. Any cool, dry place will do for storage, even the refrigerator. But that can be dangerous. Another friend, Lucy, always stored her bulbs in the refrigerator until the time she forgot their real purpose in life, absentmindedly mistook them for onions and sliced them up tidily for a Sunday supper stew.

My bulbs behave better in bowls, and half the fun is finding the right container to give at Christmas filled with paper-whites. I look all year round, usually on the bargain tables of small antiques shops. I've used old china soup plates, the deep ones that seem to have been separated from the rest of their family, vegetable dishes that have lost their lids. Sometimes I put just one bulb in a clay pot shaped like a sheep.

I first put a layer of peat moss or horticultural charcoal in the container, then several inches of pebbles or gravel. Next I nestle the bulbs in their bed, one-half to one inch apart. In a cut-glass bowl I once used another setting—first sand, then a top layer of scallop shells I had picked up from a summer beach.

I don't start my bulbs in the dark. They go into light right away. If I'm in a hurry for some cheer, I put a bowl of paper-whites by the sunniest window, filling in water about three-fourths the way up the bulb. When the flower shoots are about six inches high, I water the bulbs several times a week. And I add a tablespoon of gin to each cup of lukewarm water. This gardening cocktail stops the leggy look of the foliage, helps it and the flowers to grow stiff and straight as a Grenadier Guard.

Last year I gave our grandson Albert his first paper-white. He loved watching it grow, and this year I'll give him another. But I'm going to wait a few years before I tell him about the gin.

November 1985

I never really wonder what I'm doing in the country when it's June because I'm too busy. And it's *so* beautiful. February is when one has cold doubts. In the morning I throw down hay for the sheep; in the afternoon, some grain. But there's little else to do, as our countryside is asleep under the rough tweed of winter.

And so, when in doubt, I write. But this is the first February in two years that I haven't been writing a book, a book that was published last fall, a "memoir" of Thornhill Farm. It was a long haul.

This column, however, is a romp, my pleasure, my joy. Sometimes I must admit, a bit of a torture. But once I've finished I'm exhilarated, sometimes exhausted, often surprised. Surprised that I really did it. That may sound naive, but when I sit down to the typewriter I'm not quite sure how it's going to come out. And unlike going on stage, I'm not too sure of my lines.

But writing this book helped me understand much more about Thornhill *and* myself. Once the book was finished I thought we would be at peace again, and we are, and we are even better friends.

I once thought Thornhill was for my children. When I was a child we hopscotched around from town to city since my father worked for a large company. I wanted something more for my four children. One continuous house. We've had that, but in writing the book I realized that perhaps it was *I* who needed the childhood house. A nest forever and ever.

I seem to look at my nest more carefully these days. I walk around the rooms, find myself unconsciously rubbing the back of an old velvet rocker as if it were a child, and I find flowers in the local market for a little February cheer. The house and I are paying more attention to each other, maybe, because of the book, even giving each other a little pat on the back.

Again, I wonder if I'm doing this for myself or others. Since the book was published there have been visitors I had never met before. They call, and I find myself inviting them to tea. This amazes my husband, Tom. Although I open our house every month in my column, I am not what you might call a social animal.

But these visitors, often in their thirties, seem so interested I can't resist. I enjoy the young, and I love Thornhill. Plus a proper cup of tea. The tea I'm serving these days is Twining's Queen Mary, given to me by my young friend Margaret as a book present.

We sit and we sip and I soon notice their eyes wandering, and so we go on tour. Since most of our furniture is inherited, there are stories to tell. And I like being the in-house curator.

I once read that one can become "too umbilically" attached to a house. You can become wedded. Well, I disagree. I like our ménage à trois—Tom, Thornhill and me.

And by writing a book, especially about Thornhill, I have found a new confidence I've never had before. Perhaps it's because in my childhood house I have *finally* grown up!

February 1986

A lthough Tom has often made the suggestion, thinking it would add some spice to our dinner table, I don't *really* have to go to cooking classes. I have Mr. Ryan's. Mr. Ryan's is a rather unusual source for culinary ideas as it is a beauty parlor, *not* a cooking school, but recipes pour forth every Thursday, the day I go for my weekly restoration. I merely have to say "What shall I have for supper?" and contributions come in from every side. These country women know what they are talking about. Most are the chief chefs of their churches' covered-dish suppers.

Mr. Ryan's is in a third of an 1841 stone bank barn. Emma, its owner, calls it a "barn with a hangover," as the second floor extends out over the first. Where hay was once stored, beauty blooms by the day.

The rest of the barn houses a collection of antiques. And *I* feel like an antique when I first enter Mr. Ryan's, but Joan works weekly wonders, making me feel brand new. And while she teases my hair, my palate is equally teased by country recipes. In the summer I come home with luscious visions of peach pies and raspberry tarts, while now we are into scalloped oysters, corn pudding, even muskrat soup!

Since I've been going to Mr. Ryan's for twenty years, I feel very much at home. But recently I had to be in New York, and my friend Mary Jane decided my hair needed help. She made me an appointment at *her* hairdresser, and there *I* was at Kenneth's, where the likes of Jackie Onassis have their heads turned, where glamour reigns. It was all very intimidating.

Whereas Mr. Ryan's shop is done in gray, the shades of most of his customers' hair, Kenneth's was ablaze with flowers, showered with chintz, chaise longues under the dryers, every room a bouquet.

I was instantly put into a smock, which made me feel a little more at ease as it was the color of a grain bag. And about the same shape. Then I walked up the stairs of this handsome town house to Angela's room, a room for two.

The other customer was chic and pale with short sculptured hair and a bevy of golden bracelets that ran up and down her arm as she quickly flipped through a fat fashion magazine. She turned to me and said, "Can you imagine! My daughter left my grandson's stroller in the trunk of a taxi and she hasn't seen it since!"

I shrugged my shoulders, hopefully sympathetically. Then she told me about the play she had seen, why she was tired of glitter dresses—"They are everywhere, on anybody"—and finished off by saying she was going to cook something cozy for Alfred that night. "And I think we'll eat in the kitchen." Then it was obviously my turn when she asked, "Any ideas?"

I felt at home again when I said, "How about Maryland corn pudding?" I gave her the recipe, and soon we were chatting like old friends. And her last advice to me was, "With your ruddy complexion, I definitely think you should try auburn hair!" I'm not so sure about *that,* but I am sure of Alice Ober's Corn Pudding:

3 cups corn cut from cob (or 2 packages frozen corn)
3 eggs
½ teaspoon freshly ground pepper
2 cups heavy cream
½ teaspoon salt

Beat eggs lightly, combine with other ingredients. Pour mixture into buttered casserole. Bake at 350 degrees, one hour or until a knife inserted in center comes out clean. Serves four generously.

As I was my father's "son," I learned about sports and exercise early on. He had two daughters, but it was I, as the older, who was taught how to broad jump because I had long legs, and who played "catch" in the evening. And when I was nine he began taking me to ball games. I loved it, but the best part was just being with my father.

When I was twelve he started me in golf. "If you play golf," he claimed, "you can do business and exercise *anywhere.*" I'm not sure what kind of business he thought I was going to do, and although *he* obviously made deals on the green, for me it was just another day of fun with my father.

But a game of golf takes a long time, and these days I don't have that kind of time. I still try to exercise by playing a little tennis, a lot of running after grandchildren and occasional aerobic classes, which I love because I think I'm Ginger Rogers. Even more, I walk. And walking in the country is both pleasure *and* exercise. I can do it anytime I want, and I don't have to worry about making a point at the net!

I usually walk through our woodlands, the ten acres high above our farmhouse. I go to the woods because there is nothing like a good daydream, and among the trees it's easy to dream and wonder. I wonder where the Quakers hid their two horses when the Northern troops came through on their march to Gettysburg. I wonder how many deer banded together this winter, and in the spring I also try to catch the opening season of the wild flowers.

But this year lumbermen invaded my woods. Now they look ravaged, and I can't go back for a while. Even now the toppings from fallen trees are being cut for firewood. It makes me sad, paths blocked by once tall, noble trees, but it is a necessity, a cycle of country life. By pruning the woods we make a small profit from the larger trees, as well as give space to the smaller ones. The old, as in all things, must make room for the young.

I've adjusted, though, and now I walk from Thornhill Farm to the village of Butler and back—a total of about three miles. But I don't have much time to dream as I'm too busy picking up trash.

It's quite an archaeological study, what one tosses carelessly from a car. Going east my basket becomes filled with dark beer bottles, squashed coke cans and cigarette boxes, even car parts. Coming back toward the west the litter is one after another empty pint of vanished vodka. There's a message there I can't quite decipher. Are the Russians coming to Thornhill Farm?

If so, they may be coming by bicycle. The cars speed by, but the trim cyclists raise their hands in silent greeting. There is a certain camaraderie on the road.

There's also so much beauty, thanks to Northwest Farms, the farm neighboring Thornhill. This farm lines the road for almost my entire route. And in the springtime it's a nursery of country animals. In every pasture there is birth. Sitting in a field of buttercups is a herd of white Charolais cattle, all pointing in the same direction like sailboats in a harbor, their young beside them. Then there are Suffolk sheep and their nursery-tale lambs. And as I walk up our hill I see new fillies and colts teasing their elegant mares.

Once home I have a cup of tea and realize my father was right again. "Legs are for walking." Especially in a Maryland spring.

April 1986

A few autumns ago, when the maple leaves were as yellow as churned butter and as deep red as a country barn, we bought a sizable insurance policy. We bought a second house. A house that sits on Main Street in a small Vermont village, a house that has watched a rural world walk by for the last 170 years.

People obviously buy a second house for different reasons—some go for a cottage by the sea, others a cabin in the hills, a condo in Florida. We, however, bought this house simply because we wanted to be nearer to some of our children—Diana and Todd who have chosen Vermont forever. And so we feel we bought an annex to a continued family life, a house where grandchildren can bicycle over for an afternoon of making strawberry jam, where they can spend the night and together we can watch the sparkle of fireflies. *These* are my premiums, my priorities and why I think of this house as an insurance policy rather than a piece of property. I grew up with a lot of children—our own—and I want to be in reach for the next chapter.

Still it is a big step, certainly a new responsibility and, at times, rather frightening. I began to wonder how I was going to juggle Thornhill Farm and Main Street. Their personalities are totally different—which might be another reason we succumbed so easily. At a certain age any new spice is a tonic. The Vermont house in Hinesburg, south of Burlington, is of New England brick, square and solid. Its fine-boned facade could stand on its own anywhere. On the other hand Thornhill, funny old Thornhill, is a rambling Maryland farmhouse that we have turned into a home over the last thirty-one years. There were, I must admit, questions in my mind. Were we wise, in our emotional leap, to land in Vermont?

Todd and Diana think so, which is comforting as well as flattering. But we don't want to get in their way, be on their minds. But the partnership has worked. And for over a year Diana and Todd kept our house warm for us, living there while they looked for a place of their own.

Now they have found it, a wonderful white farmhouse with a sweeping view of their beloved Vermont mountains, and in the spring, lilacs everywhere.

Their house is just about ten car-minutes away from our Main Street. And when we returned there last July I knew we had made the right decision. We visited with our children with ease, helped them paint their new house and on the Fourth of July we all sat on our front lawn on Main Street and watched the parade go by.

It was Americana, which I love, at its best, filled with simple, old-fashioned charm. Boy Scouts and bicycles, flags and flutes, fire engines and fireworks. We were in the mainstream on Main Street as we have never been at Thornhill. And that's the excitement, a new world, new ingredients, but only from time to time.

Now I must learn, domestically speaking, how to divide my affection, put each house in its proper place. And try to remember *not* to worry about the Thornhill raspberries when I'm with the strawberries in Vermont!

July 1986

My husband, Tom, has often said, in moments of anguish, that I have never grown up. Maybe he's right. And now there is even more circumstantial evidence of my juvenile leanings.

I have just built a tree house.

Actually, my very good carpenter friend Ken Spires built it, but I designed it. It's my reward, I tell friends, for writing a book. And I believe in reward. It's probably also my excuse to be a bit extravagant. But when you get to a certain age and you've always wanted a tree house, you build one, whether you can climb the tree or not. I would like to add that I can *still* climb trees.

Our children certainly wandered in and out of family trees at Thornhill, but never settled in any particular one. They had other islands. There were occasional tents, always the barn to hide in and a small log cabin that we put together from a kit. I regret now that I gave it away too soon. But this tree house is for keeps.

My small house sits high and proud on stilts in the center of our apple orchard. Next spring it will be crowned with billowy white blossoms and this fall, when the apples ripen, I intend to stand on its deck and reach up to pick my apples. Life can be sweet.

I thought about putting it *in* a tree, but I simply couldn't find the *right* tree. None of them were really up to it. The pear tree is too old for a new high-rise, the chestnut, precious but sprawling, already blocks part of our view and the locust trees are too slender for ample support. Besides, I didn't want a tree to dictate to me, tell me where to put *my* house. Even big, bearded Ken approved of the site and tucked it in the orchard. "A tree house," he said, *"should* be mysterious." I knew then that our carpenter was really a poet at heart.

Three days after I gave him my design, Thornhill had a new miniature dwelling. Standing on four stilts, eight feet high, the house overlooks the vegetable garden and the raspberry patch, and has the best view of all of the Worthington Valley below.

I can stand up in it, and it is wider than the stretch of my arms. It seats four for lunch if you're four years old or younger, and on a warm summer night it holds two adults on its trellised deck, where the breeze is the best and you can watch the sparkles of the night. Meals are delivered in a wicker basket that is pulled up by a rope.

The house is blue, Swedish blue. And finding the right shade was almost the biggest problem of all. First I thought I'd paint it beige, the same color as Thornhill. That was too easy. Although a dependency of Thornhill, my tree house needed to have a personality of its own. Our farmhouse is sturdy, and I wanted this tree house to be a folly, an amusement.

But there are blues and there are blues, as I discovered at the hardware store. In desperation I finally mixed Cornflower with Tide Water to find the blue of Scandinavia. And at Christmas there will be a wreath, and next summer, window boxes of pansies.

So far it's been a great success for all ages. Albert, our grandson, thinks it's *his* tree house, and it probably is, but when he's not around, it's mine all mine!

August 1986

Whenever our grandchildren, Edith and Albert, come for a visit at Thornhill Farm, after hugs and kisses, we always have tea. I set out their miniature Peter Rabbit teacups, fill up the small matching teapot with apple juice, dip spoons in the jar for licks of honey. And then we all sit down and act grownup. They seem to enjoy it, but it has always been *my* idea.

Last week they came for another visit. Four-year-old Albert jumped out of the car and said in way of a greeting, "Let's have tea." Then when he said, "And *I'll* pour," I felt as if my cup runneth over. I may have started this small slice of sociability, but it is Albert who has caught its rhythm. I like to think I've started a memory.

That, I guess, is what I've always been trying to do at Thornhill, make memories. Sometimes I wonder why I care so much. Sometimes I wonder if I put too much emphasis on the "place," on Thornhill. What's really important is that you're together, no matter where. But having a place makes it easier.

Jan, a young mother and reader from Sacramento, California, recently wrote and started me thinking. She asked, "Do your children share your passion for tradition?"

I hope so, I wrote back. Christmas certainly, I told myself. You can't grow up with three Christmas trees every holiday and not feel the joy and excitement. But what about the other times? Maybe it was just too soon to tell.

Suddenly I knew when I received the news. Our daughter Beth and daughter-in-law, Diana, chose Thornhill as the place for the dinner party of their tenth reunion from nearby Garrison Forest School. Now *they* were making a new memory, a new tradition, and I was thrilled. They too had caught the rhythm.

We had seventy for dinner, and our farmhouse bulged with babies, beaux, husbands and elegant young women—young women I had once known as little girls in short blue tunics and old-fashioned bloomers. The last time I had seen them together was at their 1976 graduation in long white dresses, clutching bouquets of bachelor's buttons, their school flower.

Their bouquets now seemed to be their children. Girls I had once known holding dolls were now holding their own, their own babies. And there was a flow between the pregnant and the proud, the beaming new mothers. Especially Sabrina and her three-month-old, Evan, our houseguests. There was talk too of master's theses, theater, houses and jobs. It was a chance to catch up, a chance to go on. They liked themselves and they liked each other. Sometimes it came as a surprise. I was in heaven. Thornhill was once again in step with the young.

But I was too busy to think about the past. I was more concerned with plates, since our dishwasher, which has had far more than its tenth reunion, decided to retire that morning. But it didn't really matter. There was help everywhere. There were Diana and Beth and Mary Pitt, Jenny and Wendy, who had come all the way from Houston, in the kitchen carving the ham and turkey. We had all grown up. Now I'm looking forward to the glorious fifteenth. Same place I hope, same time, same cast. A new tradition has started.

September 1986

This fall I'm going to become a grandaunt. It's astonishing. Not that my niece Karen is going to have a baby, but that *I* am in a new category. Rather, an old one!

Being a grandmother is a different cup of tea. Being a grandmother keeps you young. But graduating into grandaunthood sounds to me a little like lavender and old lace.

This age dilemma never disturbed me before. Maybe it's because this October I'm entering a new decade, all round numbers.

I never really know how old I am until I start figuring out the ages of our children. That's a timetable that doesn't fool around. But I should have known what was happening. I feel much happier with Cole Porter than I do with hard rock, old friends are often much easier than new and although I love to travel, more and more I find I can see forever, right from the front lawn of Thornhill Farm.

I've also decided that I don't want my shape to be as round as my age. It's now or never, and so I've started attending classes called Living Thin. Thanks to our leader, Sylvia, I now can face a mirror at *all* angles, and my clothes and I like each other a whole lot better.

It's exercise and eating wisely. And if you *are* what you eat, as Sylvia keeps telling us, in the early morning I'm a half grapefruit, a shredded-wheat biscuit, a half cup of skim milk and tea. By dinner I'm fish or fowl surrounded by vegetables. In between meals my best friends, friends I see quite often, are almonds and carrots.

"I am what I am," as that song sings from the musical *La Cage aux Folles,* but I'm also fifteen pounds lighter. I actually weigh what I did in my thirties when I thought I was overweight, but it balances out as I feel better now than I did then!

I'm consumed with energy. So much so that I helped build a deck onto our Vermont house. Of course Mark and Bob did all the work, but I was there in attendance.

While the carpenters were digging the holes for the support posts, I was scavenging around picking up old pieces of broken china and glass, thinking I was on an archaeological dig. *They* thought I was a little crazy, but somehow got in the swing of things—handing me small treasures.

Then when I was making lunch, there was a pounding on the back door. There stood Mark proudly holding a tall marble tombstone he had recovered from the depths. Probably stolen long ago from the nearby churchyard, it was perfectly preserved, beautifully engraved, "Cynthia P., wife of Peter Broughton, August 13, 1838, aged 40." Macabre as it may sound, we were all thrilled. We had found a clue to the past, a mystery to be solved. Who was Cynthia? And how sad it was that she had died so young, at least young to me, and I started thinking about age again.

After lunch Mark handed me some small blue labels from the pressure-treated timber we were using for the deck. They read, "Guaranteed for 30 years against structural damage by decay." Just right, I thought. The deck and I have thirty years together with all those future grand whatevers. And I plan to have, in the time of our lives, a very good time!

October 1986

Our bedtime inventory at Thornhill includes blankets once woven from the wool of our Hampshire sheep. In springtime we hang the blankets, like banners, from the windows to air them, and in the winter they give the warmest of comfort. But over the years our source has diminished simply because our shepherds, our sons, have gone off to other pastures. As they grew older, our flock grew smaller, even faded for a while from the landscape.

But once again, a country circle has been repeated. Once again there is the familiar sound, the early-morning plaintive "baa" of sheep in the barnyard, the announcement. And the reason—we have *just* inherited a bounty of the country, bundles of wool, a flock of Suffolk sheep, eighteen of them.

This is a circle within a circle as well. Jerry, who owned these Suffolk and who died with great courage a few months ago, gave us our very first gift when we moved to Thornhill thirty-two long years ago. It is a sad thread of continuity that we hold, but one to treasure.

During the first week at Thornhill, Jerry and his wife, Frances, presented us with two handsome gray-and-white Toulouse geese. We were grateful, of course, but terrified. Geese, unlike sheep, are not the least bit shy. Quite the contrary. These strutted around the barnyard with elegant arrogance, *dared* us to come through that gate. I must admit, for all my fear, they did add style, and made us realize that at last we really lived in the country.

Looking back, I think Jerry, the old country hand, thought of it as a small joke, thought it would help toughen up those greenhorns. I still remember the gleam in his eye, the twinkle. Later another gift was to his goddaughter, Beth.

Who else, long before Women's Lib, would have given a punching bag to a four-year-old girl for Christmas? Beth, the youngest of our own flock of four, loved it. It gave her power, definitely the upper hand, especially *that* holiday.

To us, Jerry's Suffolk are just as special. The Hampshires we owned before were a mélange, looking as though they had just gamboled out of a nursery rhyme. But these Suffolk are the aristocrats, our first purebreds, their lean faces and ears black as a satin ribbon.

On Christmas Eve, Jerry often brought in the newborn lambs to show his nieces and nephews who were gathered at his farm, Western Run House, for the family dinner. The kitchen became a manger.

His sheep, now in residence, haven't quite figured out the perimeters of Thornhill. At first they huddled frightened in a corner of the barn like a huge woolly mushroom. Now they venture forth at dusk, leaving for the upper pasture, one after the other, returning at dawn.

We expected this. Sheep are bashful, timid. They don't come up to you as a pony might, licking your outstretched hand, expecting some sweet reward or a friendly carrot. Sheep have their own club, like it that way, and *now* the ground rules are a little different.

When our sons, Todd and Tommy, were younger they had a Christmas ritual. They always prepared a wonderful mush, a child-concocted "pâté" of honey and grain for the sheep on Christmas Eve. This Christmas we're making that same recipe for Jerry's sheep. We're bringing it to the upper pasture in a big tin bucket, and then together, perhaps, we'll look for the star.

December 1986

We now have a dollhouse in residence at Thornhill. "It's for the grandchildren," I told Tom. "I'm house-sitting for the future." He just smiled. He knows, he knows that I can't resist houses, no matter what size, no matter what shape. And it's true. I simply love houses.

I can't quite explain this addiction. Perhaps it's because I moved about a great deal as a child; maybe it's because a house knows its place, never talks back, is there when you need it. A nest. And whenever I travel a new road, especially in New England, I must admit I look at the old houses rather than the scenery. I want to restore every one I see, rescue it, give it back a life, a pride. Adopt it. Well, that's impossible. My plate is full.

I've done my best for Thornhill over the last thirty-two years, and we're content, settled in. And I've also just made the last tuck on that 1816 brick summer house in Vermont. At last, I thought, I'm finally finished. I can relax. No more sanding of old floors, no more searching for new wallpaper patterns. But I should have known better. Here I am making house calls again, this time in a miniature world.

There's a mansard roof, a front porch, an upstairs hall and six comfortable rooms, circa, I would like to think, about 1907, one of my favorite architectural periods. And the house was on sale already assembled, which appealed to me, an easy acquisition. And it obviously needed a mother, or in this case, a grandmother.

This house, I told myself, should be part of our real estate. And I thought of it as a leisurely project. I figured I would do one room at a time, punctuated by each visit of our grandchildren, Albert and Edith. We would do it together, take our time, something different for some winter fun.

But now that I've started preparing the rooms, getting ahead for Edith and Albert, I can't stop. It's too much fun. I never dreamed I was going to have such a good time in such a small world. And it's *so* easy. Mistakes, unlike a real house, are not costly, and are quickly repainted. A wall can be pulled down in seconds, and I never have to wait around for a plumber.

In the evenings I sit the house on the kitchen table and I urethane floors, paper bedrooms. Each morning I can hardly wait to see how it looks. There's chintz on the sofa, a brass bed upstairs, the kitchen is country pine, trimmed high with tiny baskets. In fact it's beginning to look a lot like Thornhill. But the furniture isn't inherited. It's straight from the five-and-ten.

That was an early decision. I wanted the furniture for this dollhouse to be reasonable, replaceable and child-proof. I wanted it to be fun!

And it is. I know because we've just had the housewarming, the first visit to the little house by Edith and Albert. I was thrilled. They enjoyed the dollhouse even more than I expected. We rearranged the furniture endlessly, had a wonderful time. Then Albert turned to me, and said, with the innocent wisdom of a five-year-old, "Where are the people?"

I had never thought about that. I was making a stage set, and Albert wanted a house with a heart. And so we went out and bought a family—a father and a mother, a brother and a sister. That's how they come, a set, planned parenthood and planned childhood, plastic figures, but plausible to Edith, a little girl of three, and her older brother.

Now we need more beds.

March 1987

When the first tip of the earliest lettuce leaf appears in the garden, the rabbits come to Thornhill. They seem to know. In fact, there are so many wild rabbits around that I wonder why, when our children were young, we imported white domestic ones for them at Easter. But then Easter meant a rainbow of childish modern art on country eggs, and especially white bunnies to hold and nurture and love—then cry over when they eventually escaped to join their country cousins.

Last spring we decided the time had come to have a Rabbit-in-Residence for our grandchildren, Albert and Edith, complete with an Easter Egg Hunt, the first held at Thornhill in years. The host, of course, was Albert, then four, and the hostess, Edith, just two. But it was their social secretary, their grandmother, who sent out invitations to ten young children saying, "Come meet the Easter Bunny on the lawn of Thornhill, and bring your parents."

Our daughter Louise, the children's mother, gave an early ultimatum—"no candy!" That seemed a bit harsh. Imagine Easter without a chocolate bunny! Almost like Christmas without a Claus. But I was determined to answer the challenge. I filled eighty-five garishly colored plastic eggs with small treasures from my favorite emporium, the Cockeysville five-and-ten. No candy, but fuzzy chickens, tiny teddy bears, packets of pansy seeds, peanuts, raisins, mini cars and trains. All the eggs were hidden, waiting for the right moment, along with baskets tied with rose ribbons and yellow name tags: Robert, William, Jenny, Jay, Alexander, Lauren, Brian, Robby, Nicholas, Eliza and, of course, Albert and Edith.

Signing up a six-foot rabbit to fill the borrowed bunny suit was a lot easier than filling those small Easter eggs. "I'll do it," said my husband, Tom, who although adroit at the fox-trot, had never before tried the bunny hop. *Anything,* I guess, for grandchildren. Muffie, the owner of the suit, plushy white with pink paws, warned Tom, "Try to keep cool."

The day before the party Albert and Edith dyed eggs while their mother created a ribbon tree. On the still-bare limbs of an old apple tree Louise tied bows of pastel pink and lavender, green and yellow. It was simple and beautiful, and Easter had almost arrived.

When the guests did arrive at eleven the next morning, the bunny was there. But not before he had pulled himself into his heavy suit, topping it off with a huge helmetlike head of a toothy rabbit. "I feel like an astronaut," he said bravely.

Then he hopped forward, and almost immediately half of the children burst into tears. Only Alexander, age three and raised in Zimbabwe in Africa, allowed the bunny to pick him up. But as someone figured out, "Alexander is accustomed to big animals."

Once the egg hunt was on, the tears were gradually forgotten. And as it was a warm Easter the bunny soon melted away, reappearing as Albert and Edith's "CapCap," serving punch to the parents while the children ate raspberry jam sandwiches shaped like sheep, made from our old cookie cutter.

Now what I must remember for this year is that an Easter Bunny is never six feet tall unless he's Jimmy Stewart with an imaginary friend named Harvey.

April 1987

A perennial garden, I always thought, should be like a marriage. Forever. Or at least you hope so. Something lasting to share together. At Thornhill my perennial garden and I started quite young, and very simply. Lots of peonies and two pink rosebushes. I'm still here, my husband, Tom, is still here, but my perennial garden has got to shape up—or at least stay in line and have some manners!

Every year I would plant something new, thinking I was establishing a floral insurance policy, something I could count on. I wanted it to be like an English garden—full-blown, crowded and glorious. A bit like an overdressed woman, yet with taste. But now the shasta daisies have invaded the columbine, the columbine are shading the coral bells, and I can't even find the foxglove. My garden has grown up. It is *so* busy that it hasn't time to think where it's going next. And it's all my fault.

In my naiveté I really thought a perennial garden would continue and behave. That was the *whole* idea, a family garden that would come home every year, without asking. As opposed to annuals which you have to put in every single spring, invite into your garden year after year—those pansies, those geraniums, the trim that adds the extra touch, but only for a while.

I've learned from this perennial garden, as in marriage, that weeds and worries can creep in. Small plants, as small problems, can balloon out of all proportion. You've got to prune, perhaps chart a new course. And that's exactly what I'm going to do. My old perennial garden is going to have a new life. And I've hired Frances, a young professional, to guide me. That, in itself, is a very big step.

I've never done anything like this before. Over the years it's been my pride to plant my garden at whim, decorate Thornhill just as I wished. I didn't *want* anyone else's advice. I must admit that when I make a big plunge, like covering *everything* in chintz, I call on my neighbor Minnie to give me confidence. But that was the extent of it. And here I was hiring a gardener who was still in the playpen when I planted my first peony.

Frances and I discussed and dissected my garden. She was to make a design, and I was to approve. The next day I went to Boston on business, taking in an exhibition of turn-of-the-century New England Impressionists who painted, very often, portraits of gardens and full bouquets on tea tables. That night I frantically called Frances long distance. "Frances," I wailed, "we *must* have delphinium and lupine. Somehow we've forgotten all the flowers of my youth!"

She immediately quieted me down, saying, "Dee, yours is a Maryland garden, not a New England scene. *You* may have transplanted yourself from New England, but the flowers you want will never survive Maryland summers. Trust me!"

And of course I do. We've had a wonderful time digging up the entire garden, working in bags of peat moss, dividing old plants, adding new varieties, giving the garden another chance. And like a good marriage, it's going to work.

Sometimes you've just got to compromise, make life simpler, dig those roots deeper. And then before you know it, it's spring.

May 1987

The newest bud on our family tree is a little girl named Meriwether, the first child of Diana and our son Todd, and the first Hardie born in almost thirty years! And although I probably shouldn't admit it, having a grandchild share the same last name is very special, the lineage of a family name continued.

Her first name is *far* more distinguished, but not quite as close. One of her mother's ancestors, Meriwether Lewis, helped chart the Northwest Territory in the early 1800s. That's a lot to live up to, but I'm sure Meriwether can handle it. Even as a tiny babe she would arch her head up, her dark eyes darting around, the eyes of an explorer. And now, almost a year old, when you hold her she examines you with great intent, then explores the world around her. Hmmmm, do I hear the pride of grandmothering? Not surprising, it is a role I cherish, hoping in time for even a larger supporting cast.

That Meriwether was born in October was the best present of all for her grandmother. When I dared mention to Diana that I hoped it might even be the same birthdate as mine, all I heard was a long-distance telephone groan. She was then overdue. But the package did arrive, assisted by the midwife Kathy, Diana's sister Heather and our son Todd, the new father. And although the day was not the same as mine, it's near enough and we are Libras together. *That* is a bond. We Libras have our ups and downs, but our sign is a scale of balance. I like us!

To me grandmotherhood is filled with great expectations, a luxury, an indulgence that allows you to start over again in half time. And I didn't lose *any* time in rushing to Vermont after Meriwether was born.

On the actual day of her birth I simply spent the afternoon crying with joy and relief. Then I scurried around trying to find remembrances of things past, souvenirs saved from her father's childhood here in Maryland. And when Tom and I flew to Vermont I brought along one of Todd's bibs cross-stitched by my mother and a blanket knitted by his great-aunt Alice. I also carried onto the plane a large, cumbersome toy, a life-size woolly sheep that made all the passengers smile at the impracticality of new grandparents.

I wasn't exactly a nurse-in-residence. A friend, Judy, did that, but I did market, launder and listen to the murmurs of Meriwether while Diana tried to rest. There were times, late in the afternoon, when I would stretch out on a sofa with Meriwether asleep on top of me, a tiny blanket of warmth and love. With my arms around her, I would watch darkness come early to the Vermont autumn.

Meriwether is even more portable now, and has come to Thornhill, sleeping peacefully at night in a bureau drawer near her parents' bed. Diana came up with the idea, as an old Vermont farmer once told her that whenever a new baby was born in the family, they merely pulled out the top bureau drawer. It worked, and we had a wonderful but rainy weekend together.

On Sunday after they had all flown home, Tom and I were sitting on the front lawn. The skies had cleared and suddenly there was the most beautiful pastel rainbow, arched in the colors of childhood. I'm *sure* Meriwether arranged that rainbow. Grandchildren, after all, work wonders!

October 1987

Dee Hardie has lived more than half her life in an old Quaker farmhouse, high on a hill overlooking the Worthington Valley in Maryland. But, born in Providence, Rhode Island, she still considers herself a New Englander. She started writing as a freshman at Skidmore College and hasn't stopped since—nor has she ever missed a deadline.

Dee met her husband, Thomas Hardie, then a foreign correspondent, in Paris and married him seven months later, after a courtship by mail. The Hardies had four children in five years, and now there are three grandchildren.

Dee Hardie is currently a contributing editor to *House Beautiful,* where her column, "View from Thornhill Farm," appears every month. Her columns about Thornhill have also appeared in the *Baltimore Sun,* the *Boston Herald-Traveler,* and *House & Garden.* Her first book, *Hollyhocks, Lambs and Other Passions,* was published by Atheneum in 1985.

CHRISTIAN HERALD
People Making A Difference

Christian Herald is a family of dedicated, Christ-centered ministries th
reaches out to deprived children in need, and to homeless men who are lo
in alcoholism and drug addiction. Christian Herald also offers the finest
family and evangelical literature through its book clubs and publishes a po
ular, dynamic magazine for today's Christians.

Our Ministries

Family Bookshelf and **Christian Bookshelf** provide a wide selection
inspirational reading and Christian literature written by best-selling author
All books are recommended by an Advisory Board of distinguished write
and editors.

Christian Herald magazine is contemporary, a dynamic publication th
addresses the vital concerns of today's Christian. Each monthly issue co
tains a sharing of true personal stories written by people who have found
Christ the strength to make a difference in the world around them.

Christian Herald Children. The door of God's grace opens wide to giv
impoverished youngsters a breath of fresh air, away from the evils of th
streets. Every summer, hundreds of youngsters are welcomed at the Chri
tian Herald Mont Lawn Camp located in the Poconos at Bushkill, Pennsylv
nia. Year-round assistance is also provided, including teen programs, tutorir
in reading and writing, family counseling, career guidance and college scho
arship programs.

The Bowery Mission. Located in New York City, the Bowery Mission offe
hope and Gospel strength to the downtrodden and homeless. Here, the me
of Skid Row are fed, clothed, ministered to. Many voluntarily enter a 6-mont
discipleship program of spiritual guidance, nutrition therapy and Bible stud

Our Father's House. Located in rural Pennsylvania, Our Father's House is
discipleship and job training center. Alcoholics and drug addicts are given a
opportunity to recover, away from the temptations of city streets.

Christian Herald ministries, founded in 1878, are supported by the voluntar
contributions of individuals and by legacies and bequests. Contributions a
tax deductible. Checks should be made out to Christian Herald Childre
The Bowery Mission, or to Christian Herald Association.

Administrative Office: 40 Overlook Drive, Chappaqua, New York 10514
Telephone: (914) 769-9000

Fully accredited Member
of the Evangelical Council
for Financial Accountability